FIRST ED

MW01153237

RACE AND POVERTY IN THE AMERICAS

WRITTEN AND EDITED BY **JACOB KIM**
TEMPLE UNIVERSITY

cognella®
academic publishing

Bassim Hamadeh, CEO and Publisher
Michael Simpson, Vice President of Acquisitions
Jamie Giganti, Senior Managing Editor
Jess Busch, Senior Graphic Designer
John Remington, Senior Field Acquisitions Editor
Monika Dziamka, Project Editor
Brian Fahey, Licensing Specialist
Claire Yee, Interior Designer

www.cognella.com   800-200-3908

CONTENTS

Preface and Various Acknowledgments   v

Introduction to the book   ix

1. Introduction to this Race and Poverty Class   1

2. Prior Knowledge and Perspective   9

3. Knowledge Production   21

4. Deconstruction   29

5. Resetting the Perspective and the Legislation of Morality   43

    "After Objectivism" by Renato Rosaldo   46

6. Racial Formation   63

    "Racial Formation" by Michael Omi and Howard Winant   64

7. Racialize Me   93

    Assignment: Race and Poverty   101

8. Racializing the Poor—and the Response   105

9. Economics, Greed, and Toilet Paper   117

10. The Free Market   131

11. The Free Market in Context   155
    Assignment: Race and Poverty: Voting with Your Feet   175
    Assignment: Racialize Yourself   179
    Assignment: Innovate not Regulate   181

12. White Privilege   185
    "Membership Has Its Privileges" by Michael Eric Dyson   186

13. Institutional Racism Explained through White Supremacy   209
    "Talking Race and Racism" by bell hooks   210

14. Who Makes More, Men or Women?   229
    "Employer Discrimination" by Thomas Sowell   230

15. How Much Can Be Blamed on Discrimination?   243
    "Is Discrimination a Complete Barrier to Economic Mobility?" by Walter Williams   243

16. Closing Remarks   263

Glossary   271

Bibliography   279

PREFACE AND VARIOUS ACKNOWLEDGMENTS

ONE OF THE IDEAS that will be introduced in this book is the need for students to know some details about the author (knowledge producer) to assist in the critique of the information in the book; the subjectivity of an author is important to know when hearing or reading that author's produced knowledge. This preface will serve to provide some of that information for this work. It is information I subjectively deem necessary to understand the perspective from which this information is being produced (hopefully that will make more sense after the first few chapters). In the process of sharing this information, I wish to acknowledge various people for a variety of reasons and disclose information to students to preserve my own sense of morality and integrity.

First, all royalties of this book have been signed over to Temple University's Department of Religion. It is my small contribution to the department that has bestowed the doctoral degree to my father, Rev. Sunoon Kim ('71), and myself ('03). It also conveniently takes care of any suspicion of a conflict of interest, which always arises when a professor assigns his own book as the required text for a class. Temple University and the Department of Religion have been very good to me; I am always thankful to those who have helped me and continue to extend all academic courtesies to me.

Thanks also to Cognella Inc. for this opportunity to be published. Their patience with a two full-time job-juggling academician who is married and has four children is deeply appreciated.

The ideas in this book are not my ideas, but ideas that are widely known and used in the humanities. Though the application of the ideas may be less typical, they are ideas and theories that I learned during all my years of graduate study here in America and Korea, at Westminster Theological Seminary, Seoul National University, and Temple University. Because the ideas are widely known and cited repeatedly in numerous other sources, there is little need for detailed annotation; these ideas are everywhere. There are many writers that have influenced my scholarship, such as Cornelius Van Til, Renato Rosaldo, Michel Foucault, Katie Cannon, Judith Butler, Hans-Georg Gadamer, Howard Winant, Paul Veyne, Pierre Bourdieu, Milton Friedman, Thomas Sowell, Walter Williams, and my father. Anything of value I owe to these thinkers, philosophers, and accomplished knowledge producers. Anything problematic will be the result of my own shortcomings as a writer and accidental scholar. The ideas are presented with the undergraduate in mind.

Also, it is important to know that I am, to some, a conservative Christian evangelical, the son and grandson of Korean Christians who lived through the Japanese occupation and persecution of the Christian church in Korea, which lasted until the end of World War II. My father's stories of resistance against oppression are foundational in my own identity formation. His scholarship in Christian philosophy and theology provides me with my own perspective, which makes this book possible. I am what some would call a "Jesus freak" and the senior pastor of the Korean Presbyterian Church of Huntingdon Valley, and have been since 2005.

Politically, I am Libertarian with great sympathy for anarchy. People unfamiliar with libertarianism can know simply that it favors personal freedom, voluntary participation, and the ability to live life in the way one desires without infringing on the rights and lives of others. Libertarians are a diverse group that focuses on civil liberties and shares some agreement with democrats and republicans on certain issues, but generally oppose democrats and republicans in most other things. This is particularly true when subjects concern the role and size of the government in everyday life in America. It would be an unfair categorization to identify me as simply a conservative republican Jesus freak.

I thank the many students I have taught over the years who have encouraged me and challenged me through their feedback and critique. My own struggle with sitting in class as an undergraduate continually serves as a guide for keeping each class interesting for at least some of the students, some of the time. Part of my personal goal is to provide a way for students to be creative and innovative, if that is what they want. It is always a pleasure to hear from a diverse group of former students who apply the principles learned in class in their own field, which undermines the status quo to create a productive instability in life.

I thank my church and its dedicated members who continue to put up with and tolerate a theoretically pragmatic pastor and all the baggage that is very much a part of me. The church and its members have been the object of my experimentation since I started to serve there in 1987. They have always been a ready source of feedback and information. Because of my obsessive compulsion for taking things to the extreme, our church tends to be more on the cutting edge of things, which translates to being criticized and misunderstood often. I have no regrets and trust that all things work out for the good of those who believe; I hope the congregation, too, has that same faith.

I thank my extended family for putting up with me, one who is not always around, and always just a half a step away from complete mental and physical exhaustion. I thank my parents who have supported and raised me in America and who taught me the word of God. I thank my brother Peter and his family for their understanding and patience.

I want to thank my friend and colleague Dr. Marie Dallam of the University of Oklahoma for her last minute proofing of much of this text. Her comments and corrections were invaluable and saved me from some very embarrassing mistakes. Her comments and corrections helped greatly to get my head back in the game.

Finally, and most importantly, special thanks to my wife, Elizabeth Sonmee, and my four boys, Joseph Sungtae, John Sungsoo, Timothy Sungoh, and Thomas Sungkwang, who have my love and commitment till I go to meet my maker to be judged. I thank my wife for her patience and support; it is never easy to be the pastor's wife and the mother of four boys. I recognize and appreciate her sacrifice to take care of five males in the same house. I look forward to what God has in store for us next. My boys are always on my mind when I teach and am away from home. Though it might not always be obvious, I strive to make and provide a home to which yellow kids growing up in America would always look forward to returning. It is for them and their future life in America that I teach what I teach the way I teach it, both at Temple University and at our church. Education is for the hope of peace. Hope gives life meaning and purpose; hope makes life worth living. I racialize myself as one who sometimes teaches race but also one who always tries to teach hope.

INTRODUCTION
TO THE BOOK

WHAT IS THIS BOOK GOING TO DO?

THIS BOOK WILL SERVE as a companion text for "Race and Poverty," a course offered through Temple University's General Education program. This text will introduce, explain, and develop many of the ideas raised in class. The goal of the book is to teach race theory from the humanities perspective to help students understand how race is made and used in many aspects of society today; this understanding is meant to help them make better choices in life, which will hopefully result in a better and more tolerant society. Since our society is always changing, the real-world applications and examples contained in the book may become dated. However, once students understand this perspective and the principles used in the book, they will be able to discover examples in their own lives and make the connection with the currents of oppression, exploitation, and discrimination in society as a whole.

GROUND RULES

This class and book have two underlying rules that will govern discussion and proposals to resolve issues and move forward. The first rule is that the use of force and intimidation are forbidden. In other words, no one may force, coerce, or intellectually bully another to believe or do anything they do not want to voluntarily do or believe. No method may be employed to force people to make decisions or choices that others believe are the right choices. This includes the legislation of morality, that is, the writing of laws and regulation based on narrow subjective perspective. People are free to believe what they want to believe and act on those beliefs no matter how wrong others may believe them to be. Instead, one must use persuasion and rhetoric to try to change the minds and beliefs of others.

The second rule is that double standards or hypocrisy are also forbidden for the class and its discussions about public and communal matters. When discussing issues in society and suggesting proposals to address those issues, laws and rules of society must be consistently applied and obeyed by all members of society, especially those who are in positions of government. Regulations must not give arbitrary advantage for one group resulting in the disadvantage of everyone else no matter the intent and subjective justification. In the public sphere, that is, this class and society as a whole, there cannot exist different sets of rules of justice and behavior for different types of business and different kinds of people, especially politicians.

Though double standards and hypocrisy often exist in the personal and individual aspect of everyday life, one may not impose one's perspective on others. Each individual chooses to exercise judgment in the way one freely decides; the results of those choices, for better or worse, are the responsibility of the one making choices.

These two rules are intended to protect the rights of each individual person of this class regardless of power, wealth and access to government insiders. It is a system that strives to be fair for all people regardless of location and time period. Although these are the rules of the class, it is hoped that students will see the applicability of these two principles in their everyday life beyond the classroom and for society as a whole.

METHOD: BECAUSE, AT THIS POINT, WE'RE JUST NOT READY TO "TALK RACE"

Before we embark on the difficult journey of discussing race and poverty, which eventually offends pretty much everyone, it must be stated that most people are not ready, at this point of the class, to "talk race," at least not in the way this class will discuss it. People have their own personal understanding of race, but in order to talk race as a class, the class must use the same language and perspective; otherwise, students will simply misunderstand each other and especially misunderstand the instructor.

"Deconstruction" will be used to break down existing discourses on race to establish a different field with different rules to facilitate a constructive and productive conversation.

Many classes on race begin with a "simple" definition of race and how that definition plays out in society as signified by the instructor. Definitions are given, and evidence to support those definitions is provided, about which students are later tested. There is little critical thought in this process where agreement is rewarded and dissension is labeled as closed-minded, if not racist. This process gives the impression that with completion of the class, everyone will now understand the phenomenon of race or, perhaps, the most important way to understand race. This type of race talk is done without any thought to the process through which definitions were created; that is, one does not ask, "How was this version of race constructed?" Asking this question or raising this issue does not challenge the correctness or imply incorrectness of any existing way of understanding race.

Asking how a version of race was created elevates, in importance, the process through which the various racial theories were made to the level of the definitions themselves. That is to say, the perspective is as important as what is observed and understood with that perspective. So, the starting point of this book will introduce the process that comes before the actual teaching of the various racial theories. It is a small dip into the field of epistemology (the study of knowledge).

The reason for this approach is my own personal journey and struggle to understand race. It was a struggle to find the broadest understanding of race that could apply to all situations, particularly for me, this yellow author, who sometimes travels back to his "homeland" where yellow people are dominant and in positions of power. A narrow understanding of race can, at best, only be a step toward a better and more comprehensive understanding. To reach a broad understanding of race, a relentless line of questioning the "exception" or outlier must be pursued. This takes the individual to extremes, and to the extremes is where this class and book will go. A broad understanding of race is necessary to include everyone into the conversation of race where everyone's perspective or opinion is valid as a perspective and no one is left out of the conversation. A narrow presentation of race often excludes or marginalizes many people and, at the same time, a narrow vision of race will enable some to claim the irrelevance of race to their own lives.

So, though one might think that being a colored male in America is qualification enough to legitimize a particular perspective of race, a question arises that leads to still other questions: what is the relevance of this perspective to people who are colored differently? My own perspective of being Asian in America is clearly beneficial to myself; the benefits are not so apparent for others. I have struggled with this and other underlying questions that undermine narrow explanations of race, which would then challenge any supposed relationship established between race and poverty. What does my (yellow male) vision of my own life and experience in this American society contribute to a differently colored person's struggle with the same issues, let alone the same issues of another Asian male? How does understanding the perspective of an "angry Asian man" help a poor African-American woman? How does one avoid speaking/writing for one's own benefit and profit while disregarding the effect on the lives of others? How can one claim to speak for others who are living different lives? How do I know that my perspective of race does not contribute to the state of someone else's hardship or poverty? Is it possible for me to avoid increasing the suffering of others in order for me to get what I believe is my due? The framework of this class is driven by this desire to be broadly applicable and relevant, no matter one's racialized status. To reiterate, method must be discussed first; the method is an elaboration of *how* we are going to have our conversation about race in a way that is fair for everyone in the class. In other words, this class will teach an understanding of race through which all individuals benefit; it will not engage in the vilification of specific groups of people in order for them to be plundered for the benefit of others.

It must be stated emphatically and repeatedly that this approach does not seek to invalidate any existing specific race theory. Everyone has his/her own unique experience. The goal is to understand the vast complexity and diversity of voices in order to live together in peace, no matter one's perspective in life. Often race is taught as if students are ignorant of racial understanding or they must learn what is the right and wrong way of understanding race in order to live correctly. This approach necessarily results in discord and conflict as the intellectually privileged seek to educate the rest of society who are still living in ignorance; people must be taught and they must submit to that official information. Students who are taught this narrow process of understanding race are taught to identify racists in society; these are people who are wrong, in need of correction, and often despised for their ignorance and hateful, offensive speech. This approach does not result in peace. In a strange twist, though the intent of racial instruction was justice and peace, the result is increased conflict in society. The increase in conflict occurs because students are given license to hate and be intolerant to those identified as "wrong." It is similar to the rhetoric of "tolerance." Through the process of teaching tolerance, students are also taught what must not be tolerated; life is trouble-free as long as students obey the prescriptions of tolerance and have zero tolerance towards those identified as wrong.

TOO MUCH PRIOR KNOWLEDGE

The second reason race cannot be discussed just yet is because of "prior knowledge." All of the knowledge in our heads, learned consciously and unconsciously throughout our lives until this moment, can be considered prior knowledge; tomorrow, this knowledge also becomes part of one's prior knowledge. This prior knowledge is what we know, or what we think we know, about ourselves and the world in which we live. Of course, one's prior knowledge continues to grow as s/he continues to live and learn new information in new contexts. However, prior knowledge can often hinder the learning of new ideas and perspectives and lead to classroom situations where students talk past each other rather than learning constructive information. This is because, as will be discussed further in chapter 1, people often show bias in favor of their prior knowledge. Teaching a class on race can be an interesting experience, but more often, it can become a time for people to vent or express their own unanalyzed opinions to prove how wrong the opinions of others are. Venting opinions has value and there are venues for such an activity. However, in this course, students are required to first deconstruct their own opinions prior to expressing them. Students must first understand where their opinions originated and for what reason they were introduced to and taught those ideas. Most primary and secondary students are simply presented with a single point of view, which is also represented as fact, and so many are unaware of other different and legitimate perspectives. Chapter 2 and 3 explain the process of "making knowledge," which results in students challenging their own opinions, resulting in the formation of new and more complex opinions and learning to tolerate and understand the opinions of others. It is not unlike choosing a new car to buy. Everyone has a reason and preference for buying a particular car. Few people will confront strangers for not making the same choice they made.

As just stated, prior to forming independent opinions, students must first deconstruct their own existing opinions. This process of deconstruction can often be an uncomfortable experience because information once believed as fact by students is shown to be something less than fact. So, unlike other classes on race, where only some people get upset by the personal implications of the race theories taught in that class, this class will generally offend almost everyone as almost everyone's opinion is scrutinized. After all, it would be unfair to leave anyone unoffended; just think of it as a class with equal opportunity to be offended. Contrary to the conventional wisdom of today, being offended is not necessarily a bad thing; getting upset in this class is an indication of a learning moment. Rather than avoiding these uncomfortable situations, it is better to understand the reason for one's reactions. People often have been conditioned to think and react in certain ways throughout their educations. Individuals simply follow the script they were given, even if they do not recall when they were taught the components of the script.

Through the method of deconstruction, prior knowledge will be examined to expose knowledge assumed to be absolutely true (i.e., something which is true to everyone, everywhere, all the time). Examination of the sources of prior knowledge enables us to understand why certain knowledge was taught in the first place. During this process, biases are revealed. Exposing these biases and establishing a common ground for the entire class avoids much of the conflict often encountered in other race classes. Everyone has something to learn, and everyone can engage in self-reflection. This is important because we must try to avoid hypocrisy; that is, doing the very thing for which one condemns others. However, self-condemnation is not the goal of the class, either. Productive self-reflection should be our goal.

During my years of teaching deconstruction, students are often offended; however, it is generally short lived because this class does not necessarily require a change of opinion, belief, or lifestyle. Instead, students are challenged to always see a bigger picture of society and the potential in human action and creative free choice. The goal of this class is not to teach what is right or wrong. People are free to believe what they want, no matter what others may think or say, as long as they take responsibility for their beliefs. The goal of the class is also not to teach people how to be angry or how to coerce others into agreement, but to create a setting for learning and peaceful cohabitation.

I am a former angry Asian guy. Through my graduate study on race, I learned "race talk." However, by learning race talk I became hypersensitive to social dynamics; I could and can see racism everywhere, and it used to make me angry. I was angry over perceived racism, perceived discrimination, the injustice in the justice system, and angry because of the influence of race in my own life. My anger had gotten so bad that I once told a dear and close friend and his wife, in their own home, that they were racists. Being angry all the time is wasteful, unproductive, and tiring; it is also not good for one's personal life. Being angry all the time strains relations with those around him/her. So, how does one learn race without becoming an angry person? The broad understanding of race taught in this class liberates one from this anger and makes possible the opportunity for one to live a productive and happy life. It does not require that people ignore the race dynamics in society; rather by understanding race broadly, one develops tolerance for others, including for people we dislike.

EXPLAIN RACE FOR EVERYONE

The theory of race that will be used in this class is "Racial Formation," developed by Howard Winant and Michael Omi. Racial Formation is not simply a theory of race; it is a theory of race theory. It explains why there are so many race theories and why there will continue to be more. A highlight of this theory is that it does not demonize race as evil, nor does it try to reason away race as if life could be lived without racialization (ways of perceiving/making race); that is, we live through and in race. Everyone continually makes race and lives according to those racial constructions. Racial Formation does not prescribe a single racialization or way of thinking about race; it does not attempt to become the theory through which all race is understood. It does, however, enable students of race theory to understand race on a more significant level, even deeper than the level achieved by learning many different race theories. Racial Formation allows for an explanation of how race is made and used for the benefit of some and to the detriment of everyone else. Understanding race through Racial Formation changes the typical and often-heard conversation about the relationship between race and poverty today.

Through Racial Formation, it is apparent that there are an infinite number of ways to conceptualize and explain race. This is important as one realizes that there are far too many race theories than could be known and addressed through law and regulation. New racializations are continually signified and quickly forgotten. As long as there are people in the world, there will be race. Racial Formation explains not only the creation of race, but the spread of the ideas of race throughout society. It is a tool flexible enough to explain racial situations without the limitations of time and location. Racial Formation is the broad understanding of race that this book will use to achieve a productive conversation. A further benefit of using Racial Formation is the recognition of all racial groups, including and most importantly, the smallest of all racial categorizations: the individual. This book does not seek to pit one racial group against another; rather the goal is to protect all racial groups, especially the minority of the individual. If the minority of the individual is protected, then this person is free to live as she or he wishes as long as she or he does not actively interfere with the rights and lives of others.

In other words, most race theories have certain limitations in application geographically, culturally, chronologically, and even numerically. Through Racial Formation, everyone now has a stake in the learning of race theory and in understanding the way society and individuals use it. Understanding race on the deeper level enables students to be empowered in the writing of their own self-identities and self-contexts. Racial Formation recognizes the problems associated with generalizations and empowers people to move beyond those generalizations, not because society dictated or permitted it, but because the students understand how race works.

EXPLAIN POVERTY BROADLY

Poverty is a complex and persistent issue throughout human history. The causes and character of poverty are as diverse as the people who are identified as poor. Yet, much of the impression many people have of those living in poverty is barely more than a generalization; that is, poor people are poor, and they should not be poor. It is a generalization that is so thin that the interpretation of it changes depending on the person who imagines the poor people. This section of the book tries to move beyond superficial and stereotypical portrayals of the powerless and innocent, if not ignorant, poor. It also moves past this simple depiction and imagination of the poor to a critical economic understanding of the free market and its relationship with the phenomenon of poverty and wealth. Rather than assuming stereotypical generalizations, which give people the impression that they understand what it means to be poor, this course will emphasize critical thinking in order to begin to understand the causes and complex nature of poverty today. While it can be said that there is a relationship between race and poverty, this relationship cannot be fully explained through the typical understanding of race and racism.

Though the Scottish philosopher Thomas Carlyle in 1849 called economics a dismal science, a basic understanding of economics is necessary to move beyond reactionary and emotional subjective responses, typical of race and poverty discussions. Free market economics will be the focus through which the phenomenon of action and consequences will be discussed; the attempts to resolve poverty and their results will be discussed.

There is no single way through which all people become poor, nor is there a single prescription or law that would resolve poverty for everyone. Through a better understanding of human economic behavior, students will begin to see ways of empowering people living in poverty.

Understanding free market economics not only helps students understand poverty, but also helps students understand wealth. Wealth is also not as simple as many may think. For example, many people do not know that money has a price; there is such a thing as "expensive money" and "cheap money." The price of money is the interest rate; primarily the interest rate offered by banks and other lending and saving institutions is the price of the money at that lending institution. A high interest rate means that the money is expensive to borrow because one must pay back much more than one originally borrowed. A low interest rate means that the money is cheap to borrow because one pays back close to the amount one originally borrowed. Governments and banks often manipulate interest rates for their own benefit but to the detriment of the average citizen. By covering basic economic principles, this book attempts to move beyond the simple moralizing arguments that portray all poor people as innocent victims and all wealthy people as oppressors and greedy exploiters of the innocent; these generalized stereotypes do far more damage than most people realize. In other words, there may very well be evil rich people who plot and scheme to unjustly take from others. However, to impose this stereotype to all those identified as rich implicates wealthy people who are actively engaged in helping others through legitimate business practices. Furthermore, not all poor people are innocent victims of the plans of the evil rich.

Understanding free market economics also resolves the logical problem of helping the poor; eventually, it would be desirable for the poor to be wealthy. Does a person avoid being hated by the rest of society by remaining poor? Does a person have to accept the label of "greedy" if one is successful and wealthy? Perhaps it is better to say that everyone should have the freedom to live their lives in the manner of their choosing, as long as they do not harm others in the process. This does not exclude the possibility of being the wealthiest or poorest person in the world.

WHAT IS THIS BOOK TRYING TO ACHIEVE?

It has already been stated that the goal of the book is to equip students with the understanding of the making of and use of race theories to make better choices. Students will even be given an assignment to make a race. However, what are better choices? This book cannot answer that question for each student; the goal is that each student will be able to make those choices best suited for him- or herself and not according to the desires and goals of the instructor, or anyone else for that matter. It is not and should not be the responsibility of instructors to tell students how they should live their lives. If a life of sacrifice is desired by the student, then a life of sacrifice it is. However, a student choosing sacrifice has no right to disparage or criticize the one who chooses a life of luxury. Choices should be made freely, not through intimidation or coercion.

Through deconstruction and a broader understanding of race and poverty, this course strives to equip students to understand the traditional and prevalent assumptions concerning race to make different and more creative starting points that will result in a more realistic vision of society and ultimately lead to a more productive society. To reiterate, it is not about which racial assumption or even which race theory is right or wrong because the experiences of each student is unique to that student. Due to the uniqueness of the students and the context of their lives now and in the future, they should be able to analyze, understand, and adapt to whatever situation they find themselves in. The goal is for students to be creative in the ways of overcoming racism in society today. Students will be equipped to understand racial dynamics to make better decisions for themselves and their own futures according to the unique situations in which they exist. The goal is for students and readers to deconstruct their preferences and begin new trends and lines of thinking, if they so choose. Challenging one's own bias creates a type of independence that becomes hard to predict, particularly because individuals are no longer bound by over simplified explanations of race and poverty.

This independence from the status quo, on any level, cannot be achieved through social conditioning, censorship, or force. It is easy enough to talk about racism when the implications of it are diffuse and social action is optional, but no amount of privilege can keep everyone safe and protected everywhere, all of the time. Independence enables each student to adapt and continue in a personally positive direction when the eye of discrimination is directed at them.

WHAT COMES NEXT: A FORWARD-LOOKING SOCIETY WITHOUT COERCION AND HYPOCRISY

Winant and Omi said it best when they said that race is not necessarily a bad thing suitable only for the dustbin of society.[1] Chapters 6 and 7 will explain this further and show that race-making is really a form of identity construction. The identification of people through racial categories is the product of comparing the self with others, according to signified and prescribed ways of perception. Personally, I do not know how identity would be constructed without race. This also means that attempts to eradicate race as a concept is a narrow effort to eradicate specific racializations deemed inappropriate by certain individuals. Currently society teaches that only certain racial constructions are more important or more discriminatory than others from the infinite number of ways one can conceptualize race. Society reacts by passing legislation based on this narrow vision of the world. Rather than improving the racial dynamics in the world, this endeavor only incentivizes more legislation based on other perceived instances of discrimination. The use of law in this manner is the use of force or coercion. It is using the authority of law and the threat of penalty to coerce conformity and submission to specific narrow perceptions of the world. Banning or outlawing behavior and thought in this way, no matter the intent, simply criminalizes otherwise peaceful people in a very arbitrary way. The use of coercion in this manner to change what people believe has a poor track record of success; the drug war is an example of the failure of this type of coercion.

This endeavor should be reversed and rather than proposing restrictive legislation based on narrow, short sighted perspectives, students should be taught a broad understanding of race to understand that the forces of discrimination can be circumvented through other alternate racial perspectives. In this way, free choice and action are favored over methods of coercion. The resulting free society emphasizes personal responsibility and accountability within a framework of protection for the individual. As will be seen in chapters 9, 10, and 11, an interesting by-product of a free society is wealth. Understanding the place of race in society is the primary goal of this class, but by learning race, the persistent issues of poverty are also constructively addressed.

---

1   Michael Omi, Howard Winant, *Racial Formation in the United States: from the 1960's to the 1990's*, (New York: Routledge, 1994), 55.

INTRODUCTION TO THIS RACE AND POVERTY CLASS

1

GOAL
Prepare students to think differently

DIVERSITY OR SIMILARITY: DOES IT MATTER?

THE ASSUMPTION OF THIS CLASS is that, at this point, students are not ready to "talk race" as a class. Discussion about the relationship between race and poverty is difficult to make meaningful and productive. This chapter will try to set the tone for future discussions and prepare students to be able to talk race so that everyone will benefit from the conversation and this class and book.

Studying race at the college level presents a particular challenge because people with a variety of backgrounds, different levels of maturity, and different bodies of knowledge will attempt to talk about a very controversial and complex issue. A hurdle that must be overcome in order to talk race as a class is the information or knowledge students bring to the class. This body of knowledge was primarily acquired during students' primary and secondary education. Normally, and generally throughout society, education is considered to be a good thing; it is the most promoted way to improve one's lot in life. Thus, people are encouraged to attend schools to acquire more knowledge. The nature of this education and knowledge that students bring to this class or have when reading this book will be examined.

It is common to see a favorable emphasis on diversity in many schools today. When diversity is currently invoked, many assume the conversation is about racial diversity of some kind; diversity can also be interpreted geographically, by gender, by age, and by nationality—just to name a few. In spite of all the hype over a narrowly defined idea of diversity, this class would like to point out the way most students are similar to each other. The focus on diversity can cause students to miss the great similarity they share with each other. This similarity was taught or inculcated to most students through the American public education system prior to college.

While students were learning knowledge in elementary, junior, and senior high school, they were also being **socialized** to know, think, act, and believe in similar ways about a variety of issues to become citizens of the nation. In other words, students were not necessarily taught how to think independently; rather, they may have been socialized to think and understand things in the same way as other students in their classes. Students might have a hard time realizing this shared mentality amidst all the signified diversity. The U.S. school system has taught students how to identify, approach, and solve problems encountered in life. The result is a significant amount of consensus when discussing specific contemporary and historical social issues. This is advantageous for community life in which everyone gets along with each other because they hold the same values and speak the same language. However, this also gives students the impression that they are learning the truth or the only and right method of thinking and problem solving. In other words, it is difficult to think "outside of the box" when everyone is taught to think outside of the box in the same way. Have students even left the box? In order to think outside of the box, one must first know and see the box. This class and book will try to teach students how to see the box, after which they can decide whether they wish to stay in the box or leave it.

A couple of simple, non-scientific exercises will be conducted below to illustrate to students just how similar we are to each other in the way we think. Often, we make similar assumptions, and the way we interpret problems and generate conclusions or solutions are also similar. Take a look at the following series of three numbers, and guess what the next number in each sequence would be:

- 0, 1, 2, ?
- 2, 4, 6, ?
- 3, 5, 7, ?

The answers most often given are 3, 8, and 9. The third series of numbers appear to be a series of odd numbers; in that familiar pattern, the next number would be 9. However, the third series is also a series of prime numbers (numbers that can be divided evenly only by 1 and itself), thus making the next number in the sequence the next prime number, an 11. Focusing only on the result that almost all students will say "9," one could say that those who answered with "9" were taught to identify and solve this kind of problem in the same way. Individuals often make assumptions to make life a bit easier and to make decisions and choices quickly. In almost any given situation, as soon as one recognizes similarity with an already known problem or situation, the answer for the already known problem is offered as the solution for the current problem. It is rare for students in this example to ask for more information in the data set or to offer alternative solutions to a problem (e.g., "the answer could be either 9 or 11"). Students are generally not trained to think in this way.

Another example involves math expressions:

$$0 + 0 = ?$$
$$0 + 1 = ?$$
$$1 + 1 = ?$$

The answers given here are typically, 0, 1, and 2. However, the equations could also be in binary (a number system with only 0's and 1's), which makes the answer 10 instead of 2 for the third equation. What is recognized as a simple math equation may not be a simple math equation in the way we assume it to be. Our knowledge tells us that we recognize what we see and jump to a conclusion or response. In a similar way, when people encounter a situation they have been taught to recognize and identify in a particular way, most people automatically cruise in auto pilot and react in the way they were taught to react. If something perceived appears to be something signified as racist, then the individual automatically shifts into "I have to educate this racist" mode, the mode they were taught to have. These examples are simple thought exercises to illustrate how easily people can be mistaken in their understanding of various situations. People make this kind of mistake all the time; however, they generally do not consider this to be a problem or even consider why this happens.

To go further, not only do we share a similar body of knowledge, but we also share similar ignorance for the same reasons. Because most people in America in any given era have been socialized to think and know similar things, most people in America from the same era are ignorant of similar things. This **shared ignorance** and **shared knowledge** often contributes to the impression that everything that should be known is already known when, in fact, our knowledge is simply what *we* already know and is not the whole of relevant human knowledge. To illustrate this point is an exercise in which students must name the capital of the country in question:

- The United States of America: ?
- Mexico: ?
- Canada: ?

Perhaps distance from the Canadian border is a factor, but the overwhelming majority of students in any given semester cannot name Canada's capital; thankfully most were able to name Washington, D.C., and Mexico City as the capitals of the first two countries. Canada has the longest shared border with the U.S., and the U.S. only has two neighboring countries, yet usually over 90% of my students cannot name Ottawa as Canada's capital city. The explanation for this will not be addressed in this book. The relevant point is that just as many students will make the same mistake in recognizing an equation or problem, those same students will also be ignorant of choices or information that exists already. For example, many people in America believe the education system in America is one of the best in the world, but they do not understand why this may or may not be true. To be fair, most nations in the world can be found to have a similar phenomenon of shared ignorance and knowledge.

This ignorance is not restricted to knowing the capitals of the countries of the world. Our ignorance spills into many aspects of life, including, for example, energy issues. Most people are familiar with the problems of nuclear energy; the energy is relatively cheap and clean to produce, but there are many hazardous and toxic byproducts, and there are dangers in the process of using and disposing nuclear waste. Certainly if there was an alternative that had far fewer hazardous and toxic dangers, people would know about it, right? As a matter of fact, there is a material which is more plentiful, cheaper, and safer than and almost as productive as uranium; it is thorium. The ignorance concerning thorium is likely not accidental; rather, it is highly probable that those people who profit from the use of uranium-based technology lobby heavily to promote the use of uranium while at the same time try to squash the information concerning thorium. The issue is money and people in the uranium camp stand to lose their wealth, power, and influence if the world switched to thorium. The resulting common ignorance and knowledge shapes the debate over nuclear energy. The debate becomes a matter of: should uranium-based nuclear power plants be used or not; or, how can we make the uranium-based power plants safer? Simply switching to thorium-based power plants is often not discussed. The flow and spread of information is as important as what is being promoted throughout society and by whom.[1]

BARRIER TO LEARNING SOMETHING NEW

The problem of common knowledge and ignorance is that it becomes a barrier to learning something new and different. Our knowledge coupled with our ignorance creates a bias and prejudice because one assumes to know the truth already; further learning is not necessary. Prior knowledge hampers attempts at entertaining alternative solutions, explanations, and ideas. When I was in elementary school, a brain teaser that would stump everyone posited that a boy and his father had been rushed to an emergency room because of a bad traffic accident. The doctor on duty is shocked and cannot operate on the boy because the boy is the doctor's son. So, who is the doctor? Most of us, at the time, instinctively replied "the father" only to be reminded that the father was a patient, too. We were stumped until we were told that the doctor was the child's mother. The inability to entertain the logical solution (for the time) is indicative of the problems of prior knowledge. For some reason, it was difficult to imagine a woman as a doctor in an emergency room in the 1970s. We could not get to the answer because of our bias and prejudice, in spite of the obvious nature of the answer. Today, of course, the possible answers have increased, but the point remains. One can see the same thing today when it comes to racial issues and questions. Questions that are easily answered become difficult when a color qualifier is added. For example, the question, "How do people move into affluent neighborhoods?" would be answered by, "People have enough money to buy a house in affluent neighborhoods." The same question except with a color qualifier would look like this: "How do black people move into an affluent neighborhood?" Every time this question is asked in class, I get crickets; that is, silence. The answer is, of course, the same, but the situation is complicated by many of the student's preconceived notions concerning race and wealth.

---

1   There are other directions and paths of discussion one could take in the energy debate that are equally not widely known, such as recycling "spent" uranium, as is done all over Europe; or the invention of the artificial leaf by Professor Daniel Nocera of MIT in 2008; or the ability to convert CO_2 emissions to electricity and water by Bert Hamelers and his team of researchers in the Netherlands. All three of these options are potentially far more inexpensive than the options currently pursued, which would have a direct impact on issues of poverty.

Another problem-solving brainteaser is the example of four people who need to cross a bridge in 17 minutes at night with only one flashlight. The bridge can only support the weight of two people, which means two people cross, and one person *must come back* with the flashlight. Each person crosses the bridge at different speeds; one person can cross in 1 minute, another in 2 minutes, the third in 5 minutes, and the last in 10 minutes. When two people cross the bridge they must travel at the speed of the slower person. When the person returns with the flashlight, do not forget to add the time it takes for that person to re-cross the bridge! They must cross the bridge before it collapses in 17 minutes. What is the order and pairing they must take in order to cross the bridge before it collapses?

Most students pair the fastest person with each of the other people; 1 and 10 first, then 1 re-crosses the bridge; 1 and 5 cross and again 1 re-crosses the bridge, and finally 1 and 2 make the trip over the bridge; but this requires 19 minutes. These same students often rearrange the order of the pairs, but the time required is still 19 minutes. The solution is quite simple: 1 and 2 go over first, then 1 comes back; then, 5 and 10 go over, and 2 comes back; then, 1 and 2 cross over for the last trip; this totals 17 minutes. Being stumped or requiring a large amount of time to figure this out is an indication of how difficult it is for most people to propose alternative solutions to the same problem. Race is the "problem" for this class this semester.

We must realize that consensus is not a sign of being correct or a sign of knowing what needs to be known. Just because everyone around you might agree with you does not make your opinion the correct one; one is simply perceived as not being the odd one out. Majority does not dictate truth; rather, it is just an opinion, which could be wrong. Socializing through education may produce some degree of consensus but it does not ensure understanding of complex issues which life brings to attention.

To understand "race" as presented in this class, students will be asked to put aside their socialized opinions and beliefs to entertain alternative ideas. They will be asked to think critically about all of their socialization up to this point. Though this is often encouraged in classrooms in universities, it is required in a race class. In other words, this class and book will challenge students to go radical, go to the root of their prior knowledge, and sometimes, to start the learning process all over again. It has the potential to be disorienting.

To illustrate, look at Figure 1-1.

If one had to describe the sculpture in the picture, what would people say? What do you say? Imagine that this sculpture is the object of study in some science or humanities class in the university. When it is not recognized, there is nothing with which people can relate the object, people fall back on their training and give simple descriptions with the impression that they are being accurate, that they are producing facts. However, this sculpture, by John V. Muntean (www.jvmuntean.com), is meant to be appreciated or "interpreted" by shining a light onto the sculpture in just the right angle so that people may observe the shadow it casts. When rotated with a fixed light source, the same sculpture will cast a different shadow, making three images in all; it is a 3-in-1 shadow sculpture (see figure 1-2).

FIGURE 1-1 How would you describe the object in this picture?

The point here is that basic observation and reporting may not be enough when studying something like race. Sometimes, the way to understand something complex is to do something complex. Our society's desire to reduce and essentialize extends into issues like race. One must also not confuse detail and depth of description with understanding. This class will seek to challenge students and teach them how to look at things from a different perspective to understand just how complex, uncontrollable, and unpredictable life can be. Students can continue to believe what they want to believe and continue viewing things from their comfort zone, if they choose; however, students should take care when critiquing the opinions and views of others. Things might not be as they appear, and there may even be a better way of understanding what we observe and think is true.

FIGURE 1-2 Sometimes understanding an object requires more than simple empirical description.

SUMMARY

Students are encouraged to consider that their prior knowledge may not be much more than simple socialization. This means that students may not be able to think critically in the way that is necessary to understand race today. Understanding that prior knowledge may not be the truth will enable students to overcome their knowledge bias and learn new information, especially concerning issues of race. Phenomena that were thought to be understood completely already may only be a part of what can be known.

QUESTIONS FOR FURTHER THOUGHT

1. How emotionally difficult do you think it will be to have your personal beliefs challenged?

2. How comfortable and patient are you when listening to another's perspective that you believe is completely wrong?

3. How do you approach someone who thinks she or he knows the right answer already when it may just be one of many possible answers?

PRIOR KNOWLEDGE AND PERSPECTIVE

2

GOAL

Learning that our knowledge is all based on perspective

PRIOR KNOWLEDGE

T HE PREVIOUS CHAPTER explained that education at the primary and secondary level was socialization, or education on how to behave and think in class and society. Public school education socializes students as much as it teaches information. The result of going through a standardized curriculum is that Americans have a large body of shared knowledge and ignorance. Citizens of the same country will generally believe similar things because of similar training, education, and socialization. Everything that students have learned up to this moment can be considered **prior knowledge**. This knowledge includes life and personal experiences, emotions, observations, and any formal education received over the years. Though knowledge is generally thought to be a good thing, students seeking to acquire more must always have an open mind, especially towards information which conflicts with information already learned.

People use their prior knowledge all the time to make decisions and choices, from the simple to the complex (e.g., Should I go left or right? Should I wear this or that? Should I eat this or that? Should I vote this way or that way?). Though not often considered, most people prefer their own prior knowledge because it was learned first. Because the prior knowledge got into people's heads first, it holds a type of superiority or advantage over new information. People are biased and prefer or defer to that prior knowledge. Prior knowledge is comfortable and familiar, and most people are adjusted and adapted to their prior knowledge.

Prior knowledge has little to do with what is actually right or wrong and true or false; it is simply information learned first by any given individual. So, even if someone were to hear information that is better than what is already known, the tendency is to prefer the prior knowledge for the reasons stated above. Rejecting new, and possibly better, knowledge means no change is required in a person's life because life is still understood in the same way. If one were to accept new knowledge, then other things in an individual's life might have to change, as well. For example, if one were to find out that one's best friend was lying, believing that information could require finding a new best friend; rejecting or de-signifying that information would require no change. Hearing new and different information results in a battle or a conflict in our heads; a war of sorts ensues over what to believe and what to reject. One has to weigh the benefits of adopting new knowledge against the changes required by rejecting old knowledge.

It is difficult to predict what information will be maintained by an individual; there are many factors involved as the struggle plays out. The knowledge that eventually becomes the winner of this battle is what is used for future decisions and choices. Even then there is no guarantee that the information will be used in a consistent manner.

UNDERSTANDING PERSPECTIVE

"Deconstruction" will be the tool used to minimize the conflict that arises when encountering new information. Deconstruction itself will be explained in further detail in the next chapter. For now, students must realize that the truth they believe as fact is simply a matter of **perspective**. Perspective is the individual's point of view (the subject's point of view), what is seen by someone in one position or location looking at something else. Different people in even slightly different positions or locations looking at the same thing will have different perspectives. What is viewed by the subject is an **object**. Objects are the things, information and events we study, analyze, and try to understand. They are generally something seen through our eyes. From a different perspective, the viewed object will appear different.

The process of deconstruction examines the perspective of knowledge; it is simply a way of examining, determining, and understanding what

FIGURE **2-1** What is the color of the paper shown in this picture?

perspective is being used when making knowledge. Explained this way, one realizes that disagreement could be a conflict of perspectives rather than information. If everyone had the same information with the same perspective, there would only be agreement and consensus.

We will now conduct a simple example to illustrate the basic problem of subjectivity. Look at the picture in Figure 2-1.

What color do you see in the picture? Suppose I ask students to describe what they have seen and share that information by writing a paper for publication. The papers the students write will describe a blue-colored paper. This particular piece of paper has a different color on each side; one side is blue and the other is white. Figure 2-2 depicts what I saw when looking at the back side of the paper.

If I were to read the papers students wrote and write a response, I would write that the color was not blue but was, in fact, white. This illustrates **subjectivity**. Subjectivity can be defined simply as the perspective of the one performing the observation and reporting; it implies a specific position when viewing an object. If two people are looking at the same object, and each person is located in two different locations, then the difference in

FIGURE **2-2** The same piece of paper seen in Figure 2-1, but from a different perspective: the reverse side.

location is what gives rise to difference in observation or simply subjectivity; different perspectives of the same object yield different observations and reports. The position of the subject when looking at an object determines what is seen. The information produced from that position or perspective is **subjective knowledge**, or knowledge from a specific subjective point of view. Information is often true from a single perspective; change the perspective, and the knowledge and its truth value changes, too.

What is seen by someone from a perspective is empirically obvious; that is, what is observed and reported can easily be verified by experience or simple observation and even by scientific research or experiment. This simple verification process creates reluctance for that person to listen and take seriously the observations of another person, who has a different perspective. Most people do not give much thought to perspective because most people have been trained to think in terms of right and wrong or in terms of true and false. Teaching information in the framework of right and wrong implies and assumes that there is only one legitimate perspective; the idea that there could be other perspectives is not raised and discussed.

If this were an academic debate and the piece of paper represented race, people would say things like: "I was there, I know what I saw. My perspective and voice matters more than yours." And when debate fails, people in the debate resort to attempts to discredit opposing perspectives. Often the accusation of "racist" is heard at this point. This type of impasse is a phenomenon in many classes in many departments where there are competing theories of understanding. Upper-level science classes also have this type of subjective problem. That is, differences in perspective exist in the sciences, as well, in spite of its emphasis on being objective (e.g., not everyone agrees that string theory is the next step for cosmology). Because of subjectivity, even scientific knowledge cannot claim "fact" status, or the status of being true to everyone, all the time, no matter one's perspective. Science is not free from the politicization of knowledge.

THE SUBJECTIVE TRUTH ABOUT TRUTH

Given this example of the two-sided piece of paper, we should take note of a couple of basic ideas that can be learned regarding knowledge or truth, in general. Usually, a person cannot see *every* detail from any given single perspective; however, most objects can be viewed from multiple perspectives. A person can only write from his or her perspective, conveying what one observes and already believes is significant; the subject uses the framework or thinking patterns she or he has been trained to use by schools and educators.

Limitation of observation is not just a result of perspective. Not only are students taught what and how to think, students are also taught what to notice or **signify**. To signify, or signification, is to point something out or teach something that makes that object or detail seem important or relevant. During the learning process, students are taught to pay close attention to certain details, which coincidentally results in students ignoring other details. The very process of the scientific method pre-determines what is and what is not important; the hypothesis dictates what is significant and what is not. Science has taught us to focus only on what is understood to be important and relevant while ignoring everything else. In the case of the paper, discussion has revolved around the color of the paper, and nothing has been said about the shape or size of the paper.

To be fair, in most cases, determining what to observe and what not to observe has a practical aspect; studies and research would be unmanageable

if the amount of information was too large or if there are too many variables. Though in some areas of higher math, more information is better,
the restriction and predetermination of variables for specific study allows
observers to be selective and biased in their study, whether intentionally or
unintentionally.

A simple way to understand this is if someone were asked to describe
a mutual friend, the details they include and the order in which they provide the information is a clue to what the speaker thinks is an important
characteristic and what the speaker does not think is an important characteristic. Descriptions reveal the details that a person notices or signifies in a friend or when observing someone else. Sometimes people are
aware of the significance of order and change the order they list, so that
they do not appear superficial in the description of others. What is interesting is that different people will describe the same person differently
because they notice or signify different things; the signified features are
important to that describer. In fact, if details are not important to the
describer, those details will not be noticed and, thus, will not be included
in the description; those details are not significant to the observer.

An object can be seen in different ways by different people depending
on their perspectives. The information produced by an observer is a matter
of perspective, and the disagreements people have with one another could
be explained by this difference in perspective. People even express this by
saying, "I don't see it that way." What people see when they look at the
same object can be different from person to person. The more complex the
object observed is, the greater the chance that observations and reports
will be different from each other because there are more features to select
for signification and more features to ignore.

Something else that can be learned from the two-sided paper example is that things are probably more complicated than they appear. The
example of the two-sided paper is simple to resolve, since it only has
two sides. However, life is much more complicated than this. Society,
climate change, life, race, poverty—these things are much more complex, and yet, knowledge producers essentialize and reduce things to
simple explanations. The problem is that simplification distorts the
perception of the world around us. Also, oversimplification could happen for a less noble reason. By narrowing the discussion to a single
perspective instead of acknowledging the many possible perspectives,
it is easier to persuade others to agree with what appears to be the only
valid perspective, though it will continue to simply be one perspective
among many. In other words, people share observations with others

to persuade and convince them to see things in the same way, the way the persuader sees things. This is normal; however, students and teachers must be fully aware that there are other perspectives, other legitimate perspectives, which can produce different information and result in different opinions and choices. Revisionist history, that is, looking at past events again, is an example of how a different perspective can produce different information and a different interpretation of past events. It is often the case that the new interpretation hardly resembles the old knowledge produced from earlier perspectives.

Opinions are simply expressions of one's prior knowledge, things other people have taught, which the student has learned over the years. Without knowing from where much of the information has come, many people will repeat things that may appear profound or that seem appropriate for that moment. For this reason, opinions are not applicable to this course; questions are fine, questions from subjective points of view are also fine; but opinions offered as facts are not to be considered "absolute truth;" it is all simply subjective perspectives.

For this class and for the specific task of learning deconstruction, **what** a student believes is not nearly as interesting as **why** a student believes what he or she believes. What a student believes will be dependent on the perspective that student takes; once the perspective is determined, the opinions expressed with that perspective are generally predictable. More interesting would be the reason for taking one perspective over another. In other words, the choosing of perspective may be more informative than the predictable opinions that are expressed from a particular perspective. The tool of deconstruction will bring out and try to reveal the perspective of the information that people learn. For the class and class discussion, opinions from prior knowledge will be de-signified because that prior knowledge is likely to be subjective knowledge or knowledge from a narrow perspective that can impede learning something different. The goal is for students to be empowered to make statements from their own perspective while being open to all other perspectives.

In order to do this, this class strives to teach a different perspective that all students can use with little effort and with little requirement to change already existing personal beliefs. The class will try to teach a method that puts everyone on the same page and does not prioritize any subjective point of view that would put everyone with a different perspective at a disadvantage, and it will try to consider all possible perspectives at the same time. Once the class is dismissed, what students do with that knowledge is their choice. As was said before, this class does not seek to dictate or prescribe what students should do with their lives or the choices they should make. Rather, it seeks to enable students to make decisions that are the best for them after considering risk factors and accepting responsibility for whatever might happen because of those choices. Education should not be about doing what the instructor says is the right thing to do. The information taught may or may not actually be beneficial to all students. It is more important that students learn how to make decisions and choices for themselves for their own benefit. For example, those choices can be for a life of charity and sacrifice or for a life of obscene wealth. It is for the student to decide.

To explain what is meant by "information taught may or may not actually be beneficial to all students," here is an example. When I was a graduate student studying scholarship written about Koreans in the U.S., I tried very hard to gauge where I was, relative to the prescriptions and descriptions of the authors. Much of what I read described what Koreans had to do in order to become American. Often, steps were described and explained; the process of becoming an American was detailed so that one could follow along and figure out where one was in that process of Americanization, how far along one was, how much further did one have to go, what tasks remained in order to achieve assimilation to American life and finally become American.

I realized that, though I read those books to help improve my life, I was merely making my life more difficult (miserable). The books and articles talked about Koreans generally, which meant I could relate to the information because I was of Korean descent, too. However, the details of the people in the books were not exactly the same as my own personal situation. This meant I had to adjust the prescriptions in the book to somehow make them work in my own life, but the prescriptions never worked. The information in those books not only saw different things, but it also interpreted what was seen differently. This resulted in different goals and expected outcomes, none of which were what I desired for myself.

To resolve this, I had to write, for myself, an analysis and assessment of my own personal situation with my own perspective. This is not to say that the scholarship I read previously was wrong, but rather that those books did not have my perspective and, therefore, did not "fit" my life. Sometimes, someone else's perspective may help us to get where we want or teach us to notice different things in our lives; however, that information was originally made for someone else. Students can decide to live the lives others believe is right or students can figure out their own unique take on life and then live it. The books of other writers are fantastic and wonderful starting points but should never be considered comprehensive and final. In fact, learning about oneself and where one fits in society is ever-changing because we and society are always changing. Life is dynamic, so the way we live and adapt to that life should also be just as dynamic; it should not be entirely dictated by the pages of a book written from a perspective that may no longer exist.

POLITICIZE MUCH?

Politics is the effort to persuade others to agree with one's perspective for the purpose of gaining power or influence or to execute a plan against the plans and efforts of others. Learning and teaching is a highly political activity. In the absence of absolutes (as in the discourse that uses deconstruction), there is only politics of persuasion to garner agreement and consensus. Which perspective should be used, reproduced, taught, and learned is a matter of politics. Political exercises occur in our heads as well as society.

For every view on a particular matter, there are different and opposing views. Any view or issue in education is a political matter. However, many classrooms present information simply as fact, as if there are no politics in that information; it is as if there is universal consensus on what is wrong and right. The absence of obvious politics in the learning process does not mean there is a clear right and wrong. Rather, it is likely that the political engagement already occurred in the past and has been forgotten. History is an example of this phenomenon where only the perspective, opinion, and beliefs of the winners of wars are valid. Citizens who are born after a particular war are taught only the ideology and interpretations of the winner of that war, not all of the competing ideas that existed before the war. To assist in the erasing of the political nature of information, society often destroys public evidence (statues, monuments, etc.) of those opposing views. This phenomenon also exists in and extends to the war of ideas.

One might feel uncomfortable with invoking politics here, but the struggle for dominance in society and in our heads often has little to do with right and wrong; the struggle for dominance is about "more beneficial and less beneficial." Representing a perspective as the right and only perspective is a highly political activity, one that may not have the best interests of individual students in mind.

It is important to note this political aspect of life because of what is at stake: the potential gain or loss of power, comfort, beliefs, and personal identity. For this reason, the process of deconstruction is eventually offensive to everyone. But remember, it is simply a way to reveal the perspective of one's prior knowledge; what becomes invalid for one person may be affirmed for another. Deconstruction is a tool for students to add a layer of critique when judging whether to accept or reject old and/or new knowledge. Deconstruction does not necessarily determine what is right and wrong.

SUMMARY

Our prior knowledge is a blessing and curse. We need it to make decisions all the time, but it hinders learning new, potentially better, knowledge. Students are challenged to consider that all of their knowledge is simply perspective, rather than seeing knowledge in terms of right and wrong; that is, they should entertain the idea that what is considered truth is just subjective truth or truth from a perspective. If perspective is changed, then knowledge, or what is considered truth, also changes. In order to create the perception of fact or truth, people engage in political activity to persuade others to agree.

QUESTIONS FOR DISCUSSION

1. Try to state why you make the decisions you make. What personal belief or value is reflected in the decision and choices you make? For example, why did you wear that shirt today? Why did you take the route you took to school or class? Why did you buy from that coffee store and not this one?

2. Try to ask several friends, one at a time, separately, to describe someone you all know. Note how the descriptions are different from person to person. What might this say about the values of the person giving the description?

3. How do you feel about the possibility that everything you believe is absolutely true might only be subjectively true?

4. Have you ever considered that you believe the things you believe because it is convenient or somehow to your advantage to believe that way and NOT because it is "true?"

KNOWLEDGE PRODUCTION 3

GOAL

Understand that knowledge is made, not discovered

MAKING KNOWLEDGE, NOT DISCOVERING FACTS

KNOWLEDGE DOES NOT SUDDENLY APPEAR in books without an author, a subjective source. Knowledge is made by people who observe things, draw conclusions, and then report or share their observations with others using prior knowledge as a reference. The bulk of knowledge is made through this basic process of **knowledge production**. Knowledge is not discovered in the sense that people do not suddenly find knowledge in the way that one finds gold. Knowledge producers make knowledge, and everyone can be considered knowledge producers on some level. This book is an example of knowledge production.

In a broad sense we are all knowledge producers; when people post on a blog, describe a movie they have seen to friends, name a child, or tell stories of events which occurred during a vacation, people are engaging in knowledge production. There are more formal and accredited forms of knowledge production that occur in universities and schools; these kinds of knowledge production generally yield what most people consider facts. Students are knowledge producers in training. Knowledge producing experts (instructors) train students in the art of knowledge production. From a very young age, students are taught what and how to observe, how to record their observations, and how to make reports. If one goes to graduate school to obtain a Ph.D., one receives basically a license to make knowledge independently with the authority and credentials to prove it.

The process of making knowledge can be illustrated by the simple sentence:

John sees the girl.
Subject   Object

"John" is the subject of the sentence, and he is looking at the "girl," which is the object. One might say that much university activity is summed up in this sentence: **Subjects** look at objects. People study objects, and then they write about them, and many times, that information is then shared; this is the process of making knowledge. So, for the most part, knowledge is based on things people have seen. Education is simply remembering the observations of others. To take John's perspective is to be subjective, the perspective of the subject. To be the girl is to be objective, for the purposes of this book. This is not the same as taking the object's point of view because if the girl looks at John, the girl is now the subject looking at an object, which is John.

The goal of observing is to understand and know the object through observation and study. Objects can be anything that is observed and studied by a subject; objects can be material and immaterial things. Science teaches us how to be objective as if it were actually possible. It also teaches that observers must record observations without emotion and opinions; science also operates under the belief that there is objective information, or facts. However, objects are seen from a perspective by a subject. So, though some disciplines claim that their methods are objective, it is easy to see through this simple sentence that knowledge is produced from the perspective of the subject, and the knowledge that is produced is subjective knowledge, rather than objective knowledge.

Absolute knowledge is the knowledge which is produced when observing an **absolute**; an absolute is an object which when observed is observed and seen in the same way by everyone, anywhere, at any time. So, the knowledge that is produced will always be the same. Changing perspective does not change the absolute character and knowledge concerning the absolute object. In this class it is assumed that there is no absolute knowledge. Keep in mind that for individuals in their everyday lives, there will be perceived absolutes, but they will not be universal to everyone else. In other words, for the sake of argument and discussion, it is assumed that everyone sees objects from their own unique perspective that will generate unique observations and interpretations. It is for this reason that postmodernist deconstruction itself is subjective knowledge production; this process of critique does not produce absolute truth but is helpful as a system of analysis.

Science and other areas of knowledge production in the university often ignore the subject and pretend that it is not there making the observations and producing the knowledge. This is partly achieved by standardizing the process through which knowledge is made. This creates the impression that students are making and learning facts or the truth. This approach also creates the impression that knowledge is discovered. For example, Albert Einstein did not look up into the sky and see "$E = mc^2$" (his theory of relativity) written in the stars. Because of the issues and problems he was pondering at the time, he made that expression using his prior knowledge to explain what he observed. Buddhists in Asia at the same time would likely not have produced "$E = mc^2$," not because they are dull, but because the questions they were asking, their prior knowledge, did not concern relativity. What they saw was interpreted through what they already knew, in a way that answered the questions they were asking. Their perspective was fundamentally different from that of Einstein. They were not concerned about the relative movement of stars in the way that Einstein was.

One should note that deconstruction does not help one decide which knowledge production is right or wrong, better or worse, productive or unproductive. This approach merely points out that all knowledge is made from a perspective, and when viewed and understood from that perspective, that knowledge is considered true. Different perspectives of the same object will yield different knowledge and different truths. For example, July 4th, 1776 is Independence Day in the U.S. However, in England, July 4th was the day the colonies seceded.

Forgetting that knowledge is made allows people to be dogmatic and intolerant of the ideas of others. The temptation to think one's own knowledge is true while the knowledge of others is subjective is great. It is for this reason students are reminded that though they might be tempted to be offended by the process of deconstruction, they must remember that it is all simply the revealing of perspective.

CONSTRUCTS

When knowledge is made, it is produced in the form of **constructs**. Theories, books, journals, magazines, TV shows, movies, advertisements, and ideas, as well as cars, buildings, and Legos are all constructs; that is, they were all made. Knowledge is taught to and learned by students in the form of constructs.

From the view of deconstruction, because knowledge is constructed from a perspective, it is never neutral and never absolute; it is always subjective. Calling knowledge fact or truth is possible only within the perspective of the original production. Knowledge is always produced and spread with an intent or goal of usage in mind. At the very least, knowledge was made to explain something that was observed for those who are interested. As a hammer was invented for a purpose, knowledge is made with a purpose. The saying "necessity is the mother of invention" describes this phenomenon where a need sparks the development of a method or tool to address that need. To put it in another way, normally someone does not make a hammer and then try to find a use for it; the use comes first and the tool is created to fulfill that use. Once the hammer is made, it can be adapted or used for other jobs and purposes. Knowledge is made because there is a need, use, and function for that knowledge. Notably, produced knowledge can be adapted and used for other purposes. The construct of race was made to explain something that was observed. It was made to teach others to see the same phenomenon the original knowledge producer saw in the way she or he saw it. Different people will observe and make knowledge about race, for example, and the content of that knowledge will be different according to the producer.

Though race is constructed, it does not mean that race does not exist. It is something that many people see, observe, and strive to understand. Declaring and pretending that race is not there does not make it go away or make it insignificant; knowledge producers of race are simply explaining what they see from their perspectives.

KNOWLEDGE PRODUCTION

Knowledge is constantly being made by everyone in one form or another, as mentioned above. People make knowledge for their specific needs at any given moment. As people live their lives they observe and interpret everything around them to make decisions and choices; they are making knowledge continuously for personal use. Sometimes others are interested in what other people think and believe because the knowledge of those other people seems to be better than what they have produced. In other words, our own knowledge-producing ability can sometimes not be up to the challenge of understanding certain situations and objects adequately to make a good choice.

In contemporary society, there are knowledge producers and knowledge users. As in the hammer example, the use of a hammer comes first, for which the hammer is made. Likewise, when there is a need for knowledge, knowledge is made. Of all the knowledge that is made, normally the knowledge that is most profitable and beneficial to others is the knowledge that is spread and used by many. If someone benefits from a piece of knowledge, then that knowledge is spread as truth. To repeat, everyone is a knowledge producer of some sort with various levels of skill. Knowledge that may be beneficial to others can be sold and marketed in different ways, e.g. through internships, schools, and books. Knowledge that is deemed unbeneficial by most is not spread and shared throughout society; people would not learn that knowledge even if it were free. People must feel that they have gained some sort of benefit to learn and live by newly produced knowledge.

Not all knowledge produced becomes knowledge others want to learn, for whatever reason. One might make a comparison with inventions or the research and development departments of large companies. People are always inventing new and wonderful things. Not all of those inventions are known or even used by others. Useful knowledge is made known and spread by word of mouth because of its usefulness. There are many groups of people who desire knowledge in order to do something; often that "something" involves making money. Because of the socially established beliefs regarding scientific knowledge production, people have adapted and modified the knowledge-producing process in a way to tailor make knowledge to legitimize or support a subjective point of view.

For example, driving in a car one day, the author heard on the radio news of a recent scientific study that detailed the benefits of drinking coffee. Not long after this report, he heard the same DJ announce a new scientific study about the benefits of drinking tea. This made the author suspicious enough to wonder, who goes to college to run up student loan debt to pursue a lifelong dream to study coffee or tea? If we could interview the scientist who did this scientific study while she or he was still in college, this scientist would probably not say that she or he is taking upper level chemistry classes to study the benefits of drinking coffee after graduation. It is more likely that this student majored in chemistry, was unemployed around the time of graduation, and saw an ad in the newspaper for a company (maybe even the Institute for Scientific Information on Coffee, www.coffeeandhealth.org, which produced the report originally heard by this author regarding coffee), looking for scientists to conduct not just research studies on coffee but research to find *favorable* information regarding coffee consumption. Faced with the choice of continued unemployment or researching coffee for a few years to earn a wage, the graduate would probably apply for the job, and knowledge would be made.

In this particular example of coffee knowledge production, information that provides support for drinking coffee will likely be used. If the scientist concluded that there were no benefits to drinking coffee, that information would likely be discarded; the point of hiring those scientists was to produce favorable information according to the subjective view of the coffee companies. It is well known that the tobacco companies have done this in their business history, too. Only the information produced by the scientists who said that smoking was safe was shared with the public. Can it be said that those scientists were going against their training by reporting their observations inaccurately? Perhaps, but tobacco scientists were producing information from the perspective of the tobacco companies; their job was to make information favorable for continued smoking. These examples should illustrate that using science does not resolve the problem of subjectivity and subjective truth.

This is not to say that all knowledge producers simply sell themselves to the highest bidder. On the contrary, knowledge producers who do have a problem with the sources of certain funding will not apply or accept funding. Nevertheless, funding plays an important role in the determination of what knowledge is produced and shared with others. Gatekeepers of official knowledge production use their prior knowledge to determine what information is published or not. Scientists themselves are also vulnerable to politics, wealth, and prestige because they are human.

The point is that, often, the motivation or agenda that drives particular knowledge production is hidden from view. Knowledge is presented as fact. Even the word "scientific" is often intended to signal accuracy and truth to the listener/reader so that the information is simply believed. Deconstruction must be learned to help decide whether one will subscribe to or go along with particular discourses of knowledge production.[1]

---

1 "**Bootleggers and Baptists**" is an expression coined by Bruce Yandle in 1983 to describe the unwitting alliance of seemingly opposing groups to get certain

The benefit of all this is that, if we accept that knowledge is made from a perspective with intent and agenda, students, and people in general can become open to critiquing their own prior knowledge and all new knowledge. One must be willing to examine one's own prior knowledge with the scrutiny of deconstruction to understand the resistance to learning something new and different. Upon understanding this bias and resistance, students may be better equipped to make decisions and choices that are beneficial to that student, rather than making choices that would be less beneficial and likely be to the benefit of others.

SUMMARY

Knowledge is made, not discovered. Knowledge is made in the form of constructs. Knowledge is made to be used and is biased, subjective, and has agenda. Because knowledge is biased, it is in the interest of the student to know what perspective was used to create that knowledge. This is important because people can be paid to make knowledge for the purpose of making money, which may not be to the benefit of the knowledge learner.

QUESTIONS FOR DISCUSSION

1. How might the construct of knowledge production affect the understanding of religion?

2. The concepts of right and wrong and true and false are challenged through deconstruction. How might this affect the way we interact with others, particularly people who do not share our perspective and values?

---

legislation passed through Congress. Support for prohibition came from Baptist Christians who wanted alcohol banned for religious reasons and from bootleggers whose livelihood was made possible by the 21st Amendment.

DECONSTRUCTION 4

GOAL
Evaluate produced knowledge to better understand
the subjectivity of that knowledge

THE PREVIOUS CHAPTER discussed how knowledge is made and some of the implications of knowledge production. Because knowledge is made and not discovered, knowledge is subjective and made with an agenda that benefits the people who made that knowledge and share that perspective. People may like what they are learning, but there is no guarantee that the given knowledge is best for the one learning it. This is because there may be other knowledge constructs that may yield more benefits for those same learners.

Facts are facts and truths are truths only within a perspective; if the perspective changes, so does the character of those same facts and truths. Thus, all knowledge is only subjectively true in this discussion of deconstruction. It is often the case that knowledge producers master the knowledge from a particular perspective, but that knowledge becomes irrelevant to someone with a different perspective; recall the example of the two-sided piece of paper. This also makes the entire "fact checking" phenomenon one sees in politics very curious. One might imagine a playground full of children yelling to each other that their facts are better than the other children's facts.

Because the absolute nature of knowledge is undermined, it is harder to claim knowledge of the truth when there are many competing truths in the world of knowledge. However, as has already been said, knowledge is often represented as having been discovered, which hides the subjective nature of its production; it is taught as true, rather than as subjective. Opinions become facts, and perspectives become absolutes. In light of this, the questions become: if other perspectives have the same legitimacy as the perspectives of one's prior knowledge, how does one decide and assess the value of the various knowledge productions; and if current available knowledge is not beneficial to the learner, then how does one find knowledge that is more beneficial to the learner?

DECONSTRUCTION

Deconstruction is the process of taking apart constructs (chapter 3). Understanding the subjective nature of knowledge requires taking that knowledge apart, or deconstructing it, to see how it was made from a perspective. There are probably much better and more scholarly ways of explaining and executing deconstruction, but for this class, we will keep deconstruction to a basic level. The author's own interpretation and simplification of deconstruction for undergraduate use is a series of steps and questions that will help students understand as much of the subjective nature of the knowledge as possible in order to make a better decision regarding whether to choose or reject a given piece of knowledge.

- Ask yourself, "As the reader, what is my agenda/bias?"
- Define the constructs being used.
- Who made that knowledge, and/or who paid for that knowledge?
- Who stands to gain the most if the knowledge is widely accepted and believed?
- Who stands to lose the most if the knowledge is widely accepted and believed?
- How were the constructs originally used? Has the use and meaning of the construct changed over time?

WHAT IS YOUR AGENDA/BIAS?

This is a step often overlooked. The student encountering new information already has an idea of what she or he would like to see as the conclusion or use of the produced knowledge. The student must admit to his or her own agenda prior to reading new information. Though prior knowledge has already been discussed, there is no way to lose the prejudice of prior knowledge when trying to learn something new. One can only try to account for the effects and subjectivity of that prior knowledge. For example, if someone believes that the rich get wealthy by taking from the poor and are thus undeserving of their wealth, that person would favor information that supports this belief and the methods that seek to take the wealth of the rich to redistribute to the poor. At the same time this person would reject information that does not include the plundering of the rich at some point.

Remembering that one has bias before, during, and after reading new information helps in the overall deconstruction process so that a more fair comparison of subjectivity can take place. Competing ideas from competing knowledge should be evaluated as a whole. Not only is the conclusion and use of a particular body of knowledge important, but the subjectivity and assumptions of that body of knowledge must also be considered. In other words, knowledge is not right or wrong simply because it agrees or disagrees with one's already existing bias.

People should be prepared to be confronted with knowledge that has a better perspective, explanation, and conclusion of known phenomena. Resistance to better ideas reveals aspects of advocacy and adherence that may not have been considered before. It is often the case that people develop loyalty to a body of knowledge and in the process they forget the original intended goal and use of that knowledge. For example, the 2.2 billion dollar solar energy complex in Nevada owned by NRG Energy Inc. is meant to be a cleaner and more environmentally sustainable electricity system. The fact that a bird may be killed every two minutes by the system is downplayed to focus on the appeal of solar power. In other words, in order to increase the use of solar power, other negative environmental effects are ignored. Acknowledging one's original bias assists in preventing this kind of dogmatic attitude from arising particularly in discussions of so-called religious doctrine.

DEFINE THE CONSTRUCTS BEING USED

Any and all significant terms must be explicitly defined in a way that is agreeable to all parties involved. In a conversation about difficult and complex constructs, it is easy to assume that everyone is using the same definitions and has the same understanding of those constructs. However, this is not generally, if ever, the case. As was said before, the same object could be discussed with different interpretations and meanings by people with different perspectives. One should not assume that, when a construct is used, everyone in that conversation is using it with the same understanding and perspective. Without defining the constructs that are being used, the potential of misunderstanding and having a discussion that goes nowhere increases. In order to have a productive conversation, it is helpful to define one's constructs or have people define their constructs before trying to make a point. Examples of subjectively interpreted constructs are love, art, garbage, theft, gift, greed, and fair. A simple statement like, "That's not fair," as spoken by a child, is often not a commentary on social justice; rather, it is a way of saying, "I didn't get what I wanted." Failure to acknowledge various definitions of constructs makes a conversation general, vague, and inconclusive.

In the situation of competing definitions or when participants of a conversation have different understandings of a construct, the conversation can continue only when a definition acceptable to all participants is established. If no consensus is achieved for a definition of a construct, then it is understood that the parties are not talking about the same object. If a consensus is achieved, the agreed-upon definition should have as few exceptions in application as possible. In other words, if there are many situations where the term cannot explain or be used with that agreed upon definition, then it is likely not a very good definition. With a good definition, people can realize whether they are discussing the same topic or not and proceed to conclude the discussion through the clarity of the definition. This is particularly important when discussing wealth and what is fair.

WHO MADE THAT KNOWLEDGE AND/OR WHO PAID FOR THAT KNOWLEDGE?

It is important to know about the author of knowledge. This can be done by looking at the preface or dust jacket of a book or conducting a simple Google search. Although scholarship is supposed to be objective, the subjective training of a knowledge producer can and does make knowledge production subjective. The department and theoretical background of a knowledge producer informs what they think is, and is not, important to know. Different details are signified and discussed for various conclusions using specialized methods and criteria of evaluation. For example, in the early studies of societies around the world, scholars of religion looked at those societies and saw religion, sociologists saw culture, and business/trade-minded students saw, perhaps, economic opportunity. Information that is recorded and shared about those societies differed because of the difference in perspective, which includes differences in signification, and eventual conclusions. Students should remember that the academic training a knowledge producer received shapes his or her perspective and influences what is ultimately produced.

Scholarship and research has always been expensive, requiring investors for academic study; this can come in the form of grants or a research budget in a large firm. For this reason, knowing who pays for the knowledge produced, is important. The source of knowledge produced in the form of documentaries or scientific studies is sometimes easy to trace because funders often want recognition for their generosity; one just has to view the credits for this information. For example, science related broadcasts on Public Broadcast stations clearly announce who provided funding for the project. Knowing who paid for production is a clue for possible bias in the final presentation.

As in an earlier example, knowing that the tobacco companies funded the early research on the dangers of smoking may cause consumers of that knowledge to be cautious about utilizing it. It is not surprising that, often, research studies are funded and sponsored by corporations that do business with the products that were researched. Energy companies often fund research on all kinds of energy projects. Though "expertise" in a field almost requires some degree of participation from those who actually conduct business in that particular field, the nature and influence of those business people should be carefully examined. Knowledge production is crucial in many marketing strategies.

If a wind energy company produced knowledge declaring the benefits of wind energy, then it is likely that none of the serious short comings of the project will be shared in the documentary or publication. Opponents of the coal industry would focus on specific details of the use of coal to create a negative impression of that industry but would leave out any details that would cause people to hesitate before joining the fight to reduce coal consumption.

WHO STANDS TO GAIN THE MOST IF THE KNOWLEDGE IS WIDELY ACCEPTED AND BELIEVED?

One must take care not to accept information prior to deconstructing it. It is important to know who will gain and benefit the most if people accept a perspective and its knowledge as true. Who is *supposed* to gain the most and who *actually* gains the most could be different for various reasons. Note that, though many people support a particular knowledge production because of who is supposed to benefit, it is rare for the intended target group to actually benefit, even generally. For example, when a new sports stadium is planned, many promote the construction of the stadium by claiming the revenue generated will benefit the city and the local community. In reality, stadiums rarely pay for themselves, if ever, and it is the city that is stuck with a large debt. Philadelphia was scheduled to pay off the construction costs of Veterans Stadium in 2014; the stadium was torn down in 2004. Sport teams that *occasionally* use the stadium and for which the stadium was really built benefit the most by not having to pay for the construction of their playground. Though there are others who also benefit through this arrangement, it is important to note that the average person in the city does not benefit from the stadium as was advertised.

One way to find out who actually benefits from a particular knowledge production is to see who is bankrolling that knowledge production and who is paying for the advertising and marketing campaign to raise awareness about a certain issue. This information is sometimes hard to find but can be discovered with a little research. In other situations, one can figure out who will benefit through simple logic. For example, Monster Energy drinks have been accused of being the cause of a string of deaths because of their high caffeine content. Whether or not the drinks were actually responsible for those deaths is debatable. However, if there is an energy drink ban, the beneficiaries would be companies that produce other beverages with high caffeine content, since it is easy to believe their sales would rise to meet the shifting demand; Monster Energy drink sales in 2012 totaled $2.6 billion. A Monster Energy drink ban might mean a $2.6 billion increase in other drink companies' sales. It would probably be a good idea to consider the source of the information before one decides to spend a summer trying to raise awareness of the dangers of Monster Energy drinks, since it could be coffee companies and rival energy drink manufacturers spurring the Monster Energy drink ban. In other words, the knowledge being spread claims to be in the interest of public safety, when in reality it is likely more about market share and larger earnings.

WHO STANDS TO LOSE THE MOST IF THE KNOWLEDGE IS WIDELY ACCEPTED AND BELIEVED?

Generally, because knowledge production focuses on who will benefit if it is accepted as true, few people seriously consider who might lose a great deal if that knowledge is accepted as true. As was already said, since all knowledge production is a political process, someone always loses, and sometimes it is shocking to find out who actually loses due to a certain body of knowledge production. In our previous example, the city building the stadium is supposed to gain from the construction of it; generally, the city and the people who live there are the ones who lose the most, financially speaking. Though Philadelphia was still paying for Veterans Stadium long after it had been demolished, Philadelphia constructed two new stadiums to replace it, one for football and one for baseball. The knowledge produced concerning sports stadiums used in the marketing campaigns is clearly subjective, and those who were supposed to benefit the most end up paying the most.

In the energy drink example, the losers would not only be Monster Energy drink customers, but everyone who works for that company also suffers. This is because they will lose their jobs. Additionally, consumers in general will lose as the number of choices for energy drinks decreases. It must be remembered that the threat of energy drinks from companies like Monster Energy to the general public is subjective; some brands of coffee can contain more caffeine than Monster Energy drinks. Consideration of other perspectives is recommended before forming an opinion and conclusion on a matter.

HOW WERE THE CONSTRUCTS ORIGINALLY USED? HAS THE USE AND MEANING OF THE CONSTRUCT CHANGED OVER TIME?

This final step is a historical piece of deconstruction, which tries to understand what changes and events occurred over time that may influence the current use and understanding of particular constructs. This final step might be the most difficult and time-consuming step. It is a step that requires the most amount of research and effort. Knowledge production often sets an arbitrary chronological starting point, which gives the impression that there is nothing important to know before that starting point. If something identified as a problem is being discussed, then the knowledge producer has the power to decide when a problem began and what events are relevant. It is possible that the understanding of current issues can be changed by setting a narrow chronological or contextual perspective. Simply defining how constructs are used now could ignore how constructs were used in the past or even how and why they were made in the past. Sometimes, constructs made in the past are forgotten and then revived with a slightly different meaning and use. Often the users of the revived construct are unaware of the problems associated with its original use.

Assimilation is an example of this phenomenon. The original application and practice of assimilation in the 1920s and 1930s is largely forgotten in contemporary America. Originally, assimilation was constructed for those living in America of western European descent. Though there were many people of Indigenous American, Hispanic, Asian, and African descent, they were not to be considered for assimilation to become American because their outward appearances would be noticeable for generations; in other words, it was believed that only white people could assimilate in America. Scholarship moved away from assimilationist ideas in the late 1950s and early 1960s with constructs such as "melting pot" and acculturation through religion. When assimilation was reintroduced after the immigration quota law (the Johnson-Reed Act) was repealed in 1965, the history and original problems of limited application of assimilation were "forgotten," and the construct is freely used and applied to many people, particularly people of color. The original use of assimilation was openly and clearly discriminatory by implying that non-whites can never become truly American. Forgetting the problems of a construct does not do away with the negative implications of its usage.[1]

BENEFITS OF DECONSTRUCTION

The process of deconstruction not only helps people understand the subjectivity of their prior knowledge, but it also opens up the opportunity for people to take a different perspective or even to understand why other people believe different things. Once a "deconstructer" knows the possible source and perspective of a particular knowledge production, she or he can

---

1 Jacob Kim, "Re-Writing the Silent Exodus: Reconciliation and Identity for Koreans in Diaspora Space" (PhD diss., Temple University, 2003), 72–83.

move past simple evaluations or conclusions that decide right or wrong. Instead, energy and effort are expended trying to find other perspectives that may yield more desirable or favorable results for a far greater number of people. Instead of being locked into a specific mindset, people, in general, can start to unleash a vast reservoir of creativity for better understanding or to propose better solutions to perceived problems.

Understanding the character and effect of knowledge production and deconstruction helps many to realize who actually gains or loses through a particular production of knowledge. Through this process people can choose which knowledge and perspective they will follow, knowledge that meets the needs of the learner or decision maker best.

Because everyone is a knowledge producer on some level, knowledge production is continuously happening in our minds and all around us by others, official and unofficial. This phenomenon goes largely unnoticed until and unless subjective knowledge becomes codified into law or regulation. Legislation and Regulation signify certain narrow perspectives and force choices along the lines of that knowledge; at the same time, many other perspectives fade from consideration as the regulated lines of thought rise in prominence. The topic of the "legislation of morality" is covered in the next chapter.

Knowing that knowledge is produced from a subjective perspective, individuals can understand why some details were signified and other details were not. The practice of changing perspective when a problem is encountered offers a potential that is often not considered. That potential is the unpredictable process of innovation; **innovation** can be understood as a solution proposed from a different perspective. For example, carbon dioxide (CO_2) emissions are a cause for concern for many people today, particularly because of its possible role in climate change. A traditional approach to solve this problem of CO_2 emission is to reduce the amount of CO_2 produced; this is an expensive process, which is a problem for poor countries as well as many industries that provide cheap energy. An alternative approach to reducing emissions would be to do something with the CO_2 that was produced. A group of researchers in the Netherlands developed a method to produce electricity using CO_2. This approach reduces the amount of CO_2 in the atmosphere while helping to provide energy at the same time.

Additionally, it is far more difficult to get angry about or be intolerant of the ideas of others when one understands the potential legitimacy of a variety of opinions and beliefs. Righteous indignation of some perceived moral lapse is mitigated by the realization that one's own perspective and values may not be shared by others or that the outrage is due to one's unique perspective. One's own perspective can also be the cause of another's moral outrage. For example, one may fully support the drug war and fail to understand why anyone would oppose it. At the same time, that support for the drug war can irk many others as the unjust imposition of subjective beliefs. A proponent of the drug war who changes his or her perspective on the drug war to include not only the justification for it but also consideration of the effects and effectiveness of the war on drugs could make him or her less dogmatic about drugs and drug-related policies in society. Also, a non-violent individual who is criminalized and incarcerated by the drug war could be filled with outrage at the people who support the drug war.

PROPOSAL FROM A DIFFERENT PERSPECTIVE

The real value of deconstruction is that it allows individuals to propose alternative solutions or courses of action simply by changing their perspectives. Knowledge production from a specific perspective makes sense and is logical and true from that point of view and possibly only from that point of view. However, that point of view is not necessarily the best or even the right choice or belief for everyone to hold. There are consequences to choices and perspectives that also must be considered that are often not seen because of the limitation of a single perspective.

An example would be the poor in other countries. One way of helping the poor in other countries is through the foreign aid policy of the U.S. It is commonly understood that the U.S. government gives money to poor countries so that they can buy the things they need to get out of poverty. This approach favors the government of that country, which receives the money and chooses who gets large portions of it, often without the interests of the poor in mind.

A student once told a joke that was supposedly well-known in Egypt. The joke is as follows: the President of the U.S. is in Egypt and sees a homeless man outside of his hotel. He gives a thousand dollars to the Egyptian President and asks him to give the money to the homeless man and to tell him that the President of the U.S. says, "God bless you." The President of Egypt looks at his aide, gives him 500 dollars, and asks him to give it to the homeless man and to tell him the president of the U.S. says, "God bless you." The aide looks at his assistant, gives him 250 dollars, and asks him to give it to the homeless man and say that the President of the U.S. says, "God bless you." Eventually, someone goes to the homeless man and tells him that the President of the U.S. says, "God bless you." This shows how foreign aid money rarely goes to the poor. Knowing that millions of dollars in government aid packages to other countries is largely wasted, spent on contracts to political cronies or even spent on military weapons. An alternative to the current foreign aid policy would be *private* micro-loan programs that loan money directly to poor people without the government middle man taking a piece before passing it on.

Through deconstruction we can understand how information works to the advantage of some and to the disadvantage of others, and deconstruction enables us to see just how political knowledge production really is. When there are millions and even billions of dollars at stake through government grants and awards, it is easy to see just how polarizing and political this whole process can become. To say knowledge is "political" means that what is right or wrong, better or worse, or good or bad is not as important as how profitable and beneficial that knowledge is to some powerful and influential people. It is possible that the best knowledge and perspective is adopted and used to the benefit of many people; however, given the amount of money that can be involved, this cannot be the norm. There are always people or many people who derive no benefit from particular knowledge production. Often when changing perspectives, people who enjoyed comfort and privilege through the previous knowledge production may have their perspective undermined. This is often the situation when people feel offended; people who benefit from a specific perspective get upset when that perspective is shown to be subjective and not absolute. This feeling is magnified when what has been understood as a fact-based "good thing" is actually detrimental to an unconsidered group of people.

THE OFFENDED AND DISORIENTED

When learning deconstruction, some people experience liberation of sorts. This group of people is no longer bound by the rules and moral codes that always seemed arbitrary. While some people are filled with a previously unknown feeling of freedom, many others who learn deconstruction get **offended** or disoriented. The sense is that, through deconstruction, the beliefs a person has held for many years have just been undermined, and it seems as though they are being told their beliefs are wrong. People with firm religious beliefs who were taught in terms of absolutes tend to feel particularly defensive and threatened. Still others are confused because facts that served as reference points in life are no longer there to provide context and orientation; losing context and reference can be very disorienting. The author personally experienced both freedom and confusion after learning deconstruction.

All of this is easily resolved when one remembers that deconstruction and the idea of knowledge production are simply perspectives about knowledge and learning. It is stated and presented in this way to enable examination and discussion. The deconstruction exercise can be temporary. One can always go back to one's original perspective with which one is most comfortable, if so desired. Even if one returns to one's original perspective, there is the understanding of the existence of other perspectives, which gives rise to a better form of tolerance than is currently taught in schools.

It is hoped that, eventually, when one is ready, everything in one's prior knowledge may be examined, so that knowledge "reconstruction" may take place. This book will not discuss reconstruction in detail; however, the possibilities of reconstruction are exciting. Even small changes in perspective can open up and make visible certain things that were not visible before. Rather than getting trapped in old knowledge, which is often narrow and conservative, one may introduce truly revolutionary ideas that could change the world, how it is understood, and how people live in it. A recent example is the internet. The internet has changed how people do business, share knowledge, communicate with each other, and so much more. People who refuse to change and adapt by advancing with society are in danger of becoming irrelevant, and businesses are at risk of going bankrupt.

Technology and innovation open doors all over the world in ways people could not imagine before. This innovation and change can be frightening and destabilizing to the point that people will resist and eschew change and innovation. This is always the choice people face. There will always be knowledge that does not appeal to or favor us. However, this is the political nature of all knowledge production. It should be a comfort to all that human knowledge production is never final.

SUMMARY

Deconstruction allows students to examine the source of knowledge, which may influence their decision to keep or change that knowledge. Through deconstruction, one understands that knowledge is subjective, rather than absolute, which allows for a more tolerant, critical, and creative society. While deconstruction undermines the basic beliefs of students, they always have the option to maintain a previous point of view or reconstruct their personal vision of the world. With this technique for analyzing knowledge, students are no longer passive learners but become active critics and innovators of new knowledge.

QUESTIONS FOR DECONSTRUCTION

1. Deconstruct knowledge produced regarding Walmart.

2. Deconstruct the idea of tolerance as it is often taught and applied in secondary schools today.

3. What would be the result of deconstructing one's own beliefs?

RESETTING THE PERSPECTIVE AND THE LEGISLATION OF MORALITY

5

GOAL
Establish a common perspective from which to have our conversation on race

ARMED NOW WITH THE TOOL OF DECONSTRUCTION, one could deconstruct constructs all day long. However, people cannot live on deconstruction alone. At some point, people have to start living again with constructs. Students who do their deconstructions will have to choose how they will understand and use constructs; this choosing and using of constructs after deconstruction is reconstruction, which is a lifelong process. In light of what should be a deeper appreciation of the meaning and implication of constructs, students will be better able to make choices that are progressive rather than regressive or productive rather than destructive for themselves and society. This chapter will walk through the crucial deconstruction of religion, which will help make sense of our race talk and do a bit of reconstruction by way of resetting the class perspective.

This book began with the claim that knowledge is subjective and that, as a class, talking race together is not yet possible because of conflicting prior knowledge concerning race. The conflict is great not only among students, but also between the prior knowledge of students and the knowledge production of this book. In order to make race talk possible, the perspective of the entire class must be reset so that all have the same starting point. Everyone engaged in this discussion must share the same perspective in order to see the same things and have a productive conversation. At the same time, the perspectives of individuals must not be ignored, nor should any single perspective be privileged over others. Privileging one race theory over others can only serve to sacrifice or ignore other perspectives. The knowledge production of focusing on one race theory at the expense of others runs the risk of becoming hypocritical by imposing reform or proposing change that is similar to the original problem. It would be like trying to clean something with dirty hands. What is being cleaned simply becomes a different state of "dirty," where improvement is still only a matter of perspective.

The **reset of perspective** must happen in a way that is fair and agreeable to everyone in class; the perspective must also implicate everyone in the same way. Everyone must agree to the starting point or perspective, and that perspective must be fair for everyone. In this way, discussion can proceed in a manner that does not give anyone a clear moral or subjective advantage over anyone else. Often when race theory is taught, the content of the specific theory puts some students at some disadvantage and others in a position of advantage. For example, when studying race through a color-based race theory (e.g. the binary race theory where there are only two colors, white and black), whites often experience guilt while black students feel empowered. The guilt and empowerment may be justified. The information for black students may be helpful for personal reflection and identity construction; however, the benefits for society are not altogether clear. Also, students who do not consider themselves white or black may feel marginalized or feel only included into the conversation as an afterthought. In other words, this knowledge may not speak directly to the life and experiences of those who are not white or black.

This type of knowledge production in this class is unacceptable because it is easy to sense the advantages and disadvantages of a particular perspective, which increases the probability of some students rejecting the ideas out of hand as irrelevant. Knowledge production that points out a system as being unfair while offering yet another unfair system to replace it may be seen as hypocrisy. Avoiding hypocrisy caused by subjectivity enables everyone to participate in the conversation. Everyone is implicated by a good starting point and everyone is affected by the knowledge produced by that perspective. Establishing a perspective that avoids hypocrisy fosters tolerance and inclusivity. No one is given the option to feel excluded from the conversation. This approach seeks to look at society with a broad view rather than a narrow one.

WHAT EXACTLY HAVE WE BEEN STUDYING?

Much of our prior knowledge is information about and perception of us by others. Knowledge producers study various aspects of human life so that humans can better understand themselves. Studies of society, culture, psychology, religion, politics, biology, chemistry, health and nutrition, economics, cosmology, etc. have direct or indirect relations with understanding human life. It is safe to say that this knowledge comes from the university's study of the **other**. The "other" might be explained simply as objects that are people who are not you, the one who is doing the studying. The study of the other can be explored in many ways, such as how people live, think, and function just to name a few. The study of the other is both description and contrast at the same time. People generally have a fascination and desire to learn more about others who are similar yet different from themselves. The current popularity of reality TV shows about subjectively curious people might be considered evidence of this desire to learn and observe others. This phenomenon of information gathering through non-academic sources becomes part of the identity-making process that will be discussed in a later chapter.

In the past, **ethnography**, or the study and writing about groups of people, sometimes focused on a discussion of religious practices. In his 1871 book *Primitive Culture*, E.B. Tyler discussed the basic building block of religion that every group of people in the world seemed to have. The different ways (considering factors such as geography and commerce) each society would build on top of this foundation would result in the different systems of belief found all over the world. By understanding the religious beliefs of others, it was thought that not only would the other be better understood, but also contemporary European society as well. The Renato Rosaldo excerpt below gives further examples of this phenomenon and raises a problem with this type of knowledge production. Read the following excerpt from Rosaldo and take note of some of his initial thoughts on this method of producing knowledge.

AFTER OBJECTIVISM

by Renato Rosaldo

After falling head over heels in love, I paid a ceremonial visit, during the summer of 1983, to the "family cottage" on the shores of Lake Huron in western Ontario. Much as one would expect (unless one was, as I was, too much in the thick of things), my prospective parents-in-law treated me, their prospective son-in-law, with reserve and suspicion. Such occasions are rarely easy, and this one was no exception. Not unlike other rites of passage, my midlife courtship was a blend of conventional form and unique personal experience.

My peculiar position, literally surrounded by potential inlaws, nourished a project that unfolded over a two-week period in barely conscious daydreams. The daily family breakfast started turning in my mind into a ritual described in the distanced normalizing mode of a classic ethnography. On the morning of my departure, while we were eating breakfast, I revealed my feelings of tender malice by telling my potential in-laws the "true" ethnography of their family breakfast: "Every morning the reigning patriarch, as if just in from the hunt, shouts from the kitchen, 'How many people would like a poached egg?' Women and children take turns saying yes or no.

"In the meantime, the women talk among themselves and designate one among them the toast maker. As the eggs near readiness, the reigning patriarch calls out to the designated toast maker, 'The eggs are about ready. Is there enough toast?'

"'Yes,' comes the deferential reply. 'The last two pieces are about to pop up.' The reigning patriarch then proudly enters bearing a plate of poached eggs before him.

"Throughout the course of the meal, the women and children, including the designated toast maker, perform the obligatory ritual praise song, saying, 'These sure are great eggs, Dad.'"

My rendition of a family breakfast in the ethnographic present transformed a relatively spontaneous event into a generic cultural form. It became a caricatured analysis of rituals of dominance and deference organized along lines of gender and generation.

This microethnography shifted jaggedly between words ordinarily used by the family (mainly in such direct quotes as "These sure are great eggs, Dad") and those never used by them (such as "reigning patriarch," "designated toast maker," and "obligatory ritual praise song"). The jargon displayed a degree of hostility toward my potential father-in-law (the reigning patriarch) and hesitant sympathy with my potential sisters-in-law (the designated toast maker and the singers of the praise song). Far from being a definitive objective statement, my microethnography turned out to be a timely intervention that altered mealtime practices without destroying them. The father approaching retirement and his daughters already established in their careers were in the process of remolding their relations with one another. For all its deliberate caricature, my description contained an analysis that offered my potential in-laws a measure of insight into how their family breakfast routines, by then approaching empty ritual, embodied increasingly archaic familial relations of gender and hierarchy. Indeed, subsequent observations have confirmed that the ritual praise songs honoring the poached eggs and their maker have continued to be sung, but with tongue in cheek. To defamiliarize the family breakfast was to transform its taken-for-granted routines.

The reader will probably not be surprised to hear that my potential in-laws laughed and laughed as they listened to the microethnography about (and with which I had interrupted) their family breakfast. Without taking my narrative literally, they said they learned from it because its objectifications made certain patterns of behavior stand out in stark relief—the better to change them. The reception of my tale, as became evident in retrospect, was conditioned by their family practice of taking pleasure in witty teasing banter laced with loving malice.

The experience of having gales of laughter greet my microethnography made me wonder why a manner of speaking that sounds like the literal "truth" when describing distant cultures seems terribly funny as a description of "us." Why does a mode of composition flip between being parodic or serious depending in large measure on whether it is applied to "ourselves" or to "others"? Why does the highly serious classic ethnographic idiom almost inevitably become parodic when used as self-description?

In the previous chapter I argued that during the classic period (roughly 1921–1971), norms of distanced normalizing description gained a monopoly on objectivity. Their authority appeared so self-evident that they became the one and only legitimate form for telling the literal truth about other cultures. Proudly called the ethnographic present, these norms prescribed, among other things, the use of the present tense to depict social life as a set of shared routines and the assumption of a certain distance that purportedly conferred objectivity. All other modes of composition were marginalized or suppressed altogether.

In my view, no mode of composition is a neutral medium, and none should be granted exclusive rights to scientifically legitimate social description. Consider, for a moment longer, my mini-ethnography of the family breakfast. Although classic norms only rarely allowed for variants, mine was not the only possible version of the family meal. One could have told the tale of how this breakfast differed from all others. Such a telling could include specific conversations, the intrusive potential son-in-law, and the moods and rhythms with which the event unfolded. In addition, the narrator could have assumed the father's point of view and described how the "family provider" distributed his gifts to the "starving horde." Or the tone of this account could have been droll, or sincere, or whimsical, or earnest, or angry, or detached, rather than mockingly parodic.

One plausible criterion for assessing the adequacy of social descriptions could be a thought experiment: How valid would we find ethnographic discourse about others if it were used to describe ourselves? The available literature, not to mention the family breakfast episode, indicates that a division between serious conception and laughing reception can separate the author's intentions from the reader's responses. Human subjects have often reacted with bemused puzzlement over the ways they have been depicted in anthropological writings.

The problem of validity in ethnographic discourse has reached crisis proportions in a number of areas over the past fifteen years. In Chicano responses to anthropological depictions of themselves, the most balanced yet most devastating assessment has been put forth by Américo Paredes. He begins rather gently by saying, "I find the Mexicans and Chicanos pictured in the usual ethnographies somewhat unreal." He goes on to suggest that the people studied find ethnographic accounts written about them more parodic than telling: "It is not so much a sense of outrage, that would betray wounded egos, as a feeling of puzzlement, that *this* is given as a picture of the communities they have grown up in. Many of them are more likely to laugh at it all than feel indignant." His critique of the somewhat unreal picture put forth in ethnographies about Chicanos continues with a stunning item-by-item enumeration of such errors as mistranslations, taking jokes seriously, missing double meanings, and accepting an apocryphal story as the literal truth about brutal initiation rites in youth gangs.

Paredes's diagnosis is that most ethnographic writing on Mexicans and Chicanos has failed to grasp significant variations in the tone of cultural events. In an ethnography he sees as representative, Paredes observes that the Chicanos portrayed "are not only literal minded, they never crack a joke." He argues that ethnographers who attempt to interpret Chicano culture should recognize "whether a gathering is a wake, a beer bust, or a street-corner confabulation." Knowledge about the cultural framing of events would aid the ethnographer in distinguishing an earnest speech from a joking speech. Even when using technical concepts, the analysis should not lose sight of whether the event was serious (to be taken literally) or deadpan (to be read as farce).

Lest there be any confusion, I am saying neither that the native is always right nor that Paredes as native ethnographer could never be wrong. Instead, my claim is that we should take the criticisms of our subjects in much the same way that we take those of our colleagues. Not unlike other ethnographers, so-called natives can be insightful, sociologically correct, axe-grinding, self-interested, or mistaken. They do know their own cultures, and rather than being ruled out of court, their criticisms should be listened to and taken into account, to be accepted, rejected, or modified, as we reformulate our analyses. At issue is not the real truth versus the ethnographic lie. After all, the pragmatic concerns of everyday life can diverge from those of disciplined inquiry. A person "falling in love" speaks with quite different desires and purposes than the psychiatrist who describes the "same" phenomenon as "object cathexis." Technical and everyday vocabularies differ in large measure because their respective projects are oriented to different goals. In this case, Paredes has called attention to how the "objects" of study can find an earnest ethnography about themselves as parodie as did the participants in the Canadian family breakfast. His incisive critique calls for ethnographers to reassess their rhetorical habits.

The difficulties of using ethnographic discourse for self-description should have long been apparent to anthropologists, most of whom have read Horace Miner's classic (if heavy-handed) paper, "Body Ritual among the Nacirema." (Nacirema spelled backwards, of course, is American.) In that paper, an ethnographic sketch of Nacirema "mouth-rites," written in accord with classic norms, was parodie in its application to Americans:

> The daily body ritual performed by everyone includes a mouth- rite. Despite the fact that these people are so punctilious about care of the mouth, this rite involves a practice which strikes the uninitiated stranger as revolting. It was reported to me that the ritual consists of inserting a small bundle of hog hairs into the mouth, along with certain magical powders, and then moving the bundle in a highly formalized series of gestures.

His essay thus defamiliarizes both through the narrator's position as uninitiated stranger and through the distanced idiom that transforms everyday life practices into more elevated ritual and magical acts.

Clearly there is a gap between the technical idiom of ethnography and the language of everyday life. Miner's description employs terms used by a certain group of professionals rather than the words most of "us" Americans usually use in talking about brushing "our" teeth. The article becomes parodie precisely because of the discrepancy between what we all know about brushing our teeth and the ethnographer's elevated, distanced, normalizing discourse. Unlike my account of the family breakfast, jarring discordance here does not become fully explicit in the text (despite what text positivists may think). Instead, it resides in the disjunction between Miner's technical jargon and the North American reader's knowledge that the mouth-rites refer to brushing one's teeth in the morning.

In retrospect, one wonders why Miner's article was taken simply as a good-natured joke rather than as a scathing critique of ethnographic discourse. Who could continue to feel comfortable describing other people in terms that sound ludicrous when applied to ourselves? What if the detached observer's authoritative objectivity resides more in a manner of speaking than in apt characterizations of other forms of life?

Lest it appear that no ethnography has ever been written in the manner of Miner's Nacirema mouth-rites, one should probably cite an actual case. Otherwise, the reader could regard the classic norms as a figment of my imagination rather than as the discipline's until recently (and, in many quarters, still) dominant mode of representing other cultures.

Consider, for example, the description of "weeping rites" in A. R. Radcliffe-Brown's classic ethnography about the Andaman Islanders, a hunter-gatherer group residing southeast of India:

> When two friends or relatives meet after having been separated, the social relation between them that has been interrupted is about to be renewed. This social relation implies or depends upon the existence of a specific bond of solidarity between them. The weeping rite (together with the subsequent exchange of presents) is the affirmation of this bond. The rite, which, it must be remembered, is obligatory, compels the two participants to act as though they felt certain emotions, and thereby does, to some extent, produce these emotions in them.

The reader should keep in mind that this passage describes tears of greeting between long-separated old friends. Nonetheless, the ethnographer manifests skepticism about whether or not the weepers actually feel anything. Evidently, he regards their tears as mere playacting. To the limited extent that emotions are present, the ethnographer explains them as the consequence of having performed the obligatory weeping rites.

Yet the status of Radcliffe-Brown's term "obligatory" remains obscure. Does it mean that when he witnessed weeping greeters, they always turned out to be long-lost intimates? How could he have observed greetings without tears between long-lost intimates? Or did people simply tell the ethnographer that when long-lost intimates greet one another, they weep? Despite its analytical import, the reader is left to wonder what Radcliffe-Brown means by the term *obligatory*.

Nonetheless, most anthropological readers of Radcliffe-Brown probably take his account at face value. When, for example, I told a colleague about my dissatisfaction with Radcliffe-Brown's depiction of Andaman weeping rites, she correctly followed the code for ethnographic readers and replied, "Yes, but for them, unlike for us, the rites are obligatory." Such are the costs of following rarely examined habits of reading.

The problem resides less in the use of such descriptions than in an uncritical attachment to them as the sole vehicle for literal objective truth. Radcliffe-Brown so detached himself from his human subjects that his account lends itself to being read as unwittingly parodic, and even absurd. When tearful greetings between long-lost intimates are described as obligatory weeping rites, they become so defamiliarized as to appear simply bizarre.

The idiom of classic ethnography characteristically describes specific events as if they were programmed cultural routines and places the observer at a great distance from the observed. The systematic effects of classic modes of composition were rarely explored because they purportedly held a monopoly on objectivity. The point, however, is not to discard classic norms but to displace them so that they become only one among a number of viable forms of social description rather than the one and only mode of writing about other cultures. Radcliffe-Brown's detached, dehumanizing descriptive idiom potentially offers analytical insight not available through concepts more frequently used in everyday life. The Canadian breakfast episode, as I said, suggests that distanced normalizing descriptions can be used with a deliberately satirical intent to jolt people into thinking afresh about their everyday lives.

Although my description of the family breakfast formally resembles Radcliffe-Brown's, the objectifications differ markedly in their impact. When read in accord with classic norms, Radcliffe-Brown's account appears to be the only objective way of describing social reality. It is the literal truth. My more parodic account stands as one among a number of possible descriptions. Its accuracy matters, but it objectifies more with a view to speeding a process of change than with producing a timeless truth. How social descriptions are read depends not only on their formal linguistic properties but also on their content and their context. Who is speaking to whom, about what, for what purposes, and under what circumstances? The differences between distinct forms of objectification reside in the analyst's position within a field of social interaction rather than in the text regarded as a document with intrinsic meaning.

What follows deliberately objectifies classic canons of objectivity with a view to moving not beyond conventions (which, in any case, is impossible) but toward the use of a wider range of rhetorical forms in social description. As a corrective to the literal-mindedness with which classic social descriptions are habitually read, this chapter deliberately defamiliarizes the rhetoric of objectivism (which, arguably, unwittingly defamiliarizes the everyday world) in order to indicate how short the gap is between objective characterization and objectifying caricature. My goal in thus objectifying objectivism is to speed a process of change already underway in the modes of composition for ethnography as a form of social analysis.

COMMENT

Rosaldo's writing shows the less-than-clear distinction between religion and culture; he asserts that the distinction is arbitrary and constructed. Thus, there is no such a thing as religion; the knowledge that has been produced was considered religion only because it was labeled religion and the correct religious language was used when producing that knowledge. If scholars use the correct **technical jargon**, which is also taught to students in America, then everyone will recognize religion when they see it, even if it is not considered religious by the people who practice that activity—as in the case of the "Weeping rites" above. Every field of study and every occupation have their own set of terms, which Rosaldo calls technical jargon. Technical jargon is the standardized language used in a particular field by people in that field to facilitate precise communication.[1] The language that one uses often implies the field or perspective being employed at the moment. Word choice and being able to use technical jargon also serve as credentials that demonstrate a qualification to write in that field. So, when the perspective and language of religion is used, people will see religion where they are supposed to see religion. This would also mean that if one were to use the perspective and language of culture, then one would see culture. In casual conversation, if we start to talk about rites or rituals, then we know we are talking about religion or religiously related behavior even if the behavior is not normally associated with religion. The effect is that the practice takes on a religious or spiritual quality and is understood to be practiced much like any religious practice as traditionally understood. Rosaldo simply changes the lens and re-views practices through the perspective and language of culture. He says there is

---

1 Other forms of technical jargon exist; slang and coded language among close friends are also indicative of standardized communication and credentials of authority.

no "culture-free space," which means everything should be understood as culture because there is no religion. Everything that was once believed to be a religion or a religious practice is simply a cultural practice interpreted as religion. The value of Rosaldo's approach is that everything now is scrutinized through the cultural lens. Certain practices and beliefs are not excluded from cultural study and knowledge production simply because those practices are thought to be religious.

The move this book makes agrees with Rosaldo but chooses to see things in the other way; in this book, *everything* is religion because there is no culture. In this class, in order to reset everyone's perspective, there is no **religion-free space**. Everything is religious and has religious meaning; those activities once identified as cultural were cultural only because they were interpreted as cultural. This new perspective conflicts with the prior knowledge of most students, so they must keep in mind how the appearance and the knowledge of an object can change with a change in perspective.

For the purposes of this book, **religion** is defined as a system of belief. It is something that someone believes and uses to get through the day, to help understand the world, something that can get someone excited or participating in a conversation. This set of beliefs does not have to be extensive or non-contradictory. It does not have to be profound or concern itself beyond the current moment. Anything one believes is true, even when there is no reason or proof to believe it is true, and it is part of the religion of that person. From something as trivial as "which clothes look good on me" to the "god theory" of cosmology, all can be considered part of someone's religion. This of course means that how people understand race, poverty, and the relationship between race and poverty often becomes a religious belief.

Sometimes the author will ask his class if paying taxes is a religious act. Generally the response is that it is not a religious act. Paying one's taxes has been taught today as a civil act or civil responsibility, one that has a stiff penalty for not following. This widely believed bit of information is interesting given that Judeo-Christian scripture discusses paying taxes and concludes that paying taxes does not conflict with faith. For many, the discussion and resolution in scripture makes it a religious decision to pay or not to pay taxes. Because the debate was resolved already through scripture makes it a non-issue for most people today. However, there are various sects and denominations that resist paying certain taxes because of the conflict with religious beliefs. The current debate surrounding the new health care law, the Affordable Care Act (which is a tax according to the U.S. Supreme Court), includes religious groups seeking exemption from having to buy insurance for religious reasons. For example, the new health care law requires people to pay for particular methods of birth control that are not supported by certain religious groups. Similarly, the Amish in Pennsylvania sought exemption from Social Security taxes because of the conflict with their religion; they succeeded in obtaining this exemption in 1965.

Eating food is another example where the religious associations have been de-signified for most people. Though most people tend to consider eating food as a matter of personal preference, there are many religions that either permit or prohibit the eating of various foods. There are feasts in many religions that have very specific implications to the belief structure of that religion. Most people hold to the belief that there are no restrictions when it comes to eating. To say that there is no connection with religion because most people have no restrictions regarding food is the type of arbitrary pronouncement this book seeks to avoid.

Some have defined religion as repeated rituals that have meaning or some kind of significance for those who perform them. Based on this understanding, there are many behaviors that appear religious but are not considered religious. Football games and tailgate parties can be considered religious. More important for this discussion is the largest religion of the U.S., nationalism. Nationalism is devotion and loyalty to one's country. In the same way Rosaldo described his future in-laws and recounted the content of the descriptions of other religions, if ethnographers came and wrote about the religions of the U.S., surely football and nationalism would be included, too.

As part of American nationalism people make pilgrimages to the holy places of the U.S.: the Statue of Liberty, City Hall in Philadelphia, and most importantly, Washington, D.C. The capital of the U.S. is filled with religious symbols that are not to be referred to as religious symbols in the current system. The Washington monument is a fertility symbol from ancient Egypt and the various memorials are modeled after the ancient Greek temples. The Lincoln Memorial's inscription begins with "In this temple…;" this would make the constitution equivalent to the holy scripture of nationalism. One may justifiably say that this is stretching the definition and understanding of religion to the point of irrelevance; however, not only is it consistent with the constructs employed by ethnographers who described the religions of others, but in this case this broad perspective allows students to see religion with a different perspective that does not privilege one perspective or interpretation over any other. In other words, everyone is now using the same perspective.

Certain forms of religion have been defined and signified for us. These are the traditional religions to which people say they belong. Christianity, Hinduism, Buddhism, Islam, and Judaism are all examples of religion. However, just because someone does not subscribe to one of these religions does not mean that person does not believe in anything. Scientists believe in science, atheists believe in the system of no-god; it is what subscribers believe is true. These beliefs serve as references for thought and action; beliefs help people live and function on a daily basis. Religious beliefs provide the values and morals of a person to enable that person to choose and decide what is right or wrong, true or false, good or bad.

THE BENEFIT OF THE EXTREME POSITION

The religious character of everyday life has been noticed before; Robert Bellah wrote about **civil religion** in 1967. He discussed religious beliefs expressed through life in the U.S. but these were beliefs that are not necessarily from or part of any one specific recognized religion. His writings were the center of discussion and conferences for many years. Even when this author took religion classes in the 1980s, Bellah's ideas were still influential. Bellah takes a step towards a broader understanding of religion, but this book tries to push even further by striving to include all aspects of life. All beliefs are religious beliefs. Though there are limits and practical problems with viewing everything as religion, the goal is to establish a perspective for discussion that includes everyone and excludes no one; the understanding of religion must be broad. It is a change in perspective with little regard for prior knowledge and previously existing criteria of understanding. It is a *temporary* shift in perspective for discussion to enable everyone in the class to see the same things in the same way; it is a way to theoretically see all perspectives at the same time about a specific topic. It does not mean that all the perspectives will be known, but any perspective encountered will be considered a religious perspective. By shifting the perspective and locating it in this extreme position, the entire class can see things in society that were not visible before with their prior knowledge. Locating the perspective on an extreme such as this is inclusive and not alienating for students with various individual and personal perspectives. In other words, no one can say that their own unique and private beliefs are not included in this perspective of religion; nor can anyone claim exemption

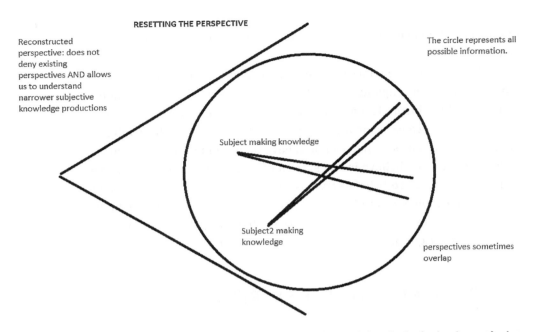

FIGURE 5-1 Resetting the perspective to an extreme one in order to be inclusive in producing knowledge.

from the discussion because that person believes they have no religion. As a class, students can learn together and have a conversation where everyone understands each other.

Figure 5-1 attempts to illustrate the reset of perspective. The circle represents the observable world and the people who live in it. Knowledge producers within that world make knowledge according to their perspective, which sees a part of the observable world. This process excludes even more of the world from consideration making that knowledge production narrow and subjectively true. If we reposition our definition to include all possible definitions, we include all subjectively produced knowledge production while including the observable world. It is flexible enough to accommodate and yield better productions of knowledge which may be introduced later.

Through the broad perspective students can see the "work" of narrower forms of knowledge production; that is, by excluding and/or including various beliefs in a narrower definition of a construct like religion, one can observe the effects and speculate over the intent and goal of that particular knowledge production. As was mentioned previously, knowledge production occurs for a purpose. The broader perspective enables the examination of the purpose, use, or agenda of the narrower perspective and its resulting produced knowledge.

Broadening the perspective in this way does not allow someone to employ a construct from a narrow perspective of knowledge to critique and criticize a different perspective as if the criticizers do not exhibit the same behavior (e.g., **religious fanaticism**). When it comes to discussing religion with this perspective, everyone has a belief that they cherish, guard, and express. Everyone is included equally in the conversation and so each person has something upon which one's life derives meaning. Often, what is most important to a person is not typically signified as religion by society. That is, society generally does not discuss nor try to regulate that particular belief of an individual. The value of that belief to that person lies dormant until the freedom to practice that belief, in the way that person desires to practice it, is taken away. It may even be mockery or criticism of a belief by others that signifies for a person his or her own belief. When a person's treasured belief is violated somehow, then the reactions of people are similar to the so-called religious fanatic. In other words, people are often under the impression that religious fanatics can only be found in traditionally signified religious organizations, such as Christianity and Islam. This allows people to talk about religious fanatics in a negative and condescending manner without implicating themselves in an exercise of hypocrisy. That is, fanaticism in religion leads to bad behavior, but fanaticism in sports is different and acceptable—even desirable. However, the various fanaticisms are not that different from each other, especially when discussing sports in Philadelphia. Philadelphia sports fans are generally notorious for their treatment of fans of opposing teams. Violence erupts all over the world in sports-related activities; for example, soccer matches in Europe are no strangers to violence.

The fanatical behavior of people identified as deeply religious can be found everywhere and in everyone; in sports, scholarship, and science, we are all religious fanatics. Even people who live so-called moderate lives can suddenly demonstrate fanatical behavior if the right mental switch is thrown. For example, parents of children who are threatened in some way will become protective in ways that could be seen as similar to religious fanaticism; in this context this fanaticism is hidden by signifying it as "good parenting." It is not that all parents will react in the same way, but rather those parents for whom their children are the focus of their lives. To say everyone is a religious fanatic is not necessarily a cause for concern because the focus and single mindedness of fanaticism, understood broadly, often leads to great benefits for society. Inventors, innovators, and artists are often consumed by their work and at the same time they "de-signify" other areas of their lives. Their fanaticism over their work may improve the lives of others in society while breeding neglect in parts of their own personal lives. Even those identified as religious fanatics may not actually be fanatics but have another motive for the decisions they make. This becomes even more obvious when the label of religious fanaticism is attached to what they did, not what they believed. What an individual decides is important or not is a personal matter as long as the consequences of those choices are accepted by the fanatic. People may share their views with others to form a community if they choose. Being a fanatic is not by itself a bad thing; it is forcing others to agree with one's fanaticism, particularly with violence, which should be unacceptable. This is not to say that fanaticism that harms others or damages the property of others should be condoned; rather, the point is that fanaticism that does not harm others or damage the property of others should not be feared. Rather, those forms of fanaticism should be tolerated no matter how disagreeable they may be to others.

THE LEGISLATION OF MORALITY

The curious realization is that, though we are all religiously fanatical, only some forms of fanaticism have been signified as religious fanaticism and are, therefore, bad. Remembering the process of knowledge production, the making of a more specific or narrow definition of religion is for a purpose. One possible reason is to shape the discussion of the separation of church and state. A narrow definition of religion enables people to decide what beliefs are allowed or disallowed in the government realm. This discussion on the "separation of church and state" acknowledges that what is meant by "separation of church and state" has changed over the years and is currently understood as keeping religion out of government. Because only certain beliefs are considered religious, those beliefs are not eligible to be discussed when creating laws of the state. At the same time this understanding allows other beliefs to be legislated by government in spite of the separation of church and state. Whether people realize it or not, it is not that all religious beliefs are prohibited and banned from the political arena; it is only the beliefs identified and signified as religious. The broad perspective where all beliefs are religious beliefs is missed because of the various narrow perspectives people have. This allows so-called non-religious beliefs to be discussed in the political arena because they do not bear the label of religion. For example, the belief that the car industry in America is somehow better than foreign car companies is a religious belief; humans caused climate change is a religious belief; diets are religious beliefs; green energy is better than fossil fuel energy is a religious belief; etc. Each belief is the result of narrow perspectives and has a moral implication of what is right or wrong.

Excising religion or disallowing religion from government is actually the act of replacing one religious belief for another; that is, one system of morals for another. The conflict between the activities of the current legislative bodies with the beliefs of various people in society is indicative of the different perspectives of religious beliefs. This is not an argument to allow everyone the ability to legislate their own interpretation of morality—quite the opposite. No one should be allowed to pass legislation based on their own morality primarily because legislation written in this way is the use of force or coercion. The **legislation of morality** is the writing and passing of laws based on the personal beliefs of a large or small group of people. The beliefs of some people are then *imposed* on everyone else through legislation, regulation, and law, especially upon the people who are unconvinced of the validity of that moral view.

Legislation of morality is coercion to the point of criminalizing different views. It is the use of force to get compliance and obedience to some arbitrary moral standard. Some people are so fanatical about their belief of what is right and wrong, they end up having that belief made into law. The law is written because in spite of efforts to raise awareness and spread a particular brand of knowledge production, too many people remain "unaware" of what is "important" and continue to do the wrong thing, whatever that wrong thing is. Because these unenlightened people refuse to do "the right thing," they must be forced to do the right thing by law; they must be coerced into doing what is best for them and society. Violation of legislation and law bring the threat of state-sanctioned punishment and violence. The arbitrary and subjective use of force with the threat of penalty and punishment is coercion. In contemporary society, people are obsessed with coercing each other into compliance with some subjective moral justification.

Note that people generally do not respond well to the use of force, and using force to try to change people's behavior is not very effective. One cannot force someone else to believe in something they do not want to believe. Think about the two-sided paper example in chapter 2. One might declare that the paper is blue and that everyone must believe the paper is blue. Those who see white will have no respect for that law. Perhaps superficially, they will give the appearance of obeying the law out of fear of the penalty; but in reality, they will teach everyone they know why it is white. Often the use of force encourages people to solidify their beliefs and become stronger adherents of their actual faith; perhaps there is a connection between this form of coercion and the religious fanaticism found in society today. The Christian church has a long history of coercion and persecution, standing on both the receiving and delivering side. History has shown that it never ends as planned.

Assuming that one's understanding of right and wrong is that person's religion, writing legislation based on one's perspective of what is moral is a religious act, the legislation of morality. In a world without the ability to legislate one's morality, one must rely on persuasion, knowing that many people will refuse to be persuaded. Legislation of morality is a short cut bypassing the work of persuasion and simply coercing the un-persuaded to submit. It is a method of intolerance where some people cannot tolerate the existence of different behavior or belief.

The effort to persuade an entire society is difficult if not impossible because of the existence of competing ideas and interpretations of situational reality. The listener always has the option to disagree and ignore the persuader's call to change one's perspective and choice. In the political system of the U.S. it is advantageous to narrowly define religion so that people can employ lobbyists (influence peddlers) in Washington to pass laws that force others to live by another's religious belief. Persuasion in the political realm today is no longer persuasion at all; often knowledge production is used for the coercion of others through legislation to believe or "convert" to a particular perspective.

All of this legislative activity is the activity of true believers of a perspective, the religious fanatics. The construct "fanatic" carries a negative connotation only in certain contexts. The subjective nature of that connotation must be remembered, and a fanatic must be understood as someone who really believes and values a certain belief. Rightly or wrongly, the religious fanatic's intent is to be moral. However, the use of force in this manner does not create a better or "more just" society. Rather, it creates a society of oppression and resentment with very little freedom. Legislating morality in this way also creates imbalance and skews the way people perceive the world and, so, skews their choices and decisions in life. The way others look at dissenting opinions or different perspectives also changes as the threat of violence lurks in the background.

As stated earlier, simply by legislating arbitrary morality, no matter how convinced one is about the goodness of that legislation, cannot and does not bring about change and compliance (e.g. alcohol prohibition of the 1920s or current drug prohibition and gun legislation). Rather, the achievement of legislation of this type is the **criminalization** of peaceful people. People who are law-abiding citizens today are suddenly criminals tomorrow when a law goes into effect. Downloading MP3s through Napster in the 1990s was a prevalent activity. Rightly or wrongly, legislation based on the morality of record companies was passed in 1998 that made this activity illegal. The morality of the record companies was expressed through lost profits but could also be expressed by saying it is morally good for the record industry to continue to exist in its current form. The legislation did not stop the downloading, but it did criminalize that activity and enabled companies and the justice system to prosecute and fine people engaged in this behavior. One creates criminals through the combination of knowledge production and legislation based on subjective moral perspective, and at the same time, society is distracted from potentially more important issues of everyday life. The religious beliefs of the few become the concern of everyone.[2] Much of the polarization in society today comes through the political process. Decades ago, victory at the polls meant little to the everyday lives of the losing party of those elections. Now, losing means being forced to live in the way the victors legislate morality. Political affiliation has replaced religion in the way people build relationships and community.

This does not mean that knowledge production, the activity, is bad or that it needs to stop. Rather, learners of knowledge production must realize that this is what is happening and consider the suggestion to end all activity that legislates based on narrow constructions of morality. Legislation must be inclusive of all perspectives and individuals to prevent arbitrary reward and punishment; society must focus more on efforts of persuasion to influence behavior. True believers must convince others of their beliefs like many traditional religions already do today; they must proselytize for followers with the awareness that there are many competing ideas against which they must make a case. The ability to legislate morality is an unfair advantage for those who understand the system and have the ability and means to participate on that level. The case will be made that poverty is one of the results of this type of legislative activity.

SUMMARY

After explaining how knowledge is made, it should be clear that knowledge production gives some advantages to some and disadvantages to others. Rightly or wrongly, for better or worse, there are people who benefit more through particular knowledge production than others, depending on

---

2 Ryan McMaken, *"More Politics means more Conflict,"* mises.org, Mises Institute, October 28, 2014.

the perspective. Taking an extreme or general position that is inclusive of everyone and all perspectives in a given field regarding a certain topic reduces the risk of arbitrary coercion and hypocrisy. Religion as defined above will be the orienting construct and perspective from which the study of race will proceed. This construct also sheds light on the phenomenon of the legislation of morality, the codification of religious beliefs that are coercively imposed on everyone in society.

QUESTIONS FOR DISCUSSION

1. Try to imagine what your real religion is; not what you were raised to think you were, but what you care about most in your life.

   a. Is it possible that the object of your belief will change according to your age and life situation?

   b. How do you feel when someone criticizes or mocks your cherished belief?

   c. Does this change your understanding of the construct "fanatic?"

2. How do you feel knowing that what you thought was true (including and especially your religion) is only subjectively true?

RACIAL FORMATION

6

GOAL
For students to learn the theory of race theories

T HE PROBLEM OF STUDYING RACE is not unlike the problem of studying religion. The same limitations of perspective and prior knowledge intrude on the attempts of achieving objectivity to understand the phenomenon we identify as race. Depending on the perspective, what is seen as race is different. If one were to change his or her location, time, or demographic group, then what is seen as race also changes. Race is not an absolute but a construct that is defined and understood according to one's perspective. This is not to say that race and racism are not real; the pain and suffering that racism has caused is very real especially to those who have suffered. Nevertheless, to move forward we must not focus on narrow reactionary responses that do not address the undercurrents of race dynamics; one may do so if one desires, but this class chooses to understand the phenomenon broadly and inclusively. In order to do this, rather than choosing a single perspective as the most important or the best explanation of our society today, this chapter offers Michael Omi and Howard Winant's theory of racial formation.

This theory does not seek to explain race from a single perspective; rather, the theory explains the phenomenon of race. Instead of privileging a single perspective of race, racial formation opens the door for an infinite number of racializations to explain all race theories. Read the following selection by Omi and Winant.

RACIAL FORMATION

by Michael Omi and Howard Winant

In 1982–83, Susie Guillory Phipps unsuccessfully sued the Louisiana Bureau of Vital Records to change her racial classification from black to white. The descendent of an 18th century white planter and a black slave, Phipps was designated "black" in her birth certificate in accordance with a 1970 state law which declared anyone with at least 1/32nd "Negro blood" to be black.

The Phipps case raised intriguing questions about the concept of race, its meaning in contemporary society, and its use (and abuse) in public policy. Assistant Attorney General Ron Davis defended the law by pointing out that some type of racial classification was necessary to comply with federal record-keeping requirements and to facilitate programs for the prevention of genetic diseases. Phipps's attorney, Brian Begue, argued that the assignment of racial categories on birth certificates was unconstitutional and that the 1/32nd designation was inaccurate. He called on a retired Tulane University professor who cited research indicating that most Louisiana whites have at least 1/20th "Negro" ancestry.

In the end, Phipps lost. The court upheld the state's right to classify and quantify racial identity.[1]

Phipps's problematic racial identity, and her effort to resolve it through state action, is in many ways a parable of America's unsolved racial dilemma. It illustrates the difficulties of defining race and assigning individuals or groups to racial categories. It shows how the racial legacies of the past—slavery and bigotry—continue to shape the present. It reveals both the deep involvement of the state in the organization and interpretation of race, and the inadequacy of state institutions to carry out these functions. It demonstrates how deeply Americans both as individuals and as a civilization are shaped, and indeed haunted, by race.

Having lived her whole life thinking that she was white, Phipps suddenly discovers that by legal definition she is not. In U.S. society, such an event is indeed catastrophic.[2] But if she is not white, of what race is she? The state claims that she is black, based on its rules of classification,[3] and another state agency, the court, upholds this judgment. Despite the classificatory standards that have imposed an either-or logic on racial identity, Phipps will not in fact "change color." Unlike what would have happened during slavery times if one's claim to whiteness was successfully challenged, we can assume that despite the outcome of her legal challenge, Phipps will remain in most of the social relationships she had occupied

Michael Omi and Howard Winant, "Racial Formation: Understanding Race and Racism In the Post-Civil Rights Era," *Racial Formation in the United States: From the 1960s to the 1990s*, ed. Pawan Dhingra. Copyright © 1994 by Taylor & Francis Group.

before the trial. Her socialization, her familial and friendship networks, her cultural orientation, will not change. She will simply have to wrestle with her newly acquired "hybridized" condition. She will have to confront the "other" within.

The designation of racial categories and the assignment of race is no simple task. For centuries, this question has precipitated intense debates and conflicts, particularly in the U.S.—disputes over natural and legal rights, over the distribution of resources, and indeed, over who shall live and who shall die.

A crucial dimension of the Phipps case is that it illustrates the inadequacy of claims that race is a mere matter of variations in human physiognomy, that it is simply a matter of skin "color." But if race cannot be understood in this manner, how can it be understood? We cannot fully hope to address this topic—no less than the meaning of race, its role in society, and the forces that shape it—in one chapter, nor indeed in one book. Our goal in this chapter, however, is far from modest: we wish to offer at least the outlines of a theory of race and racism.

WHAT IS RACE?

There is a continuous temptation to think of race as an essence, as something fixed, concrete and objective. And there is also an opposite temptation: to imagine race as a mere illusion, a purely ideological construct that some ideal non-racist social order would eliminate. It is necessary to challenge both these positions, to disrupt and reframe the rigid and bipolar manner in which they are posed and debated, and to transcend the presumably irreconcilable relationship between them.

The effort must be made to understand race as an unstable and "decentered" complex of social meanings constantly being transformed by political struggle. With this in mind, let us propose a definition: <u>race is a concept that signifies and symbolizes social conflicts and interests by referring to different types of human bodies</u>. Although the concept of race invokes biologically based human characteristics (so-called "phenotypes"), selection of these particular human features for purposes of racial signification is always and necessarily a social and historical process. In contrast to the other major distinction of this type, that of gender, there is no biological basis for distinguishing among human groups along the lines of race.[4] Indeed, the categories employed to differentiate among human groups along racial lines reveal themselves, upon serious examination, to be at best imprecise, and at worst completely arbitrary.

If the concept of race is so nebulous, can we not dispense with it? Can we not "do without" race, at least in the "enlightened" present? This question has been posed often, and with greater frequency in recent years.[5] An affirmative answer would of course present obvious practical difficulties: it is rather difficult to jettison widely held beliefs, beliefs which moreover are central to everyone's identity and understanding of the social world. So the attempt to banish the concept as an archaism is at best counterintuitive. But a deeper difficulty, we believe, is inherent in the very formulation of this schema, in its way of posing race as a problem, a misconception left over from the past, and suitable now only for the dustbin of history.

A more effective starting point is the recognition that despite its uncertainties and contradictions, the concept of race continues to play a fundamental role in structuring and representing the social world. The task for theory is to explain this situation. It is to avoid both the utopian framework that sees race as an illusion we can somehow "get beyond," and also the essentialist formulation that sees race as something objective and fixed, a biological datum.[6] Thus we should think of race as an element of social structure rather than as an irregularity within it; we should see race as a dimension of human representation rather than an illusion. These perspectives inform the theoretical approach we call racial formation.

RACIAL FORMATION

We define racial formation as the sociohistorical process by which racial categories are created, lived out, transformed, and destroyed. Our attempt to elaborate a theory of racial formation will proceed in two steps. First, we argue that racial formation is a process of historically situated projects in which human bodies and social structures are represented and organized. Next we link racial formation to the evolution of hegemony, the way in which society is organized and ruled. Such an approach, we believe, can facilitate understanding of a whole range of contemporary controversies and dilemmas involving race, including the nature of racism, the relationship of race to other forms of differences, inequalities, and oppression such as sexism and nationalism, and the dilemmas of racial identity today.

From a racial formation perspective, race is a matter of both social structure and cultural representation. Too often, the attempt is made to understand race simply or primarily in terms of only one of these two analytical dimensions.[7] For example, efforts to explain racial inequality as a purely social structural phenomenon are unable to account for the origins, patterning, and transformation of racial difference. Conversely, many examinations of racial difference—understood as a matter of cultural attributes a la ethnicity theory, or as a society-wide signification system, a la some poststructuralist accounts—cannot comprehend such structural phenomena as racial stratification in the labor market or patterns of residential segregation.

An alternative approach is to think of racial formation processes as occurring through a linkage between structure and representation. Racial projects do the ideological "work" of making these links. A racial project is simultaneously an interpretation, representation, or explanation of racial dynamics, and an effort to reorganize and redistribute resources along particular racial lines. Racial projects connect what race means in a particular discursive practice and the ways in which both social structures and everyday experiences are racially organized, based upon that meaning. Let us consider this proposition, first in terms of large-scale or macro-level social processes, and then in terms of other dimensions of the racial formation process.

RACIAL FORMATION AS A MACRO-LEVEL SOCIAL PROCESS

To interpret the meaning of race is to frame it social structurally. Consider for example, this statement by Charles Murray on welfare reform:

> My proposal for dealing with the racial issue in social welfare is to re-peal every bit of legislation and reverse every court decision that in any way requires, recommends, or awards differential treatment according to race, and thereby put us back onto the track that we left in 1965. We may argue about the appropriate limits of government interven-tion in trying to enforce the ideal, but at least it should be possible to identify the ideal: Race is not a morally admissible reason for treating one person differently from another. Period.[8]

Here there is a partial but significant analysis of the meaning of race: it is not a morally valid basis upon which to treat people "differently from one another." We may notice someone's race, but we cannot act upon that awareness. We must act in a "color-blind" fashion. This analysis of the meaning of race is immediately linked to a specific conception of the role of race in the social structure: it can play no part in government action, save in "the enforcement of the ideal." No state policy can legitimately require, recommend, or award different status according to race. This example can be classified as a particular type of racial project in the present-day U.S.—a "neoconservative" one.

Conversely, to recognize the racial dimension in social structure is to interpret the meaning of race. Consider the following statement by the late Supreme Court Justice Thurgood Marshall on minority "set-aside" programs:

> A profound difference separates governmental actions that themselves are racist, and governmental actions that seek to remedy the effects of prior racism or to prevent neutral government activity from perpetuating the effects of such racism.[9]

Here the focus is on the racial dimensions of social structure—in this case of state activity and policy. The argument is that state actions in the past and present have treated people in very different ways according to their race, and thus the government cannot retreat from its policy responsibilities in this area. It cannot suddenly declare itself "color-blind" without in fact perpetuating the same type of differential, racist treatment.[10] Thus, race continues to signify difference and structure inequality. Here, racialized social structure is immediately linked to an interpretation of the meaning of race. This example too can be classified as a particular type of racial project in the present-day U.S.—a "liberal" one.

These two examples of contemporary racial projects are drawn from mainstream political debate; they may be characterized as center-right and center-left expressions of contemporary racial politics.[11] We can, however, expand the discussion of racial formation processes far beyond these familiar examples. In fact, we can identify racial projects in at least three other analytical dimensions: first, the political spectrum can be broadened to include radical projects, on both the left and right, as well as along other political axes. Second, analysis of racial projects can take place not only at the macro-level of racial policy-making, state activity, and collective action, but also at the level of everyday experience. Third, the concept of racial projects can be applied across historical time, to identify racial formation dynamics in the past. We shall now offer examples of each of these types of racial projects.

THE POLITICAL SPECTRUM OF RACIAL FORMATION

We have encountered examples of a neoconservative racial project, in which the significance of race is denied, leading to a "color-blind" racial politics and "hands off' policy orientation; and of a "liberal" racial project, in which the significance of race is affirmed, leading to an egalitarian and "activist" state policy. But these by no means exhaust the political possibilities. Other racial projects can be readily identified on the contemporary U.S. scene. For example, "far right" projects, which uphold biologistic and racist views of difference, explicitly argue for white supremacist policies. "New right" projects overtly claim to hold "color-blind" views, but covertly manipulate racial fears in order to achieve political gains.[12] On the left, "radical democratic" projects invoke notions of racial "difference" in combination with egalitarian politics and policy.

Further variations can also be noted. For example, "nationalist" projects, both conservative and radical, stress the incompatibility of racially defined group identity with the legacy of white supremacy, and therefore advocate a social structural solution of separation, either complete or partial.[13] As we saw in Chapter 3, nationalist currents represent a profound legacy of the centuries of racial absolutism that initially defined the meaning of race in the U.S. Nationalist concerns continue to influence racial debate in the form of Afrocentrism and other expressions of identity politics.

Taking the range of politically organized racial projects as a whole, we can "map" the current pattern of racial formation at the level of the public sphere, the "macro-level" in which public debate and mobilization takes place.[14] But important as this is, the terrain on which racial formation occurs is broader yet.

RACIAL FORMATION AS EVERYDAY EXPERIENCE

Here too racial projects link signification and structure, not so much as efforts to shape policy or define large-scale meaning, but as the applications of "common sense." To see racial projects operating at the level of everyday life, we have only to examine the many ways in which, often unconsciously, we "notice" race.

One of the first things we notice about people when we meet them (along with their sex) is their race. We utilize race to provide clues about who a person is. This fact is made painfully obvious when we encounter someone whom we cannot conveniently racially categorize—someone who is, for example, racially "mixed" or of an ethnic/racial group we are not familiar with. Such an encounter becomes a source of discomfort and momentarily a crisis of racial meaning.

Our ability to interpret racial meanings depends on preconceived notions of a racialized social structure. Comments such as, "Funny, you don't look black," betray an underlying image of what black should be. We expect people to act out their apparent racial identities; indeed we become disoriented when they do not. The black banker harassed by police while walking in casual clothes through his own well-off neighborhood, the Latino or white kid rapping in perfect Afro patois, the unending faux pas committed by whites who assume that the nonwhites they encounter are servants or tradespeople, the belief that nonwhite colleagues are less qualified persons hired to fulfill affirmative action guidelines, indeed the whole gamut of racial stereotypes—that "white men can't jump," that Asians can't dance, etc. etc.—all testify to the way a racialized social structure shapes racial experience and conditions meaning. Analysis of such stereotypes reveals the always present, already active link between our view of the social structure—its demography, its laws, its customs, its threats—and our conception of what race means.

Conversely, our ongoing interpretation of our experience in racial terms shapes our relations to the institutions and organizations through which we are imbedded in social structure. Thus we expect differences in skin color, or other racially coded characteristics, to explain social differences. Temperament, sexuality, intelligence, athletic ability, aesthetic preferences, and so on are presumed to be fixed and discernible from the palpable mark of race. Such diverse questions as our confidence and trust in others (for example, clerks or salespeople, media figures, neighbors), our sexual preferences and romantic images, our tastes in music, films, dance, or sports, and our very ways of talking, walking, eating, and dreaming become racially coded simply because we live in a society where racial awareness is so pervasive. Thus in ways too comprehensive even to monitor consciously, and despite periodic calls—neoconservative and otherwise—for us to ignore race and adopt "color-blind" racial attitudes, skin color "differences" continue to rationalize distinct treatment of racially identified individuals and groups.

To summarize the argument so far: the theory of racial formation suggests that society is suffused with racial projects, large and small, to which all are subjected. This racial "subjection" is quintessentially ideological. Everybody learns some combination, some version, of the rules of racial classification, and of her own racial identity, often without obvious teaching or conscious inculcation. Thus are we inserted in a comprehensively racialized social structure. Race becomes "common sense"—a way of comprehending, explaining, and acting in the world. A vast web of racial projects mediates between the discursive or representational means in which race is identified and signified on the one hand, and the institutional and organizational forms in which it is routinized and standardized on the other. These projects are the heart of the racial formation process.

Under such circumstances, it is not possible to represent race discursively without simultaneously locating it, explicitly or implicitly, in a social structural (and historical) context. Nor is it possible to organize, maintain, or transform social structures without simultaneously engaging, once more either explicitly or implicitly, in racial signification. Racial formation, therefore, is a kind of synthesis, an outcome, of the interaction of racial projects on a society-wide level. These projects are, of course, vastly different in scope and effect. They include large-scale public action, state activities, and interpretations of racial conditions in artistic, journalistic, or academic fora,[15] as well as the seemingly infinite number of racial judgments and practices we carry out at the level of individual experience.

Since racial formation is always historically situated, our understanding of the significance of race, and of the way race structures society, has changed enormously over time. The processes of racial formation we encounter today, the racial projects large and small which structure U.S. society in so many ways, are merely the present-day outcomes of a complex historical evolution. The contemporary racial order remains transient. By knowing something of how it evolved, we can perhaps better discern where it is heading. We therefore turn next to a historical survey of the racial formation process, and the conflicts and debates it has engendered.

THE EVOLUTION OF MODERN RACIAL AWARENESS

The identification of distinctive human groups, and their association with differences in physical appearance, goes back to prehistory, and can be found in the earliest documents—in the Bible, for example, or in Herodotus. But the emergence of a modern conception of race does not occur until the rise of Europe and the arrival of Europeans in the Americas. Even the hostility and suspicion with which Christian Europe viewed its two significant non-Christian "others"—the Muslims and the Jews—cannot be viewed as more than a rehearsal for racial formation, since these antagonisms, for all their bloodletting and chauvinism, were always and everywhere religiously interpreted.[16]

It was only when European explorers reached the Western Hemisphere, when the oceanic seal separating the "old" and the "new" worlds was breached, that the distinctions and categorizations fundamental to a racialized social structure, and to a discourse of race, began to appear. The European explorers were the advance guard of merchant capitalism, which sought new openings for trade. What they found exceeded their wildest dreams, for never before and never again in human history has an opportunity for the appropriation of wealth remotely approached that presented by the "discovery."[17]

But the Europeans also "discovered" people, people who looked and acted differently. These "natives" challenged their "discoverers" preexisting conceptions of the origins and possibilities of the human species.[18] The representation and interpretation of the meaning of the indigenous peoples' existence became a crucial matter, one which would affect the outcome of the enterprise of conquest. For the "discovery" raised disturbing questions as to whether all could be considered part of the same "family of man," and more practically, the extent to which native peoples could be exploited and enslaved. Thus religious debates flared over the attempt to reconcile the various Christian metaphysics with the existence of peoples who were more "different" than any whom Europe had previously known.[19]

In practice, of course, the seizure of territories and goods, the introduction of slavery through the encomienda and other forms of coerced native labor, and then through the organization of the African slave trade—not to mention the practice of outright extermination—all presupposed a worldview which distinguished Europeans, as children of God, full-fledged human beings, etc., from "others." Given the dimensions and the ineluctability of the European onslaught, given the conquerors' determination to appropriate both labor and goods, and given the presence of an axiomatic and unquestioned Christianity among them, the ferocious division of society into Europeans and "others" soon coalesced. This was true despite the famous 16th-century theological and philosophical debates about the identity of indigenous peoples.[20]

Indeed debates about the nature of the "others" reached their practical limits with a certain dispatch. Plainly they would never touch the essential: nothing, after all, would induce the Europeans to pack up and go home. We cannot examine here the early controversies over the status of American souls. We simply wish to emphasize that the "discovery" signaled a break from the previous proto-racial awareness by which Europe contemplated its "others" in a relatively disorganized fashion. In other words, we argue that the "conquest of America" was not simply an epochal historical event—however unparalleled in its importance. It was also the advent of a consolidated social structure of exploitation, appropriation, domination. Its representation, first in religious terms, but soon enough in scientific and political ones, initiated modern racial awareness.

The conquest, therefore, was the first—and given the dramatic nature of the case, perhaps the greatest—racial formation project. Its significance was by no means limited to the Western Hemisphere, for it began the work of constituting Europe as the metropole, the center, of a series of empires which could take, as Marx would later write, "the globe for a theater."[21] It represented this new imperial structure as a struggle between civilization and barbarism, and implicated in this representation all the great European philosophies, literary traditions, and social theories of the modern age.[22] In short, just as the noise of the "big bang" still resonates through the universe, so the overdetermined construction of world "civilization" as a product of the rise of Europe and the subjugation of the rest of us, still defines the race concept.

FROM RELIGION TO SCIENCE

After the initial depredations of conquest, religious justifications for racial difference gradually gave way to scientific ones. By the time of the Enlightenment, a general awareness of race was pervasive, and most of the great philosophers of Europe, such as Hegel, Kant, Hume, and Locke, had issued virulently racist opinions.

The problem posed by race during the late 18th century was markedly different than it had been in the age of conquest, expropriation, and slaughter. The social structures in which race operated were no longer primarily those of military conquest and plunder, nor of the establishment of thin beachheads of colonization on the edge of what had once seemed a limitless wilderness. Now the issues were much more complicated: nation-building, establishment of national economies in the world trading system, resistance to the arbitrary authority of monarchs, and the assertion of the "natural rights" of "man," including the right of revolution.[23] In such a situation, racially organized exploitation, in the form of slavery, the expansion of colonies, and the continuing expulsion of native peoples, was both necessary and newly difficult to justify.

The invocation of scientific criteria to demonstrate the "natural" basis of racial hierarchy was both a logical consequence of the rise of this form of knowledge, and an attempt to provide a more subtle and nuanced account of human complexity in the new, "enlightened" age. Spurred on by the classificatory scheme of living organisms devised by Linnaeus in Systema Naturae (1735), many scholars in the eighteenth and nineteenth centuries dedicated themselves to the identification and ranking of variations in humankind. Race was conceived as a biological concept, a matter of species. Voltaire wrote that "The negro race is a species of men (sic) as different from ours … as the breed of spaniels is from that of greyhounds," and in a formulation echoing down from his century to our own, declared that "If their understanding is not of a different nature from ours …, it is at least greatly inferior. They are not capable of any great application or association of ideas, and seem formed neither for the advantages nor the abuses of philosophy".[24]

Jefferson, the preeminent exponent of the Enlightenment doctrine of "the rights of man" on North American shores, echoed these sentiments:

> In general their existence appears to participate more of sensation than reflection.… [I]n memory they are equal to whites, in reason much inferior … [and] in imagination they are dull, tasteless, and anomalous.… I advance it therefore … that the blacks, whether originally a different race, or made distinct by time and circumstances, are inferior to the whites.… Will not a lover of natural history, then, one who views the gradations in all the animals with the eye of philosophy, excuse an

effort to keep those in the department of Man (sic) as distinct as nature
has formed them?[25]

Such claims of species distinctiveness among humans justified the inequitable
allocation of political and social rights, while still upholding the doctrine of "the
rights of man." The quest to obtain a precise scientific definition of race sustained
debates that continue to rage today. Yet despite efforts ranging from Dr. Samuel
Morton's studies of cranial capacity[26] to contemporary attempts to base racial
classification on shared gene pools,[27] the concept of race has defied biological
definition.

In the 19th century, Count Joseph Arthur de Gobineau drew upon the most
respected scientific studies of his day to compose his four-volume Essay on the
Inequality of Races (1853–1855).[28] He not only greatly influenced the racial thinking of the period, but his themes would be echoed in the racist ideologies of the
next one hundred years: beliefs that superior races produced superior cultures
and that racial intermixtures resulted in the degradation of the superior racial
stock. These ideas found expression, for instance, in the eugenics movement
launched by Darwin's cousin, Francis Galton, which had an immense impact on
scientific and sociopolitical thought in Europe and the United States.[29] In the wake
of civil war and emancipation, and with immigration from southern and Eastern
Europe as well as East Asia running high, the U.S. was particularly fertile ground for
notions such as social darwinism and eugenics.

Attempts to discern the scientific meaning of race continue to the present day.
For instance, an essay by Arthur Jensen that argued that hereditary factors shape
intelligence not only revived the "nature or nurture" controversy, but also raised
highly volatile questions about racial equality itself.[30] All such attempts seek to
remove the concept of race from the historical context in which it arose and developed. They employ an essentialist approach that suggests instead that the truth
of race is a matter of innate characteristics, of which skin color and other physical
attributes provide only the most obvious, and in some respects most superficial,
indicators.

FROM SCIENCE TO POLITICS

It has taken scholars more than a century to reject biologistic notions of race in
favor of an approach that regards race as a social concept. This trend has been
slow and uneven, and even today remains somewhat embattled, but its overall
direction seems clear. At the turn of the century Max Weber discounted biological
explanations for racial conflict and instead highlighted the social and political

factors that engendered such conflict.[31] W. E. B. DuBois argued for a sociopolitical definition of race by identifying "the color line" as "the problem of the 20th century."[32] Pioneering cultural anthropologist Franz Boas rejected attempts to link racial identifications and cultural traits, labeling as pseudoscientific any assumption of a continuum of "higher" and "lower" cultural groups.[33] Other early exponents of social, as opposed to biological, views of race included Robert E. Park, founder of the "Chicago school" of sociology, and Alain Leroy Locke, philosopher and theorist of the Harlem renaissance.[34]

Perhaps more important than these and subsequent intellectual efforts, however, were the political struggles of racially defined groups themselves. Waged all around the globe under a variety of banners such as anti-colonialism and civil rights, these battles to challenge various structural and cultural racisms have been a major feature of 20th century politics. The racial horrors of the 20th century— colonial slaughter and apartheid, the genocide of the holocaust, and the massive bloodlettings required to end these evils—have also indelibly marked the theme of race as a political issue par excellence.

As a result of prior efforts and struggles, we have now reached the point of fairly general agreement that race is not a biologically given but rather a socially constructed way of differentiating human beings. While a tremendous achievement, the transcendence of biologistic conceptions of race does not provide any reprieve from the dilemmas of racial injustice and conflict, nor from controversies over the significance of race in the present. Views of race as socially constructed simply recognize the fact that these conflicts and controversies are now more properly framed on the terrain of politics. By privileging politics in the analysis that follows we do not mean to suggest that race has been displaced as a concern of scientific inquiry, or that struggles over cultural representation are no longer important. We do argue, however, that race is now a preeminently political phenomenon. Such an assertion invites examination of the evolving role of racial politics in the U.S. This is the subject to which we now turn.

DICTATORSHIP, DEMOCRACY, HEGEMONY

For most of its existence both as a European colony and as an independent nation, the U.S. was a racial dictatorship. From 1607 to 1865—258 years—most nonwhites were firmly eliminated from the sphere of politics.[35] After the civil war there was the brief egalitarian experiment of Reconstruction which terminated ignominiously in 1877. In its wake followed almost a century of legally sanctioned segregation and denial of the vote, nearly absolute in the South and much of the Southwest, less effective in the North and far West, but formidable in any case.[36]

These barriers fell only in the mid-1960s, a mere quarter-century ago. Nor did the successes of the black movement and its allies mean that all obstacles to their political participation had now been abolished. Patterns of racial inequality have proven, unfortunately, to be quite stubborn and persistent.

It is important, therefore, to recognize that in many respects, racial dictatorship is the norm against which all U.S. politics must be measured. The centuries of racial dictatorship have had three very large consequences: first, they defined "American" identity as white, as the negation of racialized "otherness"—at first largely African and indigenous, later Latin American and Asian as well.[37] This negation took shape in both law and custom, in public institutions and in forms of cultural representation. It became the archetype of hegemonic rule in the U.S. It was the successor to the conquest as the "master" racial project.

Second, racial dictatorship organized (albeit sometimes in an incoherent and contradictory fashion) the "color line," rendering it the fundamental division in U.S. society. The dictatorship elaborated, articulated, and drove racial divisions not only through institutions, but also through psyches, extending up to our own time the racial obsessions of the conquest and slavery periods.

Third, racial dictatorship consolidated the oppositional racial conscious-ness and organization originally framed by marronage[38] and slave revolts, by indigenous resistance, and by nationalisms of various sorts. Just as the conquest created the "native" where once there had been Pequot, Iroquois, or Tutelo, so too it created the "black" where once there had been Asante or Ovimbundu, Yoruba or Bakongo.

The transition from a racial dictatorship to a racial democracy has been a slow, painful, and contentious one; it remains far from complete. A recognition of the abiding presence of racial dictatorship, we contend, is crucial for the development of a theory of racial formation in the U.S. It is also crucial to the task of relating racial formation to the broader context of political practice, organization, and change.

In this context, a key question arises: In what way is racial formation related to politics as a whole? How, for example, does race articulate with other axes of oppression and difference—most importantly class and gender—along which politics is organized today?

The answer, we believe, lies in the concept of <u>hegemony</u>. Antonio Gramsci—the Italian communist who placed this concept at the center of his life's work—understood it as the conditions necessary, in a given society, for the achievement and consolidation of rule. He argued that hegemony was always constituted by a combination of coercion and consent. Although rule can be obtained by force, it cannot be secured and maintained, especially in modern society, without the element of consent. Gramsci conceived of consent as far more than merely the legitimation of authority. In his view, consent extended to the incorporation by the ruling group of many of the key interests of subordinated groups, often to the explicit disadvantage of the rulers themselves.[39] Gramsci's treatment of hegemony went even farther: he argued that in order to consolidate their hegemony, ruling groups must elaborate and maintain a popular system of ideas and practices—through education, the media, religion, folk wisdom, etc.—which he called "common sense." It is through its production and its adherence to this "common sense," this ideology (in the broadest sense of the term), that a society gives its consent to the way in which it is ruled.[40]

These provocative concepts can be extended and applied to an understanding of racial rule. In the Americas, the conquest represented the violent introduction of a new form of rule whose relationship with those it subjugated was almost entirely coercive. In the U.S., the origins of racial division, and of racial signification and identity formation, lie in a system of rule that was extremely dictatorial. The mass murders and expulsions of indigenous people, and the enslavement of Africans, surely evoked and inspired little consent in their founding moments.

Over time, however, the balance of coercion and consent began to change. It is possible to locate the origins of hegemony right within the heart of racial dictatorship, for the effort to possess the oppressor's tools—religion and philosophy in this case—was crucial to emancipation (the effort to possess oneself). As Ralph Ellison reminds us, "The slaves often took the essence of the aristocratic ideal (as they took Christianity) with far more seriousness than their masters."[41] In their language, in their religion with its focus on the Exodus theme and on Jesus's tribulations, in their music with its figuring of suffering, resistance, perseverance, and transcendence, in their interrogation of a political philosophy that sought perpetually to rationalize their bondage in a supposedly "free" society, the slaves incorporated elements of racial rule into their thought and practice, turning them against their original bearers.

Racial rule can be understood as a slow and uneven historical process that has moved from dictatorship to democracy, from domination to hegemony. In this transition, hegemonic forms of racial rule—those based on consent—eventually came to supplant those based on coercion. Of course, before this assertion can be accepted, it must be qualified in important ways. By no means has the U.S. established racial democracy at the end of the century, and by no means is coercion a thing of the past. But the sheer complexity of the racial questions U.S. society confronts today, the welter of competing racial projects and contradictory racial experiences that Americans undergo, suggests that hegemony is a useful and appropriate term with which to characterize contemporary racial rule.

RACE, RACISM, AND HEGEMONY

Parallel to the debates on the concept of race, recent academic and political controversies about the nature of racism have centered on whether it is primarily an ideological or structural phenomenon. Proponents of the former position argue that racism is first and foremost a matter of beliefs and attitudes, doctrines and discourse, which only then give rise to unequal and unjust practices and structures.[42] Advocates of the latter view see racism as primarily a matter of economic stratification, residential segregation, and other institutionalized forms of inequality that then give rise to ideologies of privilege.[43]

From the standpoint of racial formation, these debates are fundamentally misguided. They discuss the problem of racism in a rigid "either-or" manner. We believe it is crucial to disrupt the fixity of these positions by simultaneously arguing that ideological beliefs have structural consequences, and that social structures give rise to beliefs. Racial ideology and social structure, therefore, mutually shape the nature of racism in a complex, dialectical, and overdetermined manner.

Even those racist projects that at first glance appear chiefly ideological turn out upon closer examination to have significant institutional and social structural dimensions. For example, what we have called "far right" projects appear at first glance to be centrally ideological. They are rooted in biologistic doctrine, after all. The same seems to hold for certain conservative black nationalist projects that have deep commitments to biologism.[44] But the unending stream of racist assaults initiated by the far right, the apparently increasing presence of skinheads in high schools, the proliferation of neo-Nazi websites on the Internet, and the appearance of racist talk shows on cable access channels, all suggest that the organizational manifestations of the far right racial projects exist and will endure.[45]

By contrast, even those racisms that at first glance appear to be chiefly structural upon closer examination reveal a deeply ideological component. For example, since the racial right abandoned its explicit advocacy of segregation, it has not seemed to uphold—in the main—an ideologically racist project, but more primarily a structurally racist one. Yet this very transformation required tremendous efforts of ideological production. It demanded the rearticulation of civil rights doctrines of equality in suitably conservative form, and indeed the defense of continuing large-scale racial inequality as an outcome preferable to (what its advocates have seen as) the threat to democracy that affirmative action, busing, and large-scale "race-specific" social spending would entail.[46] Even more tellingly, this project took shape through a deeply manipulative coding of subtextual appeals to white racism, notably in a series of political campaigns for high office that have occurred over recent decades. The retreat of social policy from any practical commitment to racial justice, and the relentless reproduction and divulgation of this theme at the level of everyday life—where whites are now "fed up" with all the "special treatment" received by nonwhites, etc.—constitutes the hegemonic racial project at this time. It therefore exhibits an unabashed structural racism all the more brazen because on the ideological or signification level it adheres to a principle to "treat everyone alike."

In summary, the racism of today is no longer a virtual monolith, as was the racism of yore. Today, racial hegemony is "messy." The complexity of the present situation is the product of a vast historical legacy of structural inequality and invidious racial representation, which has been confronted during the post–World War II period with an opposition more serious and effective than any it had faced before. The result is a deeply ambiguous and contradictory spectrum of racial projects, unremittingly conflictual racial politics, and confused and ambivalent racial identities of all sorts.

COMMENT

My own personal interpretation of racial formation follows as I summarize, highlight, and elaborate. Omi and Winant define **race** in the text above as "a concept that signifies and symbolizes social conflicts and interests by referring to different types of human bodies." They go on to say that "selection of these particular human features for purposes of racial signification is always and necessarily a social and historical process." This process is **racial formation**; the "process by which racial categories are created, lived out, transformed, and destroyed." Rather than a biological understanding of race, or a simply empirical understanding of race, Omi and Winant connect the process of identifying race with how it is used or operates in society. They explain racial formation as having two parts: the **racial project** and **hegemony**.

The racial project is "simultaneously an interpretation, representation, or explanation of racial dynamics and an effort to reorganize and redistribute resources along particular racial lines." Hegemony is defined as "the conditions necessary, in a given society, for the achievement and consolidation of rule ... hegemony was always constituted by a combination of coercion and consent. Although rule can be obtained by force, it cannot be secured and maintained ... without the element of consent ... consent (is) far more than merely the legitimation of authority ... consent (is) extended to the incorporation by the ruling group of many of the key interests of subordinated groups, often to the explicit disadvantage of the rulers themselves."

RACIAL PROJECT RE-CONSTRUCTED

It is important to note that, for the knowledge producer of this book, the racial project is not limited to any one single type of defining characteristic. Although the author read and understands Omi and Winant as limiting their racial projects to phenotypes, there is no need for that limitation as *any perceived* characteristic can be used as a racial marker and function in the way traditional racializations function. This understanding of race through any signified characteristic includes all possible explanations of race without privileging any single racial project over another. In other words, one does not need to determine which racialization is the only way to understand race. The characteristic does not need to be a permanent one; the characteristic simply has to be a characteristic that other people can recognize and understand once it is signified. In fact, once a characteristic is signified, certain pre-existing social connections and social dynamics will be noticed. Perhaps because of the perceived prominence of "color" as being a major racial marker in the U.S., the condition of phenotype by Omi and Winant was necessary. This process of racial formation, if limited primarily along the lines of phenotype or skin color, loses its value as an explanation of race once one changes perspective. For example, in some areas of sub-Saharan Africa or in remote areas of China, everyone is the same skin color; yet, there are social dynamics identifiable as racializations, but utilizing a different characteristic (e.g., tribal affiliation or dialect). To clarify, when everyone around you is black or yellow, then color ceases to be a characteristic usable to signify the "other" or to distinguish one person from another.

Omi and Winant say that race signifies and symbolizes social conflicts and interests. By redefining the construct **conflict**, it is easy to see social conflict and tension arise in all areas of life. Conflict does not necessarily mean violence or even hostile behavior; it can simply mean and represent difference. In the context of race, the othering process is the process where one identifies characteristics that are different from the self to an "other." The characteristic that is noticed is not always the same. Every time we look at someone, we make that person an "other" by noticing something that is different. This is not necessarily bad; in fact, it is part of the way personal identity is constructed. **Identity** is the understanding of one's self and includes society's perception of that person through the language of race; in other words, we construct our identity through difference. The connection between race and identity is explained further below. This helps to explain the expression, "they all look alike." One hears this expression when people see different groups of people for the first time; "all Asians look alike;" "all African Americans look alike;" and "all Anglo Americans look alike." Initial observation focuses on generalizations of difference; it is only later after further details are signified that one no longer believes this is true.

Again, notice that the reconstruction of the construct "conflict" is necessarily broad to include all possible subjective understandings of "conflict." If one were to distinguish between mild and severe conflict, who would decide the criterion for that? What is conflict for one person may not be conflict for another. This book has already discussed the process of narrowing a definition to create types of difference for a specific agenda of knowledge production. Narrowing of definition is done with the purpose to signify certain conflicts in a way that privileges one perspective over all others; it is essentially the process through which one can create an arbitrary moral high ground. This process coincidentally opens the door to accusations of hypocrisy and possible double standards, which is an important aspect of race and racism.

In order to avoid the problem of double standards and hypocrisy, attitudes and behavior must be treated uniformly. Thus, if one maintains that a particular racism is intolerable, then all racism is intolerable. If some racism is tolerated, then all racism has to be tolerated. If action must be taken against a kind of racism, action must be taken against all forms of racism. It should be immediately apparent that legislation against all forms of discrimination would make everyday life impossible as we know it now; thus, legislation based on subjective understandings of race should not be written. This also means that people must learn to tolerate the beliefs and perspectives of others, especially when we disagree with or dislike those beliefs. This does not mean that practicing racism, which results in harm and damage to others and their property, is acceptable. Harm or damage to others and their property must be resolved where the guilty party is held responsible for any damage. However, if racist attitudes do not result in the direct harm of an individual nor does it destroy another's property, then one adjusts accordingly by the situation. If for example a car dealer is openly racist against a certain type of person, then a buyer would simply look for a car from another dealer. Of course, the fallout might be that many people would stop buying cars from the openly racist car dealer—potentially putting him out of business, but the discriminated person still has a car that was bought from another dealer. In this situation neither legislation or the use of force was required to resolve the situation.

Recall that the othering process has no limitation with regard to usable characteristics for racialization. Difference in height, weight, body type, mental ability, hair color, and eye color are familiar racializations. We can go on to include clothing, hairstyle, body art, uniform, occupation, idiosyncrasy, citizenship, etc. The list of definable racial projects or racializations is infinite. The list is infinite because we live in a dynamic society that is constantly changing and introducing new categories with new advances in technology and human behavior, enabling even more ways of making race. For example, the racial project of "blogger" did not exist twenty years ago.

Notice that the list of characteristics that can be used to "make race" includes items normally excluded from lists of other knowledge producers. The justification for using these markers is the standard of how seriously people take those characteristics. The measure of the seriousness of a characteristic is not the duration of the characteristic, nor is it biological. The criterion is life or death. Can one lose one's life over a characteristic, even a temporary disposable one? Unfortunately, yes, one may lose one's life because of a temporary characteristic that has nothing to do with skin color. For the person who loses his or her life, that "insignificant-to-some" characteristic is deadly serious. Here are some examples. In Cambodia in the 1970s, people were killed for wearing glasses because it was seen as a sign of education and exposure to Western influences. U.S. military officers in Iraq or Afghanistan are targeted by their uniform or the vehicles in which they travel. The Bloods and Crips are two rival gangs in Los Angeles, California, that are distinguished by the color of their clothing. One may lose one's life because one is wearing the wrong color. That is pretty serious and something that should be hard to ignore. Clothing might not be serious to some people in certain contexts; however, people often kill each other because of the clothing they are wearing, which is usually taken off at the end of the day. Spying is a very serious offense and is characterized by pretending to be someone else. Identical twins often try to find something that distinguishes one from the other, even if it is just birth order; for example, in the case of two Korean women who were identical twins; one of them always referred to the other as "elder sister" in the Korean language. The older sister always called her twin by the younger sister's first name. They both have friends with larger age gaps but call those friends by their names rather than using the word for sister, as is the custom when a younger female addresses a female who is older. The twins not only signified their birth order but took on the traditional roles of older and younger sister. The more two people are similar, the more sensitive and particular the racialization of the othering process becomes. Additionally, in Korea, dialect and hometown become significant racial markers in a country where language and phenotype are similar.

With great respect to Omi and Winant, the author modifies the **definition of race** as a category of people based on *any* characteristic that can be used to create an "other." Anything may serve as a racial marker and be signified in a way that becomes recognizable by others. To put it another way, race is made by naming, signifying, or identifying a characteristic and putting people into a category based on that characteristic, *even if it is only a single person that qualifies to be put into that category.* The racial project or racialization can be called "making race." Put in this way, just as Omi and Winant state, race is not necessarily an evil that needs to be eradicated from society; there is a stigma and negativity attached to the construct "racism." However, **racism** is to identify someone through a single category, expect that person to act according to that category, and treat that person differently because of that category; but then, are we not all racists? For example, I recognize and distinguish my children over the children of others; my expectation of my children is clear as I remind them frequently, and I do not treat my children in the same way I treat other children because they are my children. I have racialized my children, and I treat them differently based on that racialization. I treat other children differently because they are not my children. If there is a food shortage, I will not share my limited food supplies with other children; I will only share that food with my family. I am, therefore a racist, in the strict sense. Here, the discrimination can be viewed as positive, yet it is racist by definition. It is interesting to note that in a time of food shortages, my lack of sharing with others could be seen as bad by others who have no food. This could also be presented as an example of parental love and care or even sacrifice. Therefore, eradication of racism should not be the goal of race-talk as it includes subjective knowledge production that might be considered a social good. To criminalize only certain kinds of racial discrimination is hypocritical; in this type of narrow thinking, one can only establish double standards that many will feel obligated to disrupt and disobey.

Instead of perpetuating the signification of narrow racial knowledge production for the purpose of legislating morality, the *de-signification* of racial projects in public and political discourse is suggested as an alternative activity. Perhaps this is different from what many other knowledge producers in the field of race theory are saying; others believe that racial awareness must be raised and signified. However, this author says that while awareness on a personal level is important and necessary, on the political level, most race-making, commonly understood, is counterproductive, as it often becomes a legitimation of violence and conflict. Recall the earlier discussion regarding tolerance; by teaching tolerance, one also teaches intolerance. People who do not conform to the teachings of tolerance cannot be tolerated. Identifying certain kinds of racializations as bad encourages and sanctions violence against those people with those characteristics. Once one adopts the subjectivity of tolerance, then many will even celebrate when horrible acts of violence are committed against the signified bad people. Whether they really were bad people who deserve the violence and hate thrown upon them does not seem to matter to the proponents of tolerance.

One must not think that, by having a broad understanding of race that results in an infinite number of racial categories, we have reduced our discussion to meaningless banter. Rather, it must be remembered that the standard of what is bad and good is subjective; so to simply ban racist behavior is a problematic activity because banning racist behavior includes banning behavior that is perceived as a social good to some in a subjective way. The knowledge production surrounding legislation often does not consider repercussions and consequences beyond a narrow subjective perspective. At the same time, the bad behavior that was initially signified and legislated against does not stop and continues in spite of the raised awareness. One cannot write a law and expect that people will change their beliefs; legislation of morality rarely works, if ever. For example, prohibition of alcohol and drugs are two well-known attempts to legislate morality; neither achieved their goal of stopping the relevant activity. In contemporary race-talk, only negative aspects and application of racism are signified as if these are the only racializations that matter or even exist; this type of knowledge production is confusing and is open to abuse and distortion. In fact, so-called positive racializations do not always play out in ways that benefit everyone. There are often unintended consequences that come from the efforts to do good things for others. As the definition of religion was broad in order to make visible and signify important behavior and actions that would otherwise have been ignored, so also the definition of race is broadened in the most extreme way possible to make visible important issues that would otherwise go unnoticed; unnoticed because focus is concentrated only on certain specific racial projects. As a matter of fact, with this perspective it becomes clear that race making is extremely diverse in expression, purpose, function, and understanding. This is true on not just a personal individual level, but on the global scale as well. Race making is an important part of personal identity as well as corporate profit seeking activities.

Another way of expressing racism is by the construct discrimination. **Discrimination** is making a distinction between different things to determine which is better or preferred when making a choice. There are many occasions where being very discriminatory is a social good. Shoppers who are careful and wise are complimented by being called discriminating shoppers. When I feed my children, I do so because I have discriminated against all other children in the neighborhood. Sleeping with my wife and not your wife happens partly because of discrimination. At what point is discrimination bad, and by whose standard and subjective perspective is the criteria made? Is it that all forms of discrimination are bad, or is it that some people do not agree or like how other people discriminate? It becomes a matter of political knowledge production. The process of legitimizing some forms of discrimination while criminalizing others is typical of hypocritical double standards, which are unacceptable in this class. Imagine if parents told their children not to be discriminating when it comes to selecting a life partner; anyone would be good enough because everyone is equal. Many people would have a problem with this piece of parental advice. To not select someone based on some arbitrary characteristic could be considered, to some, racism in the typical sense if the characteristic cited was already signified as race. However, a personal preference is a personal preference. The preferences that matter should be the concern of the one making the choice, not of others, because the one making the choice must live with that choice; furthermore, how a parent teaches a child to make choices is the responsibility of the parent. The way a parent teaches his or her child to discriminate will depend on that parent's prior knowledge.

What should not be forgotten is that choices involve cost and sacrifice. In order to obtain something, one must pay a price. Assuming a limited amount of resources, one cannot have everything; one must sacrifice one choice in order to have the other. This is not to be confused with the idea of a "zero-sum game" in that giving and taking always balances to a zero sum. Rather, people should understand the costs associated with the choices they make and they should also realize that this cost must be paid by the one making the choice; choice is ultimately made because the choice was deemed worth the cost to that individual. Legislation of morality or the writing of arbitrary legislation based on subjectively produced knowledge often erases the cost of short-sighted and irresponsible choices and shifts the loss or cost on to others. It is often the case that when choices are made without consideration of cost, not only are outcomes less than favorable, but who has to pay and how much they have to pay are often a surprise. The Social Security program is a good example of this phenomenon. The program is based on a racialization of older people living in the U.S. and proposes to do what appears to be a good deed; that is, provide for people in society stereotypically portrayed as weak or poor. The government maintains that it will provide monies for this race of people; this reduces the incentive for people to save for retirement. In other words, the cost of not saving for retirement is reduced. The cost does not disappear; rather the cost is now put on the future generations who are working today to pay the benefits of those who receive today. Unless the program is reformed or modified in some way, people under 25 years of age are unlikely to see any payout from the program as it is "bankrupt." Note how the racialization for a social good coincidentally results in a social bad for people not included in that original racialization.

THE PROBLEM OF RACE: GENERALIZATION VS. SPECIFIC

Though everyone makes race most of the time, all race-making has the problem of **generalization** vs. **specific**. Part of the way humans learn is through generalization or through the use of broad strokes to explain and understand phenomena. It is the creation of reference points to generate context and orient a person in life; racial categories are generalizations about groups of people. However, people do not live on the level of the general; rather, we live in the specific. The individual is the specific that stands in contrast with the generalization. For example, I love my mother— not all mothers, but my mother. When people live in the specific and use generalizations, they discover that generalizations do not allow them to understand differences in detail. Upon closer inspection, generalizations are often true, but only to a point, a single characteristic. Generalizations are adequate for orientation but wholly inadequate for subtle decisions and responses. Actual individual decisions must be made on the order of the specific with consideration of detail and uniqueness. The same is true when one tries to go from the specific to the general. Potential problems arise when our experience with the specific informs and influences our understanding of the general category. At best going from the general to the specific or from the specific to the general can only be a partial under-standing of the entire category.

For example, males and females are all human, but males are not females; senior citizens are all older people, but they are not all male. The extreme expression of individuality is our name (or social security number). Each person is different to the point that each of us has a different name. However, society does not throw away generalizations for the sake of the individual or because of the uniqueness of the individual does society do away with generalizations; rather, we come to an understanding that generalities are generalities, which are true only to a single defining trait or characteristic. On the level of the individual, differences are many and significant.

When getting to know an individual, generalities are simply inadequate for the task. One can know what an Asian is in racial terms, but it does not mean one knows all Asians, nor should one assume Asians are all the same in every way. Each Asian person can be seen in many different ways; nevertheless, society cannot function in certain ways as a society if the individual is prioritized over any generalization. That is, the uniqueness of an Asian person does not eradicate the generality of "Asian."

Racializations are subjectively true, but they are also subjectively false; this is not unlike the "**fuzzy logic**" idea in probability math and philosophy. In fuzzy logic, ideas are both true and false at the same time. This notion of being true and false at the same time is relevant to this discussion of race because perceptions of race are not absolute; they are subjective. This means that any racialization is both true and false at the same time because of different perspectives. When getting to know an individual, one does so initially through several recognized characteristics. As more labels and characteristics are learned that can be applied to that person, one sees the uniqueness of that individual. The individual is the category of one, the smallest minority. Even on the level of the individual there are still more details, which increases our "expertise" regarding that person; perhaps this is the time one can invoke the construct of intimacy, intimacy in the sense that one person knows another on a level of detail that is exclusive and private. Keep in mind that just which details are considered exclusive and private are still subjective.

All people are individuals and all of us fit into more than just one category; humans are all unique in many ways, not just one or even several ways. Humans are individuals who others seek to understand, oppress, exploit, befriend, or love. Humans are more complex than objectification leads us to believe. Each and every one of us carries an infinite number of racial markers; which one is signified at any given moment is dependent on who is looking at us and making race. To ascribe a single race onto a person or to imagine that there is only one racially significant racial marker per person is to draw a **caricature** of that person. That is, to signify only one of the many characteristics of a person, as if that is the only characteristic that matters or is important to know is to distort that person's identity; the caricature is a little bit true but is mostly false. Knowing an individual by only one racial marker is to sacrifice all other markers and deny their potential significance for the individual.

RACE AND IDENTITY

This brings us to the issue of race and identity. Many race theories would, for any individual, prioritize one racial project, racialization, or understanding at the expense of other racial projects. For example, if I am to self-identify as "yellow," then am I always yellow? When I go home my children do not proclaim that their yellow father has come home; at home, I am simply "awesome and amazingly funny dad." Yellow is not a racial marker that is always or even regularly invoked. At the same time, this does not mean that yellow cannot be one of my racial markers because many people still will see me as a yellow. Sometimes, for people who see me as yellow, in order to see a different racialization, they must be primed or taught to see something different.

In the late 1990s, I attended a conference session where a presenter said that Koreans will be assimilated to American society when they can speak English fluently. I raised my hand and asked everyone to look at me. I said that I spoke English fluently, I was punctual, I dressed like an American, my mannerisms were pretty much American, so I guess I could call myself an assimilated Korean person. Everyone in the room nodded in agreement, and I felt like some people were congratulating me in their minds for finally achieving the correct and prescribed dream that immigrants are supposed to have. I then said that I was not assimilated because I had to prove to everyone that I was assimilated. The rules of assimilation are that you would know just by looking at me that I was assimilated. I accept that there are many people who will see what they want to see when they look at me from their subjective location. I know that, over time, the impression or perspective people have of me may change, but I do not expect it or count on it, nor am I disappointed in anyway. I understand that unless I write my own identity for myself, I can only be what others see me as or what knowledge producers tell me I am. If I try to follow the prescriptions of other knowledge producers, I can only try to live up to the expectations based on some arbitrary caricature. This is unacceptable to me. I must make knowledge for myself; this knowledge is, broadly speaking, my own personal identity.[1]

Each individual's **identity** is not a single dominant racialization that we live in all the time; rather, our personal identity is the sum total of *all* racializations into which we can be put—all racializations, including the racializations we dislike, reject, and find offensive in addition to those we like to use to think of ourselves and the labels we accept from other people. For example, if I were at a family reunion, and I were to preach a sermon, at the moment everyone is looking at me, I would be many things all at the same time, and I am not really defined by any single one of them. This combination of racializations is my identity for that moment. In that family reunion, I am a son, husband, father, cousin, uncle, brother, man, Asian, Korean, preacher, nephew, tall, short, old, young, etc. all at the same time, and yet, I am not wholly any single one of them; I am not defined by any single racialization. This is the nature of racial identity generally speaking; we are always many races all the time, but each of us are always an individual.

To restrict the racial identity of an individual to a single category is to create and impose a caricature upon that individual. Details of the individual are ignored or even unnoticed because of the force of the generalized racialization. People who are invested for whatever reason in a particular racialization "police" that racialization inside and out and become enforcers of that racialization; they would use expressions like betrayer, traitor, or self-hater. In reality, generalizations can only be a little true some of the time.

HEGEMONY

Omi and Winant write in the excerpt above that hegemony is "the conditions necessary, in a given society, for the achievement and consolidation of rule ... a combination of coercion and consent ... the incorporation by the ruling group of many of the key interests of subordinated groups, often

---

1 An alternative view on immigration and assimilation and adaptation to life in America involves changing the criteria of acculturation. Instead of using exclusionary racial projects to determine if a demographic group has achieved "American" status, one should use different criteria; for example, financial independence, employability, and the ability to raise a family. If characteristics of this sort are signified instead to determine acculturation, then Asians have long since been acculturated.

to the explicit disadvantage of the rulers themselves." This cannot be more true, since racial projects are also **special interest groups** found in the political scene. By raising awareness of a category of people, lobbyists can now go to Washington, D.C. to use the political system to express and obtain the things they desire through the use of legislation. In other words, special interest groups use the coercive power of the government to gain an advantage for that particular interest group alone at the expense of others. Those in government cooperate with the requests of special interest groups because this only increases the power and reach of government while giving the appearance that government listens to the people. The use of coercion with the threat of violence through the rule of law, based on arbitrary legislation of morality, leads to increasing exploitation and oppression via the special interest group. Special interest groups function within this hegemonic system affirming and submitting to the injustice of the system because they can gain from it. The objectives of the special interest group are met through the political process; thus, the process is given the consent of the special interest group. The racialization that benefits most from this arrangement is the race of politicians. Their position, power, and ability to write laws are affirmed to the detriment of the general public through this process of hegemony. The "politician" racialization includes most of the racial projects that have traditionally been understood as oppressed. With the racial perspective of this book, it is clear that oppression and discrimination are still openly practiced in the U.S. but in a way that renders them invisible to most people.

This hegemonic process explains how race-making knowledge production is performed for profit and part of the reason why race-making will never stop. In spite of the moral outrage over some particular and specific racial projects, people hypocritically continue to embrace, use, and condone racial projects when there are tangible benefits to do so. Knowledge production assists in this process by endeavoring to persuade people to see phenomenon from a specific subjective perspective to legitimize the legislation of morality, that is, the use of force.

On the one hand, people must racialize particularly to construct personal identity. On the other hand, to elevate and codify any single racialization over all others opens the door for everyone to have their signified racialization codified to the detriment of others. This process is basically hypocritical and eventually undermines society's ability to determine and maintain a consistent and fair justice system. Laws become a farce as serious crimes are punished lightly, if at all, and victim-less crimes are pursued with extreme prejudice. Further elaboration of this dynamic will be discussed later in the discussion of the free market.

SUMMARY

After reconstructing racial formation, students should understand that our racial identity is not limited to a single racial category, but that our identity includes and incorporates all racial categories applicable to us. Racial categories or projects are based on any recognizable and teachable characteristic. There are an infinite number of categories and each person can be put into an infinite number of racial categories. Making race is part of being a human and understanding who we are in society. However, race-making is a personal affair and the attempt to codify any specific, subjective understanding of race has unintended consequences. Society uses race-making in the political realm through special interest groups and lobbying groups. In this way, various groups accept the race-making process and attempt to use it to their own advantage.

QUESTIONS FOR DISCUSSION

1. What is identity, and how is it made?

2. Can you think of certain "racisms" that are positive in intent or beneficial for society?

3. Is it possible to ban racism? If not, why not? If possible, then how?

RACIALIZE ME 7

GOAL

For students to understand from where much of our source
material for race-making and identity come

HOW DO WE RACIALIZE?

AS PREVIOUSLY STATED, there are an infinite number of racial projects
that can be and have been made. Racial projects are continuously
being made, destroyed, remade, forgotten, and normalized. When does it
begin, where does it begin, what is the source of information for racial
projects, and how are racial projects known in similar patterns from person
to person all over the country? When an individual begins to racialize is
beyond the scope of this book, but the other questions are more manage-
able, and answering them is the subject of this chapter.

Racial understanding is founded on subjectively perceived differences
and characteristics in the other. In other words, creating the other is the
process of simply recognizing someone as distinct and different from oneself by signifying specific characteristics. This chapter argues that the
racial projects all around us are the basis of one's personal and individual
identity. This identity is dynamic, shaped and reshaped as people perceive
the other. As people learn and internalize more racial projects their identity
is modified.

Everything around us screams racial projects. Every time we open our
eyes, we racialize the world and the people in it. Omi and Winant's racial
formation takes place over a long period of time. However, with the advent
of the Internet and TV, the transmission, teaching, learning, and practicing of race is amazingly fast. Some ideas, such as the Occupy Wall Street's

racialization of the 99% vs. the 1% needed only a couple of weeks to be learned and used by many people all over the world. Racializations like the Occupy Wall Street movement tie a growing body of knowledge production to a signification of some social conflict. With the help of the news media, racial projects can be normalized in a matter of days. Occupy Wall Street protests appeared all over the world in many major cities.

Key to this is the idea of TV. TV is responsible for spreading the general understanding of many signified racial projects. Because many people watch TV, they will have been introduced to similar racial projects that allow society to have some degree of consensus or shared knowledge.

What is TV? Since being invented in early 1928 when images were transmitted for the first time over the airwaves, TV has become much more than originally intended. Not only has TV programming expanded, but the way we can access that programing, the variety, and the forms have diversified to the extent that it is hard to be far from TV at any time of the day. TV can be understood as images transmitted without geographical limits to a large number of people; it is the medium through which many are introduced to different kinds of people who they would not otherwise have the opportunity to meet. Types of people and types of social situations are packaged together to teach viewers about the different kinds of people who live in our world. TV can be accessed via satellite, cable, phones, and gaming systems. TV can also range from traditional big screen of movie theaters to online streaming platforms.

When watching TV, people may think they are only watching entertainment or news programs. I maintain that they are also watching and learning race. Through the various shows, people learn race, or different categories of people. People learn about many different types of human bodies, which are racial projects.

TV programs, especially sitcoms, are snippets of racial discourse connecting types of people and their idealized or imagined behavior patterns. Viewers make the connection between what they saw on TV and the life they live on an everyday basis. This means that anyone, at any time may make a connection between what is observed in life with what was seen on TV. This is making race. The types of race and racial projects that are made are as numerous as TV programing can make. Racial projects include geographical origin, philosophical and political leaning, accent, religion, tribal affiliation, dialect, behavior patterns, and our own understanding of morality, etiquette, and emotion. That is, we understand and learn what is good and evil, rude and polite, and funny, sad, or awkward through TV.

TV signifies varieties of people who may hold the fascination and curiosity of viewers. Reality TV shows teach society about people most of us never knew existed: hoarders, talented people, people who can dance, etc. Movies teach us about mean girls, drug users, bullies, nerds, jocks, and goths, among other categories. People can be members of multiple groups, easily shedding one identity and racialization for another.

Racialization not only teaches us about different kinds of human bodies, but it also teaches us behavior codes and etiquette in particular situations. Sitcoms give viewers a situation in which different people act in a variety of ways; people process the images viewed with the assistance of the laugh track and other sound effects. In this way, people learn proper behavior codes according to situation. The first funeral, wedding, and bar experiences for most people has been through TV. Because people have no reference with which to compare the images being viewed, those first images seen on TV become the basis of future encounters with that race or situation. When people find themselves in a recognized situation, they decide how they are going to act based on their memories from TV. TV information becomes part of our prior knowledge. This is a global phenomenon as shows and movies are sold overseas. Hollywood movies give people who have never been to America glimpses into the caricatures of the kinds of people in America. It is well known that "Baywatch" was one of the most popular shows worldwide for many years, so for people who had never been to the U.S., Baywatch became synonymous with America.

TV is full of information, information that teaches people social archetypes, or racial archetypes, such as heroes and villains. TV teaches family dynamics through family shows, from *Father Knows Best* to *Modern Family*. As the values of society change over time, so do the racializations portrayed. Viewers watching these racializations create their identity. As individuals watch and notice the different kinds of people, viewers self-identify with or reject various racializations for themselves. People do not always simply accept racializations as they are portrayed; often racializations are tweaked or modified to create new variations of existing categories. Some categories serve as inspiration for even more outlandish or regressive categories. Viewers pick and choose, accept and reject, recognize or learn new categories all the time while being entertained.

As time goes by and the scope and range of our daily encounters surpass the racializations seen on TV, the appetite for more diverse and complex characters increases. In other words, once TV established itself in society as a source of knowledge, viewers now continually express a desire for more complex TV characters to reflect the complexity of actual life. There is a desire to see new kinds of people, shocking people, curious people, and interesting people through our TVs. This is a reflection of our lives and the world in which we live. Life, society, and people are complex, dynamic, and different. Viewers demand the familiar, and this expectation must be mixed with a heavy dose of different. Characters on long-running serial sitcoms or dramas must be developed further than before, and viewers watch them as old friends. Many of the racializations are romanticized and some become caricatures of life. In the end, the foundation for the idea that people can create their own unique identity is there. Recall that racializations are racial projects or generalized categories of people constructed through the othering process. Race-making happens all the time because people are constantly defining and redefining their own identities as they live in a dynamic society.

Perhaps this is what creates that fascination of meeting new people. People learn racializations all through their childhood, and when they start going out into the world, they meet people. Some of these people have traits they have heard about and studied through their favorite TV shows. When they finally meet someone of a particular and familiar category in life, people often pretend as though they know all about that kind of person. They might think "I know about goths because I watched a show that had one and she was a forensic scientist, so I know what goths are like." Then when we meet one in person, we are shocked to learn they are *not* as the show portrayed them, which actually can make them interesting or boring.

Viewers can also self-identify and imitate what they see, or they can modify and personalize the racializations to create uniqueness so that they are not confused with others in the same category. In this way, people not only categorize others, but people categorize themselves according to the images seen. As was mentioned before, the sum of *all* racial projects that could be attributed to us is our identity. We are, at once, all of them, but none of them individually. Not just the ones we like, but the ones we dislike and reject, as well. Though we have an image of how we would like to be seen, people rarely see us as we want them to see us. Instead we are seen based on the subjectivity of the viewer.

The beauty and power of racial formation is that, at the end of the day, we can choose to say who we are for ourselves, in spite of the fact that society will try to impose how it wants to see us onto us. We need not follow the knowledge production of others, but should pursue our own subjectivity for our own personal benefit, instead of the benefit of others. Recall, we have already said that the knowledge production process benefits the knowledge producer, first and foremost. To accept the knowledge produced about us by others is to accept categories others impose upon us; it can be a good or bad category depending on the subjectivity of the person. Rather than having only the option of accepting the knowledge production of others, this book encourages students to make knowledge for the self in order to maximize the benefit of that racialization. For example, we, as viewers of TV, know what other people will come to expect of us based on the racializations that can be imposed on us. Depending on what those racializations are and how people feel about them, people will either distance themselves from those racializations or try to create their own unique expressions of those racializations. Personally, I never wanted to be the typical Asian pastor with the typical Asian pastor accent, saying the typical Asian pastor type things. It is not that they are necessarily bad characteristics, but they were racializations that did not appeal to me in any way. Also, many people do not want to be just like everyone else who share a characteristic. There were many other racializations that I wish people would signify more than the ones I knew people expected when they looked at me. In fact, many people wish to be identified with and by particular racializations, racializations that others would not expect. In other words, by default one may not like the categories imposed on them by others, so they actively seek to redefine themselves through the inclusion into other categories.

Humans in general, perhaps because of the way people have been trained to think, need to categorize people. Categorization not only establishes a sense of self and identity, but it also enables people to know how to act toward others. Distinguishing friend from foe, family from stranger, is a basic part of life.

Consistent with the theory of racial formation, all racializations have politics attached to them. Racial projects all have some sort of political connection. A good example of this is the androgynous character "Pat," a sketch from *Saturday Night Live* and the film *It's Pat*. The basis of the humor stemmed from the quandary of whether Pat was Patricia or Patrick, and people wanted, even needed, to know what Pat's gender was. Viewers find humor in this character because they recognize the need to identify the gender in others, for whatever reason (even if that reason is socially conditioned). This ambiguity was at one time the source material for humor in comedy shows; however, today gender ambiguity and racial ambiguity are valued in the modeling and entertainment industry.

For whatever reason, people often *need* to know what one's racial category is. Our brains are wired in such a way that we have a strong desire to categorize. People will first try to place the other into known racial projects within our prior knowledge. This phenomenon is an indication of the presence of an already established idea of what it means to be black or white or male or female, etc. Not all racial projects can be identified individually; many do not last long enough to get a name or are identified by enough people to even be known. Some are so contextually narrow that some categories would only exist in small situations and venues, but all attitudes on race are indicative of the presence of a racial project. Racialized society is extremely complex, and there are many racial projects that interact with each other to form our racial consciousness. A person can maintain several racial projects at the same time, each showing its influence at the relevant moment. Signifying one racial project as important and crucial to understanding social dynamics is interesting but subjective. Privileging any racial project as more important than other racializations happens at the expense of other racial projects. Signifying only a few at a time distorts identity formation for the individual as discussed in chapter 6. One's identity is not a single racial project but all racial projects combined, and the primary source material for this identity-making process is TV.

SUMMARY

TV is the medium through which many different racializations are transmitted, taught, and introduced to people all across the country. Because of the entertainment aspect of TV, these racializations are a caricature of reality. Nevertheless, the information people learn through the TV becomes the foundation of our prior knowledge when meeting people. When people are met in various social situations, there is a need to racialize them to understand how one is to behave appropriately towards them. To accept the caricatures as truth would be a distortion.

QUESTIONS FOR DISCUSSION

1. Ask yourself how you know how to act in various social situations; was it through your parents or through TV that you learned these behaviors?

2. Why do children of immigrant cultural and ethnic backgrounds often feel embarrassment because of their parents' behavior?

    a. Why do normalized Americans notice the behavior of people who were not born in America?

    b. How might these attitudes affect the way people choose to live or construct their personal identity?

RACE AND POVERTY:
MAKE A RACE

ASSIGNMENT

WHAT: Name a race or racialize a group of people found or presented through or within a specific broadcast or illustrated published "event." That is, identify a group or type of person in your event as a race; use that group or individual from your event to make a broader generalization of others who are members of this race. This is what we always do unconsciously; this is racialization or making race. This paper requires you to consciously racialize others, or organize others into racial categories. Then explain what that event teaches you about the race named and what that race or racialization teaches you about yourself.

WHY: A racialization or race is a category of people. When we look at other people, we describe them and give different types of people names or categories. This is racialization or the act of making race. This paper will require you to racialize people through the medium of something visual (broadcasted or illustrated printed event).

HOW: Events for this paper are published, printed graphic (pictures) advertisements, commercials, movies, documentaries, and episodes of TV series. The easiest strategy for completing this assignment would be to watch an episode of your favorite TV show or recall your favorite movie. Identify and label a type of person in that broadcast event. Then, explain what that event teaches you about that particular racialization or race.

DETAILS: Two (2) double-spaced pages *max* (650 words). You may write the paper in a simple reporting style as one would write a science experiment lab report. In other words, creativity, style, profundity, and grand conclusions are not required or expected. This is an exercise to apply the ideas of race learned so far. The point is that this is an unconsciously habitual activity everyone performs. It is the basis of most racial projects produced by other knowledge producers for the purpose of legislating morality.

NOTE: Refrain from using the word "racist" or any of the usual knowledge production that describes racist behavior. This is primarily because this paper is technically racist. You are making knowledge by creating and generalizing groups of people based on simple superficial observation.

YOU MUST HAVE YOUR TOPIC APPROVED BY THE INSTRUCTOR.

A simple email will suffice. This is to ensure you are on the right track. Some topics are harder than others, and some topics do not apply to this assignment.

FAQ

Date due: As discussed in class or as indicated on the syllabus.

WHAT QUALIFIES AS AN EVENT?

An event is anything observable that depicts live, non-fantasy humans; for simplicity's sake, this semester we are limiting the range of topics to broadcast or published media.

- Examples: a TV show, movie, advertisement, commercial, magazine ad, etc.
    - » This makes it easy for the instructor to see what you are racializing; the instructor can easily search for the student's event if it the instructor is unfamiliar with that event.
- The following events do not qualify for this assignment:
    - » Cartoons
    - » Science fiction characters, since you will never actually meet a Vulcan, zombie, or clone trooper
    - » Fantasy characters
    - » TV shows and racializations already discussed in class
    - » Racializations that already have an established discourse; e.g. African American studies, Latin American studies, Gender theory, Queer theory, etc.
    - » News stories, or reports seen through any news media

WHAT QUALIFIES AS A RACE OR RACIALIZATION?

A race or racialization is an intentional grouping of a kind of person. Usually, it is done by color, gender, age, etc. You must identify and/or create other categories that would not normally be considered racial categories by others. Some examples would be geeks, secret agents, survivors, and game show contestants.

WHAT IS MEANT BY "TEACHES ABOUT THAT RACIALIZATION?"

The event through which you observed the racialization teaches you something about that racialization. When you observe or watch shows you are learning (rightly or wrongly) about different kinds of people. What are you learning?

- For example, any James Bond movie teaches me about the race of British secret agents who are athletic, attractive, rugged, etc.
- "Ice Road Truckers" is a reality TV show about ice road truckers. By watching the show, I feel as though I now know what ice road truckers are like.

SO I CAN'T WRITE ABOUT "BLACK" PEOPLE?

You cannot name your race "black," but you may talk about hip hop artists and in the description of that racialization say that they are usually black.

WHAT DO YOU MEAN "TEACHES YOU ABOUT YOURSELF"?

When you racialize the other, you are also contributing to your own sense of self, either positively or negatively. What does this racialization (the race of your paper) teach you about you? Do you want to be like that race, imitate that race, or distance yourself from that race? What kind of attitude do you now have for members of that race? For example, do you feel admiration, disgust, fascination, etc.?

HOW DO I WRITE THIS?

- Clearly state your event.
- Clearly state the racialization within that event.
- Explain what you learned about that race through the event.
- Conclude by commenting why you chose that race and what that might say about the way you think of yourself.

RACIALIZING THE POOR—AND THE RESPONSE

8

GOAL
For students to understand that the poor are racialized, categorized, and stereotyped, to the detriment of the poor

T HE GOAL OF THIS CHAPTER is to deconstruct the construct of "the poor." That is, this chapter will analyze the people who are identified as being "poor." Though it may seem that there is a lack of compassion being shown to the poor in this chapter, it will be suggested that it is a misdirected compassion that has caused and fueled the growth of poverty in the first place. The goal is to arrive at a better understanding of the issues in order to propose or allow for a more productive and useful course of action to a serious global issue.

RACIALIZATION OF THE POOR

Take a moment and racialize the poor. Describe poor people in the way you imagined the poor were like prior to taking this class. Think for a moment, and consider whether your description fits all, most, some, or none of the people who are poor. Just as any other racial category, people are taught what to think about certain topics in society. Poverty and the poor are among those ideas pre-taught to people in order to have specific kinds of conversations. Accuracy, inaccuracy, right or wrong are ideas not in focus with this type of knowledge production.

There were no qualifiers to the initial task of racializing the poor, so it would be interesting to know what students have imagined. Do students imagine the poor of the U.S. or of other countries? How do the poor in the U.S. compare with the poor in other countries? Though sometimes the student reading this book grew up poor, the higher probability is that most college students in America imagine poor people according to the images they have seen on TV and in magazines. Some of the characteristics of the poor mentioned are as follows: they are unemployed, lazy, exploited, black, dirty, unintelligent, uneducated, pathetic, helpless, and hopeless. There is no clear unifying concept or idea, and most people do not agree as to what the poor look like.

Knowledge is often produced by signifying and identifying generalized groups of people according to the perspective and goal of the knowledge producer. The poor are often essentialized and generalized in order to propose certain forms of legislation. It is really not so different from any other racialization. In fact, to be consistent with the understanding of the racial project, the **poor** is a racial project. Like all generalizations, the racialization of the poor is not false, but it is not true either. The reality is that the racialization of the poor suffers from the same problems as other racializations. The generalization ignores the individual and the uniqueness of a poor individual's situation and context. Further, the racialization ignores what an individual might actually need in order to get out of that category of the poor. The advantage of focusing on the generalization of the poor is that now, simplistic "one size fits all" solutions related to the redistribution of money can be generated.

Poverty (the state of being poor) is diverse and complicated. It is described in relationship with other issues of society, such as health-care, welfare, education, and employment. The desire to do something, while admirable, is not enough to do what is needed for the benefit of most poor people. In other words, consistent with knowledge production, proposals would benefit the proposers and a small group of people more than the generalized poor. Some of the poor may benefit from reductionist descriptions and reactionary policy but the majority will not.

THE POOR AND HELPING THE POOR

First, it is assumed in this argument that the eradication of poverty is not possible, primarily because people are always finding new ways to become poor. Assuming that, as long as money—in whatever symbolic or material form—will always be needed in the global economy, people in the U.S. will always try to devise ways of accumulating more and/or find themselves with none. Some people will gamble for more at the casinos, poker tables, and lotteries; others will lose money through failed business ventures. Some lose their life savings to bad investments, and others will never have saved any money at all. People might lose their jobs because of modernization or because they were incompetent. Some people might not be able to find better work, and other people never looked for work. Sometimes the classification or criteria (e.g. annual income) used to be considered poor makes someone poor. There are many different reasons why people might be and have become poor. Becoming poor may not be the critical issue that needs attention in this book; instead, how long one remains in poverty is the issue that is more important for this book.

With so many different kinds of poor people in different circumstances, there cannot be a simple solution that is helpful to everyone in the same way. In the U.S. the basis of most government assistance pushed onto the poor is related to the **redistribution of wealth**; take from those who have too much, and transfer to those who have too little. Because the government itself has no money, it must first tax people and then use that money for whatever program it enacts.[1] The various tax schemes in place supposedly target the wealthier of society for the benefit of the poor of society.

There will always be poverty because with any change in society, the definition and understanding—that is, the racialization of the poor—will change, too. If one were to successfully take millions from the wealthy of the country through taxation and give that money to the bottom 20% of the country, does the society no longer have a bottom 20% that year? The 20% of people that were previously above the bottom 20% become the new bottom 20%. There will always be a bottom 20%, but just who is in the bottom 20% is never really addressed. The Department of the Treasury published a report that shows that half of the people in the bottom 20% got out of the bottom 20% and only 25% of the very top 0.01% remained there after 10 years, from 1996 to 2005.[2]

Further, the money required to pay for many of the programs designed to help the poor are actually paid in part by the working poor through taxes.

---

1   Often when taxes are not sufficient, government borrows money from other countries to fund and pay for programs it promises to provide and so imposes the cost of largely ineffective programs onto future generations in the form of the national debt. This process of borrowing money from other countries through currency manipulation will not be covered in this book in detail.

2   *Income Mobility in the U.S. from 1996 to 2005: Report of the Department of the Treasury*, November 13, 2007. www.treasury.gov/resource-center/tax-policy /Documents/incomemobilitystudy03-08revise.pdf

These programs are often utilized by those who are not as poor and even utilized by the wealthy. An example would be the state university system; these schools were conceived as a low-cost alternative to private colleges and universities. Taxes are collected from everyone who works in the state. Poorer people generally and statistically do not go on to higher education and are paying taxes for a greater part of their lives, which pay for services they will never use. Middle class families often see the lower tuitions of the state schools as a bargain and are overrepresented at state universities. This example is not an argument to discourage people from taking advantage of a system that already exists. Rather, it should be used as an argument to rethink how society attempts to assist the poor.

One might suggest raising taxes only for the wealthy; this kind of suggestion is indicative of a racialization of the rich and a lack of understanding of money and human behavior. As has often happened already, some wealthy people who refuse to pay high taxes simply become the citizens of a different country to avoid paying taxes.[3] This results in decreased overall revenue for the U.S. because the government is deprived of the taxes that would have been collected if the taxes were never raised. If the wealthy were prevented from moving from place to place or prevented from changing their citizenship, then many wealthy people would simply be more creative in hiding their assets and money from the taxman.[4] It is also not just the extremely wealthy who engage in tax evasion. Tax evasion (or tax avoidance) includes such behavior as ordering products online or making purchases in another county or state if, in this way, one can avoid paying taxes for the same product. Of course, most people who engage in this type of behavior do not think in terms of tax evasion; they believe they are simply getting a bargain. Criminalization of tax evasion is the effort to force people to pay their taxes. The coercive nature of tax laws and of many other regulations is hidden through various creative knowledge production endeavors. Using police to enforce tax laws to protect revenue streams has become more visible today. The very high profile death of Eric Garner in July of 2014 occurred when police were enforcing cigarette taxation in New York City.

---

3 Kay Bell, *Dump citizenship to avoid taxes?* May 3, 2012. www.bankrate.com; Robert W. Wood, *Trending Now: Giving Up U.S. Citizenship*, May 9, 2013. www. forbes.com; note that businesses have engaged in this practice for years, most recently *Burger King* in 2014.
4 The recent repatriation effort to bring money earned overseas back to the U.S. through a tax holiday is a testament to the amount of money being kept away from the hands of the IRS; Emily Stephenson and Patrick Temple-West, *"Senators weigh tax 'holiday' to help fund highway repairs,"* June 10, 2014. www.reuters.com.

The point of all this is that people cannot be forced to work diligently only to have to give away what they earn with no direct benefit for themselves. Further, the expectation that people will generally submit to new tax lawsthat require them to pay more money to the government is naïve. Simple solutions do not consider the responses of living, calculating beings. Tax evasion by these types can be portrayed as being immoral behavior, but the underlying principle of taxation is plunder. Plunder through taxation may not be any less immoral than trying to avoid being plundered. People acquire property and assets in a variety of ways, thus making it hard to generalize how rich people became rich. What is generally true is that taxation is coercive and therefore immoral; failure to pay results in fines and imprisonment.

WHO ARE THE POOR?

The only thing that could be said about the poor that could be somewhat true is that "the poor are poor," which is really not helpful. Official knowledge producers like the Institute for Research on Poverty determine who is poor and, therefore, define poverty according to annual household income. Again, it is easy to see the knowledge production aspect of this information. Criteria are arbitrarily determined and applied to people in a way to produce results that may or may not accurately explain the phenomenon. There are many problems one could raise concerning this criterion, and the institute's own website acknowledges this.

In addition to glossing details of just who is poor and how they became poor, there is the problem of the **welfare trap**. People who are close to qualifying for welfare programs are encouraged to work less in order to qualify for benefits; then once on welfare, it is difficult to live a life without welfare because of the loss of substantial benefits outweighs potential gain in wages. For argument's sake, if we say that the poverty level for a family of four is $23,492 per year in 2012,[5] technically speaking, a family of four earning $24,500 per year does not qualify to be counted among the poor and would not qualify for any federal or local assistance.[6] However, the actual quality of life might not be too different from someone who qualifies

---

5 Institute for Research on Poverty website, "What are poverty thresholds and poverty guidelines?" www.irp.wisc.edu/faqs/faq1.htm.
6 Similar problems exist with the current "Affordable Care Act": Craig Eyermann, "More Perverse Incentives in ObamaCare," August 2, 2013. www.mygovcost.org.

for assistance. People who qualify for assistance become careful not to go over the line and be disqualified for receiving that assistance; the system then discourages higher productivity and incremental improvement in life. This government assistance for people below the poverty line is a significant amount. In New York City, a single mother with two children can collect $38,728 per year in total benefits, which is more than the starting salary of a teacher in that state.[7] One might make an argument for higher teacher wages, but most would think this is only fair for a family in need. However, this overlooks the change in incentives for families. Not only is education for a better income a more difficult and less attractive option to take, welfare money has an adverse effect on two-parent families. Walter Williams points out the destructive power of government assistance on African American families over the past 60 years: welfare incentivizes single-parent over two-parent homes.[8] An excerpt from Williams' book will be read in chapter 15.

Once one is on government assistance, to give up the assistance would require a significant increase in earning capacity to equal what the government was providing. The amount of assistance received sometimes means that the chance of earning $10,000 per year more is simply not worth the effort. This is the trap; considering all benefits available to qualified recipients, a single mom is better off with a $29,000 job and welfare than taking a $69,000 job.[9] The likelihood of many long-term welfare recipients to be eligible for a job that pays $70,000 is not high. It becomes easier to stay on government assistance rather than getting training to get a better job. In 33 states, welfare recipients receive more benefits per year than people holding jobs that pay $8 per hour. Twelve states offer more than a $12 per hour job.

Wage is the price of the labor to do a job; when the cost of the labor exceeds the value of the job itself, people lose their jobs. When the price of labor is forced higher through legislation, many employers

---

7   Total benefits include housing and medical benefits in addition to other state and local welfare benefits; Michael Tanner and Charles Hughes, "The work versus welfare Trade-off: 2013; An Analysis of the total level of Welfare Benefits by State," Cato Institute, 2013.
8   Walter E. Williams, "Race & Economics: How much can be blamed on Discrimination?" (Hoover Institution Press Publication), 2011.
9   James Pethokoukis, "Why a single mom is better off with a $29,000 job and welfare than taking a $69,000 job," July 12, 2012, www.aei-ideas.org; and Clifford F. Thies, "The Dead Zone: the Implicit Marginal Tax Rate," Mises Institute, November 9, 2009.

must cut the number of hours employees can work.[10] This situation is well known to many including prominent politicians who spin this welfare trap and trade-off in wages as a good thing and claim that cutting back on hours worked or even quitting one's job is a desirable activity. Politicians like representative Nancy Pelosi (D-Ca) and senator Harry Reid (D-Nv), have declared that this type of activity addresses the dreaded problem of "job lock." Job lock would be the situation where people are trapped in an unsatisfying job. These politicians go on to say that working less or not working at all enables people to pursue their personal pleasures. Ending job lock and providing assistance through the government does not directly address the issue of who benefits and who pays for all of these programs while assuming that this policy is a mostly good policy. In other words, how does the government pay for all of these programs that often encourage people not to work and stay in school? The government must obtain its revenue through the taxation of working people. Who pays those taxes and for whose benefit is often not explained in detail.

The preoccupation with creative uses of taxation to benefit the "poor" results in the legalized and regulated exploitation of the poor through other racial projects. For example, if we were to racialize the country by age and not by color, then younger people are almost all in the bottom 20% of society. Students who are in college are counted among the poor, though many of them are not poor in the same way that other people are poor in the U.S. Student loan debt adds to the confirmation that many young people are among the poor. Older citizens in the U.S. are often racialized as poor and thus need social security in order to make ends meet. However, in order to pay social security benefits to the wealthiest age racialization in the country, the older population, taxes are collected from the poorest age group in the country, the young. To add insult to injury, it is also no secret that, unless social security is reformed, these young people will never see a penny of what they have put into the program and yet are helping pay for the benefits that older and wealthier Americans enjoy today.

This is not to say that we must forget about taking care of older people who need help. Rather, the older generation of society might be better served by other methods. The current system exploits the young for the sake of the old; whether this is intentional or not is irrelevant. Social Security is one of the programs that is talked about when discussing the

---

10   Michael D. Tanner, "In Fighting the 'Job Lock,' Democrats Opened a Poverty Trap," March 1, 2014, www.cato.org.

national debt. Many believe that the national debt is in the neighborhood of $18 trillion in 2015. However, this does not take into account the **unfunded liabilities** of the government. The unfunded liabilities are those programs and benefits that were promised to people that have no funds available to pay them; they include programs, such as Social Security, Medicaid, and government worker retirement benefits. The plan was to use future tax revenue to pay for the debt of the future. These unfunded liabilities are looming as the baby boomers begin to retire; depending on whose numbers are used, future debt is anywhere between $86 trillion and over $200 trillion.[11] This debt is unsustainable and was incurred through the efforts of society's knowledge production–driven attempts to help the poor, whoever they may be. Almost everyone in the country is becoming poorer in the attempt to make some people not poor. Short-term benefit for some must be weighed against the long-term detriment for the many.

To emphasize, this book is not saying society must ignore the poor. This book is also not saying the poor must learn to take care of themselves. Rather, what is being said is that the programs in place have the opposite effect of their original intent. America is becoming poorer through the policies and attempts to help the poor; there are more poor people in the country today and benefits for the poor are subjective at best. In other words, the redistribution programs are not working. The rising number of people living below the poverty line in this country stands in stark contrast with the decline in poverty rates around the world (see below).

A DIFFERENT PERSPECTIVE

Giving poor people more money and benefits as a method of assistance is popular because goods and services in society are becoming more expensive. The details of this increase in cost will be addressed later, but for now, it is enough to say that things are getting more costly. What if society could implement a system where prices would come down? The poor would be able to buy more without having their income increase. A quick beginning to long-term solutions might be to strive to have lower prices in society's market place, without government involvement and price fixing measures.

---

11   Chris Cox and Bill Archer, *"Why $16 Trillion only hints at the true U.S. debt: hiding the government's liabilities from the public makes it seem that we can tax our way out of mounting deficits. We can't."* November 28, 2012, online.wsj.com.

Further, this process will result in more opportunity and increased living standards for all people, not just the poor.

In addition to this, lowering the cost of these goods and services would not add to the national debt, nor would it require an increase in taxation. To understand how this might be possible requires the lesson in economics presented in the following chapters.

There is evidence that poverty is on the decline worldwide and it is not through the efforts of government programs and benefits; rather, it is the decrease in the role of government that has resulted in people being not as poor as they once were.[12]

BUT ISN'T IT ALL JUST KNOWLEDGE PRODUCTION?

It is conceded and recognized that all of this information is knowledge production. As has already been said, knowledge production happens with intent. There is a purpose and reason why knowledge is made. This book is no exception. However, this book does not seek to identify behavior that must be eradicated based on some subjective knowledge production. The knowledge production of this book proceeds from the perspective of the individual; if the goal of this knowledge is the protection of the rights and property of the individual, then everyone will be able to benefit from this knowledge production. Knowledge production is fundamentally biased because of its subjective nature. Rather than protect some at the expense of the many, or the many at the expense of the few, the goal of this knowledge is the protection of all. It is primarily for this reason that the extreme, all-inclusive single perspective is favored, as all ideas are now treated and evaluated in the same way in order to prevent hypocrisy and action built on double standards.

The current popular and dominant attempts to rectify and compensate for the past that fill the prior knowledge of many in society are an admirable and desirable activity. This is not a simple or inexpensive activity. It is not simple because of the unaccountable actions of thinking and calculating human beings who continually make the consequences of public policy unexpected and counterproductive. The good intentions of those who produce knowledge to help the poor are praised. However,

---

12 "A fall to cheer," www.economist.com, March 3, 2012.

good intentions are not enough when the results of the policies are detrimental to the very people who were supposed to benefit the most.

Racial projects have credibility in contemporary society but are often used to accuse and blame a lifestyle, an individual, an industry, or a country of discriminatory or unfair practices. People invoke the need for regulations and laws to stop the immoral behavior. People desire to legislate morality subjectively. Though many of the true believers of subjective knowledge production have the goal of helping the objectified poor, others see opportunity through regulations to enrich themselves (note the discussion in chapter 3). It should be easy enough for most, if not all, to agree that if there was a way for everyone to have the opportunity to enjoy a high standard of living, this would be a good method to follow. This book advocates knowledge production that fosters the quickest route out of poverty for everyone because anyone might find themselves in poverty one day. In order to get on this road, we must deconstruct another racialization: the racialization of the rich.

SUMMARY

The poor are often discussed through generalized racial categories that ignore the unique and specific situations of the individuals categorized as poor. Compassionate policies to help the poor have only worsened the problems for most and for society as a whole. Perhaps it is time to move away from current policies based on racialization and redistribution and focus more on how to make living well, cheaper.

QUESTIONS FOR FURTHER DISCUSSION

1. Is tax evasion (which includes buying online without tax when and where applicable) wrong?

2. Is there a difference between a business trying to avoid paying taxes and an individual who tries to avoid paying taxes? (Imagine owning a small business that is being heavily taxed.)

3. Aside from sales tax, income tax, social security, Medicare, city, and local taxes, are you aware of other taxes you are required to pay?

ECONOMICS, GREED, AND TOILET PAPER

GOAL
Clear the air for a couple of maligned constructs

P ERHAPS BECAUSE there is so much negative prior knowledge about the field of economics, all too frequently the discussion regarding poverty and wealth ignores and is ignorant of basic economic principles. It might also be that the economic principles that people do know and favor are those principles that enable preferred knowledge production concerning wealth and poverty. This knowledge is used for the legislation of morality. Chapter 9 and 10 are not meant to be comprehensive in any way; rather, it is meant to explain, in brief and in a manner fit for a humanities course, some of the basic and necessary economic principles of the free market according to the Chicago and Austrian school of economics.

ECONOMICS

Many people do not realize that economists and economic principles have been racialized or categorized as a uniform body of boring people and boring ideas. While it is true economists study the economy, there is by no means a consensus in the knowledge and theories produced; there is a lot of subjectivity in the science of economics. Recall that knowledge production is basically a political process for general material gain for producer and subscribers. What should be understood is that the construct **economy** implies limited supply of certain resources. If there were an unlimited amount of resources and supplies for everything and anything, then there would be no need to discuss economy; there would be no need to discuss conservation and economic uses of oil, water, and air. However, one *must* understand economics because there is a limit of how much there is of certain resources that have multiple uses and applications with varying degrees of importance. For example, one could make a bowl out of gold, but because gold is very rare, it would be an extravagant use of that resource, and perhaps, that gold would be better used as currency or as a conductor of electricity in electronic goods.

Put in another way, **economics** addresses the issues surrounding priority and relative value of limited resources. The choices people make are based on each person's perspective on priority, deciding what is more important than something else, what comes first in the order of things to do, or things to acquire, or things that are required. Priority also involves trade-offs, sacrifice or cost; in order to have one thing, one must give up something else. In a world with unlimited resources, there is no priority, only preference. This is because there is no cost. In a world of limited resources, particularly in regard to time and money, everything has a cost; cost and price can be measured in many ways that are not universal. For example, working two jobs for more money costs a father time with his family. The desire to do good things for other people must be tempered with the realities of economics and the unpredictability of human action and choice. One must remember that how each individual in society understands priority is unique and that it is impossible for any one or any group of people to set and decide priorities for everyone else in society without coercion.

In India there is a movement that seeks to make access to food a human right; it is the "right to food" movement. In 2013 the National Food Security Act was passed in India to guarantee food for everyone. However, simply declaring that everyone has a right to food does not mean that everyone will have food to eat; in fact, it means that many more people will likely go hungry. Why that happens seems to be a mystery to many well-intentioned believers of the "right to food" racialization in India. Political declaration and desires often, if not always, ignore the reality and unpredictability of human behavior and response to incentives, not to mention priority and cost. As the government regulates the process by which people will have access to food, behavior of all the people implicated by this legislation from growing to eating the food will adjust their behavior based on the changing situation. It is a fallacy to believe that people can be controlled like pieces on a chessboard, doing what they are told when they are told. Policies and declarations such as these also ignore the limitations of infrastructure and commerce that result in waste and food shortages. Human beings are thinking creatures, and each person responds to incentives according to his or her own context and prior knowledge. People act according to what they believe is best for them at that moment. In this situation, farmers will likely overproduce certain crops to receive the guaranteed government payment, but will deliver the goods to government drop off points rather than the market place. In other words, the food does not go to the places where it can be eaten without delay, extra steps and effort. This is further complicated by lack of storage facilities and weak transportation and distribution infrastructure, which in turn result in waste and food scarcity.

WHAT IS GREED?

Before jumping into a discussion of the free market and what it has to offer, a construct needs to be deconstructed: the construct of greed. The construct is used so frequently and often that most people believe they know what greed is. Often, when the construct is used, tempers flare, and people are socialized to understand that the greedy one is the bad person. Deconstructed, greed simply means wanting more than what one has right now. Because everyone always desires more or better, everyone is greedy.

So far, this book has deconstructed religion, race, and poverty. Through knowledge production, most people have subjective knowledge about each of these constructs. This does not necessarily mean that the understanding people have is wrong; it just means that it is mostly not true. People understand constructs from their own perspective. However, perspective is biased, and different perspectives yield different truths. Before proposing "free market capitalism" as a way to address the interesting relationship between religion, race, and poverty, the construct "greed" will be deconstructed.

Because of their prior knowledge, most people regard greed as a bad thing; not only what the construct supposedly describes, but the word itself. Perhaps this impression and prior knowledge is because "greed" is subjectively and narrowly understood. Most people would define greed loosely as wanting "more than one really needs." Greedy people are racialized as rich people who are never satisfied with what they have, greedy people constantly want more at any cost. If it means that other people have to suffer for the greedy person to fulfill their greedy desires, then so be it. Consider how many children's movies teach greed as bad, and how many villains are greedy; it is not surprising that so many people have a negative view of this construct. Most people think they understand "greed" and what it is, but it is all only knowledge production.

There are nagging questions that bring out the arbitrary and subjective nature of this discussion. How much is more than one really needs for life? By what subjective standard should the concept of "need" be understood? Whose subjective level of satisfaction is enough to satisfy everyone? Do the standards ever change with inflation or deflation? What does one do when one has enough? How does this change from country to country or state to state?

If all of life was based on simple needs, then the concepts of varying degrees of quality and improvement would not exist. Any good or service that can be exchanged for money would have only one level of quality, the level of what people need. In a hypothetical situation, if the level of need for everyone were arbitrarily established by someone entrusted with that responsibility, the individual would fail to establish guidelines that would satisfy everyone in society. This kind of arbitrary setting of standards does not permit anything beyond the base level of need. To have something more than what was determined as how much one needed is to be greedy regardless of the reason. This also means that improvement or upgrades are unnecessary because it is beyond what is needed. This kind of mentality carried out to its logical conclusion results in a regressive society, where more and more people become poor. It is an attitude or position that is inflexible and inadequate to adapt to the ever-changing demands and needs of society.

ANOTHER LOOK AT GREED

If one listens carefully to people who use the construct "greed," it is often *someone else* who has too much or is greedy; it is usually not the person speaking. No matter how much the person speaking makes, it is perfectly acceptable, in that person's mind, to use the word greed. News anchors on major networks making 12 million dollars a year are completely comfortable talking about greedy business people. Obviously, those reporters are not greedy; they are just being paid what they are worth. It does not seem to occur to anyone that perhaps those business people might be paid what they are worth.

If only people who have too much are greedy, does this mean that poor people are never greedy? Many poor people desire wealth. Rags to riches type stories are popular because many people living in poverty may desire that type of life. Is their greed not maligned because their greed is unrealized? Why are poor people who become rich suddenly greedy, or was it that they were always greedy but with no money? The fact of the matter is that poor people are just as greedy as rich people; it is just that they have not been able to make the kind of money that attracts the kind of attention that rich people attract. The knowledge production about greed is all very subjective to the point of meaninglessness. The only thing we know for sure is that the one who accuses another of greed likely has less than the one accused. Beyond that, there is no usable information gained by using the construct. The real purpose of calling someone greedy is often to get everyone else angry at that racialized person. Society already believes that greedy people are bad. If a trusted knowledge producer identifies and racializes someone as greedy, then that person is bad. This is the classic othering technique employed to get a consensus for action; many times the action is legislation of morality; more specifically, it becomes an effort to punish or control those identified as greedy.

Though there are many types of greedy people; most people think of wealthy people when they think of greedy people. It must be remembered that "wealth" and "rich" are racializations. The people in those categories are signified by a single characteristic. But, not all rich people have the same character and live the same kind of life with the same principles and ethics. Some wealthy people acquired their wealth unfairly, and others acquired their wealth by working hard. Legislating morality against all of them would be arbitrarily discriminatory, hypocritical and counterproductive; it sacrifices the individual for the sake of a category. In fact, legislation of morality often results in a windfall of profits for large businesses. For example, legislation of morality in the form of regulation often serves as barriers against competing businesses. This results in more people buying products from the protected company; protected companies are companies that already exist when regulation is passed. The automotive industry benefits greatly from this type of regulation and taxation; domestic cars appear to be comparable in price to foreign cars, Japanese cars in particular. Restaurants often lobby against food trucks in many cities around the country. Stiff restrictions for food trucks protect traditional brick and mortar restaurants against the perceived competition.[1]

Not only is the construct "greed" not informative, productive, or helpful for poor people, it also increases the amount of anger in society. Good people are supposed to dislike the evil greedy people of society. It is not unlike any other racialization where people are reduced to a single characteristic; it is believed there is nothing else that might be important to know about them. Those people are greedy, so they are bad, and something must be done about them. This results in hostility and anger to be directed only at the wealthy of society. This book would argue that those people who have acquired their wealth through cronyism or corporatism might be deserving of this negativity. Cronyism or corporatism is the practice of giving favor in the form of subsidies, contracts and tax breaks to one's friends or to favored corporations by government officials. Not everyone who is wealthy achieved their wealth in this manner and so may not be deserving of this type of negativity. Usually the knowledge production concerning greed does not make this distinction.

Furthermore, this type of knowledge production allows the knowledge producer and anyone who uses this knowledge to take a moral high ground from which they may pronounce what is and is not acceptable for all. Not only is a certain kind of person criticized based on a caricature of their life but this knowledge production creates the all-knowing perspective through which all double standards and hypocrisy are hidden from view and through which coercive regulations and laws may be pronounced.

To avoid all contradictory or vague knowledge production, **greed** will be defined as wanting more than what one currently has. This means that if you want a higher salary, a bigger home, a better car, better clothes, or to attend a better school, or attempt to have a better quality of life, then you qualify to be racialized as a greedy person. Understood this way, poor people are also greedy. In other words, the desire for more is not confined to people who already have more than most. Defining greed in this way also recognizes the reality that everyone is greedy, if not about everything then about something. This discussion of greed implicates pretty much everyone; it is not just that person over there, who someone else thinks has too much. This desire for more or something better is practically a universal; what is not universal is the understanding of what is "better" or "more of

---

1   Baylen Linnekin, *"Chicago's Disgusting New Food Truck Regulations: The Windy City's treatment of mobile food vendors is a case study in how to stifle entrepreneurship and innovation in the name of protecting powerful, entrenched interests,"* Reason.com, July 28, 2012.

something." Nevertheless the desire for something better for self or others is a natural part of being human. It is not a bad characteristic at all.

Some would raise the objection that if everyone is greedy then no one is greedy; that this perspective is also meaningless; there is no point to this exercise. Remember that the extreme position is for the sake of perspective; it is a temporary perspective taken before reconstruction. This extreme perspective of greed includes all possible subjective definitions, applications and racializations of greed; this allows everyone to share and use the same perspective. Assigning guilt and assuming a moral high ground is not possible with this perspective (e.g. you are greedy and I am not). The view from the extreme should make it impossible for one person to look at another and call that person greedy or to arbitrarily declare that one person's greed is somehow better than or less worse than another's greed; this perspective avoids the possibility of hypocrisy and establishing a double standard. From this perspective, the dynamics of greed should be examined and understood.

With this reconstruction of greed, the eradication of greed is not necessary; society, this class, and this book do not need to design a way to eradicate, pretend to eradicate, or try to mitigate the bad effects of greed. Instead, greed is recognized as a part of human nature. To say, at any point, that someone is too greedy is basically saying "If I can't be rich, then you can't be either" or "You can't be rich, but I should be rich."

Even if greed was not part of human nature, and thoughts of greed were unnatural to a human, one still cannot impose one's own belief of what is too much on others. The use of force to elicit compliance to an arbitrary and subjective standard is unacceptable. If one is able to pass legislation based on the belief that having too much (however much that is) is bad, then no one needs to ever accumulate more and to accumulate more would be criminal no matter the situation or explanation. If another person wants more because that person grew up in a house with continuous financial problems, and the only way they can deal with those childhood memories of hardship is by accumulating more, then why should they stop? What right or authority does one exercise to forbid and prevent others from having peace of mind on their own terms? If one has four children and hopes that they will all attend university, is it fair to say that, at some point, a certain amount of savings is enough, without knowing the effects of inflation and what money will be worth in the future? Who is responsible for the education of those children, the knowledge producer who would prefer to restrict the accumulation of wealth, or the parent who realizes that college tuition is not the only expense that must be covered? What about other expenses a knowledge producer could not possibly consider as part of deciding how much is what is needed by anyone? There are too many variables that cannot be accounted for in any piece of legislation, so arbitrary establishment of regulations should not occur.

For example, when my wife said she would marry me, my father bought the engagement ring. It is a common traditional Korean practice where the father of the groom pays for the engagement ring for the bride. This suited me fine because, as a full-time student most of my life, I had no money. My father pulled me aside and reminded me that if I were to have children, I would be responsible to do the same for them. I now have four sons.

Knowledge producers who arbitrarily determine "need" can only consider needs and expenses they already signify for themselves. Human life and the economy are unpredictable; prosperity today is not a guarantee of prosperity tomorrow. In this way, the effect of regulations or the legislation of morality should start to become visible. Regulations are promoted as declarations of what is right and proper through minimum or maximum standards, and standards of safety for the protection of the public. Instead these regulations, in reality, are protections for various businesses and industries that restrict and strip away the freedom of choice for the individual, especially the freedom to rise out of poverty. Regulations preserve the status quo and seek to prevent "undesired" change in society; that is, the change that threatens those in power. Without these regulations or restrictions it is much harder to maintain market dominance for a long period of time. Thus, there are some who believe they can prevent change in society through legislation; and there are those who embrace change as a part of life by discouraging increases in legislation and regulation.

There are two constructs that can make the issue of regulation or the legislation of morality difficult to accept. They are the constructs of **liberal** and **conservative**. A conservative is one who seeks to preserve the current state of affairs or the status quo. Change is generally bad in the mind of a conservative. A liberal is someone who recognizes that change is part of life. Human beings through their independent actions are unpredictable and should be allowed their free expression and practice. What is confused is how change is prevented or allowed to take place; regulations, laws and the legislation of morality often serve to preserve the status quo. In spite of the rhetoric surrounding various legislations, most regulations prevent change and narrowly define what is and what is not acceptable. So, those people who continually propose regulations to control human behavior are conservatives. Liberals are those who will not stand in the way of innovation and human freedom or independence; they will rarely pass regulations to control any behavior. In the U.S. both the Republican and Democratic parties seek to pass regulations about a variety of issues; both parties are in many ways conservative parties because, as was already stated, regulations have the effect of preserving the existing structure of society, in spite of the way those laws are sold to the public. For example, "Net Neutrality" is a legislative move that supposedly will make the internet more accessible to people and less open to corruption and manipulation by large corporations. By declaring the internet a utility the Federal Communications Commission (FCC) may now write regulations that it deems best for everyone. In reality it will further preserve existing cronyism against competition and change that would benefit users of the internet. One just has to speak with people from Asia to know that internet service and speed is far better in Asian countries than it is here in the U.S. In other words, the adoption of Net Neutrality preserves the existing state of the internet while bringing it further under government control. Government control means that the cost of using the internet will also increase.[2]

INTRODUCTION TO THE FREE MARKET VIA TOILET PAPER

From the perspective of this book the two most important characteristics of the free market are **voluntary cooperation** and **competition**. Everyone in the free market must be free to make decisions based on their own individual subjectivity; there can be no coercion especially through legislation. This works as long as everyone accepts responsibility for the consequences of those free choices. Competition is the second characteristic and it is a crucial aspect of the free market because competition creates incentive for everyone to constantly improve their lives by any subjective perspective. This desire to improve one's life often means innovation that revolutionizes aspects of society to the benefit of the poor. These two characteristics of the free market determine the field upon which people may apply their subjective greed. The free market employs different constructs to describe what others call greed; they are **self-interest** and **incentive**. "Self-interest" is to act in a way that will benefit the actor. This means everyone acts in a self-interested or selfish manner. It is this self-interest that all of us have,

---

2 Nick Gillespie and Todd Krainin, FCC Commissioner Ajit Pai: Net Neutrality is a "Solution that won't work to a problem that doesn't exist," Reason.com, February 25, 2015.

that protects each of us in the free market. In other words, our desire to protect ourselves is an incentive (the motivation based on self-interested calculation) to always seek the best quality at the best price or our desire to ensure continued prosperity is the incentive to continue to produce the best product at the best price. Instead of passing arbitrary legislation that criminalizes one type of greed among many, the free market works by allowing everyone to live according to their self-interest while respecting the rights and property of others. This results in a mostly stable society. The way self-interested behavior can result in a relatively balanced and peaceful society without government interference can be illustrated through the following example of toilet paper.

Toilet paper is a product that most people use and take for granted. Suppose that, in a fictional city, there are two merchants who sell the same kind of toilet paper for the same price; it is brown, rough, and $5 per roll (which, at the moment, is obscenely expensive). Customers buy their toilet paper from the store that is most convenient in location; other than that, the price and quality is the same. Suppose that Seller 1 wants to make more money, which he can do if he sells more toilet paper. He realizes that if he lowers his price to $4, he will have more customers, sell more toilet paper, and make more money. When Seller 1 lowers his price, his competitor realizes that unless she does something, she will be out of business; so Seller 2 matches the lowered price and wins back some of her customers. She also introduces a new line of toilet paper that is white and softer. Seller 1 responds by introducing a similar product line but also introduces a variety of colors. Seller 2 then offers quilted toilet paper with more sheets per roll. Seller 1 subsequently introduces scented toilet paper. Then, Seller 2 buys a factory to control and streamline production, which enables her to sell toilet paper at $0.50 per roll. Seller 1 does the same and offers wet wipes. Now customers can choose from a variety of toilet paper at a much lower price because of the self-interest of the sellers. The entire scenario required "greed" from everyone, the competitors and the consumers of toilet paper. The people buying toilet paper want to use their money in the most selfish way, that is, to spend as little as possible to get the most possible.

The sellers have lost a lot of sleep in this process but are happy because they are still in business and making money. Customers love this process because now they have a better quality and selection of toilet paper at a much cheaper price. Even lower income people no longer have to worry about having enough toilet paper. As we said earlier, one of the important issues of poverty is the price of goods and services. If the price of goods and services can be brought down, then a lower income would be less of a problem.

This is a simplified example of how the free market is basically supposed to work. As a rule, through competition and voluntary transactions, quality improves as prices drop; people will rarely voluntarily spend more for less quality goods. The market is able to function and reach stability without the help of a governing body. Everyone was acting on their own self-interest without regard to the well-being of others. In other words, though people were acting on their own greed, everyone in society benefited from that greed. In this example, as in life, consumers are also greedy; they want to spend as little as possible and keep as much as possible after the transaction to buy other things or to save for another day. Smart and discriminating shoppers look at competing stores and buy from the store that, for them, is the better bargain. The customer's desire to save money pushes sellers to find ways of lowering their prices through increasing productivity without sacrificing quality. If one goes shopping for toilet paper today in the local Wal-Mart, one will see the variety of options; this is the result of free market dynamics. Some may think that lower prices would mean lower quality; however, this is not true. In spite of all the price manipulation by government through regulation, there are areas of the market where this is evident; computers, Blue-ray players and televisions also follow this same pattern primarily because those areas of life are less regulated than others. Less regulation means more competition in everything for everything.

In spite of this free market dynamic, some people are still unconvinced and believe that a corporation's pursuit of money will incentivize it to engage in shoddy work. This would rarely happen in a free market because of the issue of liability. The company is responsible for any damage that it may cause due to its business choices. If an oil pipeline were to leak onto the property of individuals, each person can seek damages against that company. Liability would be astronomical. There is no way to make money if a business engages in less than top quality work. There are cases where large corporations did engage in shoddy practices resulting in the damage of many people's property; however, they were not punished in the way the free market supposedly predicts they would be. It is likely (as in the British Petroleum oil rig spill in the Gulf of Mexico in 2010) that government regulations were in place to protect the corporation against excessive liability. In other words, the government interfered with the market, which in turn led to harm for many. Often government failure in catastrophes is downplayed and the blame is shifted onto the greed of capitalism.

Government is incapable of managing markets. Venezuela's government tried to resolve its toilet paper problem by declaring a set price for toilet paper, which made it unprofitable to produce and import toilet paper. This resulted in toilet paper shortages in that country. Declaring a lower, more affordable price with complete disregard for market forces did not make toilet paper available to everyone, rather, the manufacturers could not afford to produce and sell it at that price and so many had no toilet paper; there were shortages at most if not all of the stores that sold toilet paper. It is not that there was no toilet paper to be sold, but that sellers were unwilling to sell the paper at the lower price. The government succeeded in creating a black market for those goods as people began to hoard toilet paper in order to sell at the price closer to the actual market value. Most recently the government of Venezuela has taken military action against toilet paper factories (September 2013). In spite of military intervention, people still do not have enough toilet paper. **Price fixing** or setting a fixed price on a good or service usually results in either shortage or waste. In Venezuela's case, because the price of the paper was set too low, there were shortages. Often when prices are set too high, the government guarantees payment at the higher price point; this results in over production and waste.

The cell phone market is another good example, for now, of how the market works. Cell phones, when they first hit the market were expensive and massive in size. Through innovation and competition the prices of cell phones have dropped while the quality and variety of the product has risen. There are a tremendous number of different phones to choose from with different levels of quality and price to match anyone's budget and preference. That variety was not the result of government action but of many people living self-interested lives. In the free market, no individual's priorities are the priorities for everyone else; no one decides anything for everyone else. It is a complex result of competing interests that no government could possibly predict or control.

If government intervenes and attempts to give an advantage to one group over another, unpredictable and often undesirable consequences arise. When that happens, the original overreach of the government is forgotten and government once again declares that it will do the right thing to solve the problem. The recent housing crisis in 2008 is an example of this kind of government sleight of hand. This crisis is discussed further in the next chapter.

SUMMARY

Greed and self-interest are not absolutely bad characteristics of people; these constructs are only subjectively bad. Through economics one can understand the benefits of these constructs. The dynamics of the economic market are too complex for any group of people to control. The attempt to control the flow of goods and competition between businesses results in undesirable situations in society; the knowledge production against an expression of greed gives advantages and disadvantages to people based on their subjective position. Greed, or self-interest, leads to competition and voluntary transactions that result in lower prices with higher quality; this is beneficial for everyone. It is greed that makes the free market possible and relatively stable. Greed, often thought to be a bad thing, is the protection and incentive needed to keep the free market moving forward.

QUESTIONS FOR DISCUSSION

1. Products in society that have a wide selection of styles and choices with decreasing prices are likely to be operating without excessive government regulation. Take note of those goods and services where there is little choice and variety and where the price always rises. What do they have in common with each other?

2. How is greed a good characteristic of people in the free market?

THE FREE MARKET 10

GOAL
To understand the free market as a
perspective of Race and Poverty

THIS BOOK OFFERS THE FREE MARKET as a possible approach to understand and work out the issues of race and poverty in America, if not the rest of the world. Racism and poverty exist in the free market; but the market itself may be able to handle those issues in a much more effective manner than current approaches involving the legislation of morality and the redistribution of wealth. The free market offers an area of no coercion because, in the free market, there is only voluntary cooperation through **voluntary transactions**; the use of force is not permitted in the public market. The exclusion of force includes government legislation and regulation that are generally coercive in nature; that is, the government cannot be used to legislate morality in the free market. The role of government is to primarily protect the property of the individual, including one's body. **Competition** in the free market generated by the self interest of the consumers preserves stability within it. The racialization of the **consumer** allows for subjective knowledge production that is equally valid for every individual consumer. In other words, no one gains an unearned advantage over anyone else through this racialization and knowledge production because everyone is a consumer. A consumer is one who consumes goods and services produced by him or herself and by others. The perspective of the consumer will be the broad perspective used to include everyone into the conversation equally. In the previous chapter, the construct "greed" was deconstructed to reveal the lack of productive content within that construct; everyone is greedy. No single person's greed is better or worse than another's greed. Doing away with what seems to be the primary critique of the free market and keeping in mind the example of toilet paper from the last chapter, let us proceed with a basic humanities introduction of the actual workings of the free market.

THE FREE MARKET

The free market is a constructed place that prioritizes voluntary cooperation and competition. The free market's constructed space is simply any place where goods and services are voluntarily exchanged for payment and where businesses compete with each other for customers. The free market does not need a specific physical location to exist; it can exist anywhere transactions are made, even virtually on the internet. The voluntary cooperation prioritized in the free market means that people are free to participate or opt out; free to work or not work; free to compete or not compete; free to share or not share; free to be selfish or selfless; and free to choose goods from competing businesses. In a voluntary society, one is free to do what one wants but must also take responsibility for the choices she or he makes and cannot harm or damage anyone else and anyone's property, which includes labor. In the free market, anyone can sell anything to anyone at any price people are willing to spend voluntarily. In other words, forcing others to buy or sell some product or not to buy or sell some product is strictly prohibited. One may choose to buy something, but that person cannot force other people to buy the same product, especially through regulation and legislation. The use of force here is the public use of force. That is, in a private company or home, rules may be established according to the custom and beliefs of that family or business. Nevertheless, harming another individual or destroying someone else's property still has legal repercussions. One does not have the right to abuse one's family because each member of the family is an individual. Each family may live by whatever doctrine, dogma, religion, or political belief it desires. However, the focus of this book will be confined to issues of poverty.

Although anyone can sell anything they want at any price, people must *want* to buy the product at that price. If no one wants to buy the product, for whatever reason, no one can force anyone else to buy it. If one wants customers to buy a product, then one has to sell something others want to buy for the given price. Some things do not have a price because they are too valuable; other things have no price because they are too cheap to charge anyone (e.g. the Mona Lisa is priceless, but air is free).

This means that the market cannot prevent competition, that is, the buying and selling of any product to anyone. The market, and any governing body, may not prevent sales, nor may it impose arbitrary restrictions on the buying and selling of goods, e.g. through taxation. If someone is unable to sell one's products, then that seller must improve or innovate their offering to the market in order to attract consumers. This is the nature and character of competition. Because, at this point, the reader may be imagining children buying heroin at the local grocery, the ideas of responsibility and liability will be touched. Depending on the transaction, both buyer and seller have responsibility, and the seller has some measure of liability. Because the free market functions with these concepts, buyers and sellers take care and caution in every transaction. Sellers would be less likely to sell heroin to children and parents would be sure to teach their children about the dangers of drugs. Instead of passing responsibility to others (particularly to government agencies) through the use of regulation, that creates a false sense of security and safety, buyers and sellers are forced to consider choices and options carefully. Responsibility would fall on the buyers and sellers. In the cases of negligence, misrepresentation, or damage, one would go to court. Court cases would not be decided through arbitrary, morality-based legislation that is passed by elected politicians. Instead court cases would be decided through historically based property, contract and tort law. This kind of law was not legislated but it is a case-generated law that evolved over time through the settlement of actual disputes. That is, historical experience taught people how to resolve differences, which allowed them to continue to live together and cooperate.[1]

The free market is free from government regulation and legislation, but this does not mean there is no law. The law utilized in the free market addresses damage and negligence through case generated laws. Standards of quality and safety are not arbitrarily imposed by government bureaucrats who either know little about the products or harbor subjective agendas for personal gain. Instead standards are determined by the producers of those goods. The standards set by actual producers would likely appeal to customers because producers are continually trying to increase sales. Even if several businesses decided to set a quality maximum (expressed as a minimum standard), competitors need only produce a product with a higher standard to attract consumers who want a better quality product.

Within this framework, businesses must compete with each other for customers. In order to attract customers businesses must provide goods

---

1   John Hasnas, *"Have Markets Failed,"* video lecture to ReasonTV's Headquarters in Los Angeles, May 26, 2013.

and services at a fair price; fair prices would be prices that people are willing to pay. As long as there is competition with other businesses, quality and price will be fair. If, for example, a company or several companies agree to sell a product above market price (overcharge), a competitor only has to maintain a lower price to break that incidence of price manipulation. Even if every business agrees to artificially raise prices on certain goods, the market allows for **innovation** and creativity to undermine and break that monopoly or oligopoly on those goods at those prices. An example would be the movie rental business. There was a time when renting a movie was unknown and movies could only be viewed via TV or the movie theatre. When renting movies became possible, one had to go to a store and physically pick and take home a tape. Rentals moved away from tape to disc recordings of many varieties. That market was dominated in the Northeast by Blockbuster Video. That business was undermined by video delivery services such as Netflix. Delivery of movies by snail mail is being replaced by streaming media via the internet. The presence of competition breeds innovation, which in turn is important to keep prices low and quality and choice high. It is difficult to maintain market dominance in a market that fosters innovation and competition. Many fields of life in the U.S. do not enjoy this type of innovative and competitive climate but are heavily regulated and controlled. **Regulations** represented as protections for consumers result in protection for existing and established businesses whose interests are opposed to those of the consumer.

NOT FASCISM OR CORPORATISM

The free market construct being proposed here is not to be confused with two other systems often conflated with the free market brand of capitalism, fascism and corporatism. The construct, **fascism** is commonly misunderstood to be the opposite of capitalism, but because many do not know what free market capitalism is, many also believe that the system they advocate is not a fascist system, when in fact, it is. In fascism, though industry is in the hands of private individuals, the industry itself is controlled by the state. In other words, the various industries are not really independent businesses that are competing against each other. Instead, they are often instruments of the state to facilitate the agenda of those in power; sometimes they exist as long as they submit to government demands. The conditions in a fascist type market are unfavorable for the consumer because there is no real competition between rival companies; goods and services are sold through coercion, direct and indirect. Because the corporations are owned by private individuals, many mistakenly think that what they observe is a free market capitalist system. An example of government controlling the pricing of products produced by private companies is the 2014 decision by a federal court to have a "monitor" from the US Department of Justice in the Apple Computer company to "supervise all the company's pricing decisions."[2]

Corporatism, or **crony capitalism**, is where corporations and government collude with each other in a symbiotic-type relationship. Large corporations ask for, help write and benefit from government regulations in exchange for political support for politicians. Politicians pretend to be against corporations and pretend to be for the interests of the consumer when they push for various regulations.[3] In this system competition is prevented or severely hindered and coercion is expressed through hegemony; people are taught that certain choices are the right choices to make; e.g. the "buy American" marketing campaign. The Food and Drug Administration often bend to the wishes of large pharmaceutical companies to prevent competition from start-up and foreign drug companies. One case would be with regard to the drug "Iressa," which can cure cancer for some people. Rather than allow further testing to continue in America, the FDA removed it from the market as it did not serve the interests of large pharmaceutical companies and the many cancer treatment facilities across the country.[4]

In a corporatist or fascist society, some rich people get richer and many poor people get poorer. This is primarily because certain kinds of people and businesses are protected and maintained by the regulations of society that the politicians passed in the name of protecting the consumer. It is interesting that when wealth gaps appear and are extreme, capitalism is blamed instead of the corporatist or fascist arrangement between business and government. These two economic forms are often conflated or confused with free market capitalism. In the free market, the role of government is to protect the individual, not corporations. The individual consumer

2   Dara Kerr, "*Apple loses bid to yank court-appointed antitrust monitor,*" February 10, 2014, news.cnet.com.
3   Peter Schweizer argues that politicians use extortion to extract money from corporations in return for favorable legislation in Washington. Peter Schweizer, "*Extortion: How Politicians Extract Your Money, Buy Votes, and Line their own Pockets,*" (Houghton Mifflin Harcourt Trade, 2013).
4   Jim Epstein, "*A Miracle drug cured Ed Levitt of Stage IV lung cancer, then the FDA withdrew it from the market,*" December 3, 2013, reason.com.

is most important in the free market rather than certain corporations or special interest groups.

PRICES

Price acts as a messaging system that communicates interpreted data to many people constantly. It is interpreted data because unregulated prices are reflections of a world of different priorities. As was discussed in the previous chapter, many resources are limited in supply and availability. Because many resources have multiple uses that require differing quantities, suppliers of resources adjust prices according to demand. They may not know why demand is increasing in one industry or decreasing in another, they just know they must adjust their prices accordingly. Small changes in price may lead to small changes in the cost of manufacturing products. Dramatic change in price can spark the search for alternative materials for that product. For example, when crude oil spikes, research for alternative fuels increases; research for natural gas, solar or wind power to name a few. End users or consumers do not need to know if a resource they normally use is being sought after by another industry. Their concern is the price. The price informs buyers of the relative value of the products they are purchasing. Because money is also a resource that is limited, consumers have to choose between, for example, buying the next gaming system, saving for future tuition, or purchasing tonight's meal.

Prices are important for individuals. Prices tell people what to buy, how much to buy, what to produce, what not to produce, who to work for, and whether to work at all; prices even inform college students on which major to declare. Through prices, individuals can make decisions based on their own abilities, priorities, and needs, and their decisions affect prices, as well. This becomes a complex dance of constantly changing variables, actions, and reactions that no person or government could possible calculate and predict, much less manage; prices are constantly changing 24 hours a day, 7 days a week, 365 days a year.

Government policies attempt to control and manipulate prices through edict, law, or tax and ignore this dynamic of price. Government regulations are developed based on subjective knowledge production, which concerns itself with only a single use of a multiple use resource. The interconnectedness of prices and the behavior of people do not mean that the area of life targeted by the legislation will be the *only* area affected by the price control. For example, when the price of sugar is regulated through import restrictions to protect domestic sugar farmers in America, any product that uses sugar may rise in price. Some product manufacturers, unwilling to raise the price of their product, substitute corn syrup for sugar because corn syrup is cheaper than sugar; this leads to most manufacturers switching to corn syrup to remain competitive. Sugar farmers in the U.S. make an average of 3 billion dollars a year more with the restrictions, and each consumer must pay about ten dollars more per year for their purchases; the average consumer does not notice the cost, and corporations reap the profits of their ability to legislate morality through their connections in Washington D.C.[5] Corn farmers (who are also subsidized by or receive money from government) benefit from this arrangement too as demand for their corn increases. Corn farmers, in turn, pass these increased costs to the consumer. Because corn is also a multi-use resource, the increased demand in one industry affects price and demand in other industries; so other prices will be affected by any changes to the production or cost of this commodity. A major alternative use of corn is corn feed for farm animals; these farm animals are a source of food for many. When the price of corn rises, the price of corn feed also rises. When the price of corn feed rises, the price of the animals that eat the corn feed rises. In this way, most food products that use corn and corn-related products increase in price. In addition to the increase in price, it is likely that some farm owners will seek alternatives for feeding their livestock.

It is easy to see the ripple effect of price control, which most people cannot predict nor manage. In the free market, "no policy" is better than "any policy." In other words, when government passes arbitrary policy to favor certain industries or because the regulation sounds compassionate, there are many negative consequences that hurt consumers and the businesses that received those benefits in the first place. In this sugar industry example, eventually, cheaper imports will be sold in the U.S., and when that happens, domestic farmers won't be able to compete; they will either adapt at high cost or go out of business. The years of protected commerce has hampered development in methods for the U.S. sugar farmer. It would have been better for no government intervention, which would have forced farmers to develop better farming methods to compete with the foreign sugar, and Americans would always have had cheaper sugar. One might

5 "Why is there Corn in your Coke?" November 19, 2012, LearnLiberty.org; Ernest C. Pasour Jr., "U.S. Agricultural Programs: Who Pays?" The Independent Institute, November 1, 2008, www.independent.org.

even say that the use of corn syrup would not be as prevalent today had the government not protected domestic sugar.

Many different people are affected by arbitrary policies, but the poor are adversely affected the most by the rising cost of many goods. It is interesting to note that the poor are often used and invoked when price policies are debated and legislation is proposed. In the case of sugar farmers, the image of the poor family farm is employed to evoke sympathy and generate support for continuing farming subsidies. True or not, the lower income person in the city must pay more for the same products because sugar farmers are now protected against competition. The working poor pay taxes, which go for programs that include farming subsidies. The poor are supposed to be the beneficiaries of this type of welfare policy, not an industry or other racialization. From 1980 to 1998 each sugar farmer received $3 million annually through this legislative policy.

THE PRICE OF RACISM

Not only do goods and services have prices, but our choices have prices as well. For example, if a person has a preference for buying German cars, then in the U.S. that person will likely not only have to pay more, but will have fewer choices than someone who has no preference at all. Someone who prefers to shop at small local stores will probably expect to pay more than someone who shops at a big box store like Costco. What most people do not realize is that discrimination or racism, too, has cost; choices based on our own personal standard of discrimination, that is, racism, have costs. The market accounts for this discrimination/racism in ways that most people do not understand. The costs of racism are misinterpreted by those who are unaware of the basic principles of economics. In other words, people should have to pay for their preferences. It is this ignorance of the cost of choice that allows so many to be convinced that legislation is the only way to account for and counter racist behavior in everyday life. Rather than trying to coerce people to change their beliefs through ineffective legislation and regulation, in a free society, people should be allowed to make free choices, even choices that subjectively may appear to be bad or racist choices according to some arbitrary standard. For the individual making the choice, it is not a bad choice; it is a free choice based on that individual's preference. This freedom to choose should be protected not because society is insensitive, but because the market works out and resolves this type of arbitrary discrimination. Also, legislators cannot predict the consequences of policy, no matter how well-intended they might be.

For example, if I am the kind of racist who only wants to serve Asians at my fictional restaurant, then I have to pay for this discrimination by having fewer customers. In other words, I have to turn away potential customers and word will spread that I discriminate against non-Asian customers. Other entrepreneurs with restaurants near my own that serve anyone will draw all non-Asian customers in addition to Asians who are uncomfortable with my discriminatory policy. Additionally, they may pay higher wages to their workers because they have more customers and they can afford to do so. Because they pay better wages, I will lose some of my better workers because they can earn more with my competitors. Eventually, I would be faced with the choice of either serving everyone including non-Asians or closing as more and more of my customers patronize my competition. I may still be a racist, but I am going to serve anyone, with a smile, if I want to stay in business. The end result is what is desired by most people: restaurants that serve everyone. The racist feels the pinch quickly and legislation that might have had unintended consequences was not written. Also, it is possible that the market has softened my anti-non-Asian feelings because I now realize those non-Asians are keeping me in business. Coincidentally, this dynamic increases social tolerance of the other; hostility towards the other bears a price that is often too high for most people to pay. Racism, in general, tends to be very costly. Many people in the free market realize that arbitrary racism is so costly that it is not worth maintaining. In other words, discrimination that includes factors not relevant to the products of the transaction increase the cost of the transaction without a corresponding increase in quality of the product. A consumer gets less for his or her money in this transaction. This principle of cost holds true for large businesses and businesses in small towns. The color of the skin of the people going to a restaurant matters little when compared to the customer's ability to pay for the food and whether they will recommend the eating establishment to their friends.

What bothers most people is the way in which this end result where restaurants serve everyone was achieved. It seems like "bad" racism or racism that has been taught as intolerable is condoned and normalized. In situations such as this, people feel that someone should be punished. In spite of the effectiveness of the market in dealing with this form of discrimination, many still push for legislation to force equal treatment. People are unaware that, by legislating morality in this way, one removes the cost of racism and so protects the racist and his or her racist beliefs. Regulations often hide and mitigate the cost of being racist, while being ineffective in changing people's beliefs. For example, equal pay for equal work laws remove the cost of racism by creating a situation where there is no difference between hiring a colored person and someone who is white. From some perspectives, the question of fairness is raised, and the demand for equal payment for the same job is legislated. Before this legislation, however, it was cheaper for a business to hire more blacks than whites, simply because they are cheaper to employ. To make this easier to understand, think of the hiring process as employers buying labor. If something is cheaper, you can buy more of it, in this case, labor. By removing the difference in price, one removes the cost of discrimination and makes white labor the same price as colored labor, so racist employers may not hire any colored people. The regulations remove the penalty of being a racist and actually encourage more racism in society. It is a widely known piece of knowledge that colored unemployment rises as white unemployment declines with rules such as this. It seems that many expect the unemployment rates to remain unchanged with legislation resulting in a benefit for colored workers. One example of such legislation is the minimum wage law. **Minimum wage legislation** is known by some as the most racist law in America. Prior to minimum wage laws, black teen unemployment was always lower than white teen unemployment. Today, with continually rising minimum wage levels, black teen unemployment is nearly double white teen unemployment rates.[6] Rather than trying to coerce certain so-called acceptable forms of behavior and thought, it would be more effective to force people to have to pay for their racism. Arbitrarily signified discriminatory practices are generally more expensive that non-discriminatory practices. In other words, it is less expensive to be less racist. Freedom is preserved and more of what was desired in the first place is the result.

It is worthy to note that slavery is not possible in the free market. **Slavery**, by definition, is not voluntary. The buying and selling of slaves flies in the face of the idea of private property, which includes the self; simply, one cannot buy and sell the property of others without the owner's consent; slaves rarely give their consent in this regard. Slavery also is extremely expensive. There is no need to buy a slave when one can hire day laborers.[7] Simply put, because there are cheaper labor sources other than slavery available, the free market would not have supported slavery in America, at the very least, in the 1800's.

---

6   Walter Williams, *Race & Economics*, (Standford: Hoover Institution Publication, 2011), pg. 43.
7   Theodore Allen, *The Invention of the White Race, Vol. One: Racial Oppression and Social Control,"* Verso, 1994, pg. 16.

Part of the reason it did persist for so long in the U.S. was because it was a practice that was protected by law. In other words, the very government charged with the responsibility to protect the property of individuals failed.

The **market itself discriminates against bad business practices** (including slavery). Some racist business practices are costlier than others. It is far more practical for people to allow the market to punish those practices that are counterproductive and need to be weeded out of the market. Legislation and regulation reinforce, strengthen, and legitimize certain racist practices to the detriment of society as a whole.

I want to preface the next example problem by saying it is a hypothetical situation using an actual historical event; it is a "what if" type problem. A comparison will be made between the free market perspective and the traditional perspectives taught in schools today. The problem question is: "Why did Rosa Parks (a civil rights heroine) have to sit in the back of the bus?" The answers one might hear are the standard answers taught to most children in the U.S.: it was the racist bus policy that stated blacks had to sit in the back of the bus if a white person wanted to sit in the front. A free market view would indicate the problem originated when the argument was made to have the city control public transportation through one company; in other words, there was only one bus company allowed to operate in the city. The proponents of this legislation most likely produced knowledge that highlighted various benefits of having no competition in the transportation industry. In reality, this was the creation of the worst kind of monopoly; a **government-run or controlled monopoly**. It is the type of monopoly that most people imagine when they think of evil monopolies, though they do not realize it.[8] The knowledge production by those legislators was fundamentally racist because it favored everyone affiliated with the bus company against the interests and to the detriment of consumers. Because the monopoly was protected by law, Rosa Parks had no choice but to ride that company's bus. In other words, government monopolies tend to be mismanaged, inefficient, increasingly costly, inconsiderate to customers, and yet still stay in business

---

8   When people imagine an evil monopoly, most would likely imagine a large private corporation; but this is more the result of knowledge production usually produced by competitors. The fact that there is competition means that a corporation cannot be a true monopoly. If that corporation has a large enough market share to give the impression that it is a monopoly, it may mean that it is producing a product that everyone is buying voluntarily because it is the best product. Government-run monopolies are actually what people are taught to hate. This is because the government monopoly makes competition illegal and so consumers are forced to buy the product that is offered, no matter the quality and price. In fact, the quality of government monopolies falls short of what could be achieved by independent corporations through competition and innovation.

because competition is illegal. If competition was allowed, then rival companies seeking more riders would pursue policies that would make operation cheaper, more efficient, satisfying and fair to all riders. This does not mean that racism is eradicated; rather it means that people are held accountable for the choices they make. Because certain racist choices offend and drive away potential business that may lead to bankruptcy, business owners focus on serving their customers well, no matter their color or gender.

Marriage is also an exercise in racism or discrimination and demonstrates how discrimination is costly; another construct for discrimination could be "pickiness." I firmly believed that I should marry the best person for me. I was going to exercise extreme prejudice in my choice because I would only get one chance to get it right, since divorce is not a voluntary option for me. This meant I discriminated against all men, non-Christian women, and non-Korean women, as well as all women unwilling to live with my folks and me for a year after marriage. Of the few women remaining, many of them discriminated against me for various reasons, but mostly because I was going to be a pastor and the fact that we had to live with my parents for a year. The price paid was steep, and I did not get married until I was 33 to the best person for me. It was my choice and the price paid was mine to pay. It would have been unusual and intrusive for a third party or a government regulation to tell me who the right person to marry would have been. No one was going to have to live with my wife for the rest of their life except me. As long as one is willing to pay the price, that person should be allowed to pay that price.

The construct "racist" has been deconstructed to add positive and productive connotations in the use of that construct. In addition to the subjective negative uses of racist, there are positive uses and expressions of racist. Usually people do not use the construct "racist" in situations similar to the marriage example; rather in addition to picky, people use the words loyal, love, and devotion as alternatives signifying the positive aspect of discrimination. That is one may choose to interpret pickiness or discrimination as a negative trait, however, this type of discrimination can also be characterized as exclusive devotion or love to one individual. It is a subjective activity to believe one's racism is better or worse than another's. Given that the cost of any racist trade-off is extremely high, people are naturally forced by their own beliefs to make adjustments for a better life. Consideration of what is a double standard enables one to see the logic and meanings beyond the typical subjectivity of a body of prior knowledge.

It should be a comfort to know that the market is extremely discriminatory against unproductive ideas, resulting in failure of those unpopular ideas. After all, what is business but the application and expression of ideas? Bad, unpopular, and costly ideas will have few subscribers. This is the same dynamic that takes place in the market of products. This reality of the market ensures the broad atmosphere of high quality and safe products for consumers to consume. Though some may object and point out that some producers may opt to produce products that are unsafe and are of low quality, the observation is subjective. In other words, everyone is free to buy what they want to buy according to their situation. A low income family may not be able to afford the "best" or most expensive option on the market and so may buy a lower priced, lower quality option. Lower price and lower quality does not necessarily mean unsafe. Producers and sellers have some measure of liability or responsibility for selling the products and likely will be clear about the risks that come with lower priced options. For example smaller cars are generally cheaper than larger cars. Part of the difference in price is the tradeoff in safety of the larger car. To ban the sale of smaller cars simply because they are not as safe in certain situations as larger cars may make sense to some people. However, the decision to buy a smaller car should be left with the buyer. If cheaper cars were banned then fewer people would have access to that mode of transportation.[9]

One might raise the issue of market failure as an objection to the natural regulatory process of the market. In other words, it is imagined that there are situations when the market by itself is unable to manage corruption and politics. Though the socialized reaction today is to have government step in and manage where the market has failed, the result is that actual government failure replaces the fear of potential market failure. Government regulatory failure can be much more devastating than the market could ever be through its own self-interested pursuits. For example, the British Petroleum (BP) oil spill in the Gulf of Mexico was brought on by government regulations that encouraged oil companies to drill in deep water. Oil companies do not have (at present) the technology to drill in water a mile deep. Oil companies require insurance coverage to help pay for damage caused in the event of an accident. The liability for drilling in deep water is unlimited and so no insurance company would cover that type of drilling; because in the event of an uncontrollable oil spill from a deep water rig the cost of the damage is potentially infinite, no insurance company would be able to cover that expense. Insurance companies are businesses, too. Because oil companies would be unable to secure insurance coverage, they would not drill in deep water. The government held drilling licenses for the gulf and

---

9   U.S. Customs and Border Protection website, *"Prohibited and restricted Items,"* *www.cbp.gov.*

realized no one would buy those licenses given the potential for unlimited liability in the event of an accident. The government then passed the 1990 Oil Pollution Act, which capped liability at $75 million; in other words an oil company would be responsible for only $75 million in damage. This is a small figure compared to the potential billions a company could make before a major accident. With the passage of the act in 1990, many oil companies now drill in the Gulf of Mexico. In the free market, BP would not have been drilling in the Gulf at that location because the government would not have been able to pass a bill that would cap liability; if the company wanted to drill in the gulf, it would have had to develop the technology to make drilling at that depth safe. Because liability was capped by the government, not by the market, corporations were encouraged to engage in behavior that the market would have disallowed.[10] This dynamic is known as a **moral hazard**. By capping liability the government encouraged and incentivized high risk behavior, that is, very bad decisions.

The BP oil spill example should illustrate the effect of government regulatory activities. For the sake of argument, if we posit that the result of both market and government failures were the same, then the difference would be that consumers paid for the government failure and the damage it created. In a free market system, BP would have been responsible for all damage and cleanup costs without limit.

THE CONSUMER

The perspective of the free market is the perspective of the **consumer**. In other words, the basic racialization of the free market is the consumer. A consumer is a user of products and services that s/he acquires in the market. Everyone who lives in the world is a consumer because everyone needs to buy food, clothing, and shelter. A consumer can be rich or poor, male or female, black or white, tall or short, old or young; everyone must use goods and services to live in society. Many people produce goods and services that other people consume, but everyone consumes products; such products include food and knowledge that must be produced by someone. The consumer racialization covers everyone and, at the same time, preserves the individual preferences and choices of a person, even within the racialization. Another expression for the racial group consumer is **general interest**, that is the interest of all consumers as a whole. Consumer and

10 Hasnas.

general interest (the specific and the generalization) are much more broad and inclusive racializations than most others; in fact, they include everyone. The racialization of consumers avoids the problems associated with narrower perspectives that establish hierarchies and systems of privilege. Any other racialization that can match this type of generality without ignoring the specific individual is a good starting point to understand the free market aspect of many areas of life. That is, not only are physical goods and their producers in competition with each other for consumers, but ideas and beliefs are also in competition with other ideas and beliefs for consumers; e.g. religions, economic schools of thought, scientific schools of thought, etc. Because poverty is an issue to be addressed in this book, then the consumer racialization lends itself easily to this topic.

The consumer makes choices often independently of any particular racialization and according to his/her individual preference at that particular moment of time and space. To reiterate, racialization generalizes and usually does not speak for every individual in that racialization. Most people in a particular narrow racialization may prefer to eat bread, but then some member of that group may be on a carbohydrate-free diet. The typical racialization is incapable of taking that detail into account, but the free market and the racialization of the consumer allow for each person to buy according to his/her individual wants and needs. One might even say that typical racializations are only descriptive of a group at a specific point in time; it does not enable accurate predictions of what individuals within that racialization will choose over time or even how society's view of that individual would change over time. The original food pyramid is a great example of how generalizations imposed on everyone is problematic when it assumes that everyone is the same and the individual is ignored. The racialization of consumer avoids the limitation of other racializations and has no expectation other than consumers consume. The food pyramid supposedly teaches good eating habits for everyone; however, it originally did not take into account different dietary restrictions or beliefs of many in society; e.g. vegetarians.

In this way the consumer racialization generalizes and yet preserves the uniqueness of the individual. In other words, the individual is not lost in the racialization. To protect the freedom of the consumers in general is to protect the rights of all individuals. Individuals also are liberated from the idea of **collectivism**; the idea that individuals belong to and are identified through a group or a particular racialization. One does not need to be affiliated with the right group of people in order to be protected. Rather one is free to associate with anyone one wants because no matter the association, the consumer as an individual is already protected. Also individuals do not have to wait for the political process to work itself out to express opinion and be represented. Choices in the free market are gratified immediately, most of the time. It might be argued that the "consumer" is the most ideal kind of racialization.

In the free market system, consumer satisfaction dictates the behavior of sellers. If customers are not satisfied by a product, they will not buy that product. The color of the customer is less important than his/her ability and willingness to pay. The race of the seller also is less important than whether s/he has products others want to buy. To maintain patronage from consumers, businesses must provide the right combination of service, quality, and price; this is done with the understanding that competition may choose, prioritize, and market similar products in different ways. As in the example of toilet paper, a small improvement in one company's product is enough to start competition among producers for customers. Having sellers competing for the patronage of consumers is a desired and necessary aspect of the free market because this not only requires producers to constantly improve their product but it shifts control to the general interest or consumers as a whole away from smaller special interest groups. If a company makes something that breaks easily while another company makes long lasting goods, fewer people would buy that product that breaks easily and instead would buy the longer lasting product. Thus, companies must be careful about the products they sell. They have the motivation or incentive to produce and sell a safe and reliable product, since they are liable or legally responsible for any damage or harm that might result through the use of that product. The cost and process of testing and guaranteeing safety becomes the responsibility of the producer and seller, not anyone else. Often in some of the less regulated areas of commerce today, third party evaluators and testers exist to rate and review new products for consumers without government oversight. In fact, it is likely because of the lack of government oversight that these evaluators and testers exist. The government does not **subsidize**, that is, help pay for this behavior nor does it impose minimum standards for product quality and evaluation. Yet, the service of testing and evaluation are free to the consumer in spite of the high quality of information. For computer components, for example, sites such as www.tomshardware.com provide just the kind of service discussed here.

An objection to this type of arrangement would be the "asymmetry in knowledge" argument. The seller (or buyer) may have more knowledge than the other party and take advantage of the other's ignorance. However, this situation is mitigated or managed in the market through various methods. Independent organizations may exist for the purpose of reviewing new merchandise for potential customers as in the example of computer components. Other areas of business have the same system in place that prioritizes consumers rather than producers. The computer/console gaming industry distributes advanced copies of games to testers and reviewers to generate buzz and interest for the product once it is available. Companies like www.gamespot.com and www.tomshardware.com must focus on consumers otherwise they will no longer be able to sustain the necessary internet traffic to stay in business.

Also, some products that have been in the market for some time are reviewed by people who already bought the product; customer reviews are a common aspect of online shopping; these customer reviews provide a wealth of often accurate information for traditional shoppers as well. Smart and discriminating shoppers take advantage of this information to make more informed purchases. The liability of safety and protection are still with the seller and producer.

In our society today, the government pretends or poorly attempts to perform the activities of product selling companies. These government agencies often establish guidelines or minimum safety standards to give the impression to consumers that products are safe. This practice benefits corporations because products only have to satisfy the minimum safety standards. Products may satisfy the minimum safety guidelines but this does not mean the products are safe. One example is the flame-retardant chemical, Tris. The Consumer Product Safety Commission issued in 1973 enforced the "Flammable Fabrics Act" of 1953 and required children's sleepwear to include flame-retardant. The chemical Tris was used for this purpose; however, 4 years later, after realizing it was a carcinogen, it was removed from the market.[11] Furthermore, regulations cannot account for cases of human error. Many accidents are due to human error rather than equipment failure. Regulatory agencies cannot protect consumers from themselves, all the time.

Often when failures by regulatory agencies occur, most of the blame is put on the companies that made the product while the role of the agency is downplayed. Shifting blame away from regulatory agencies allow for the agencies to continue to exist and grow in size and power. Their budgets come from tax payers that are forced to pay for inconsistent and often politically and fiscally motivated service. Regulations also dictate to

---

11   Milton and Rose Friedman, *"Free to Choose,"* New York: Harcourt Brace Jovanovich, 1980, pg 212–213.

producers what should be produced and how. In a system where regulatory agencies pass many rules and requirements the market is no longer free.

Pricing, the messaging system for consumers in the market discussed in the previous chapter, becomes distorted as companies must spend more to comply with arbitrary requirements continually being passed by government agencies. The price distortions created by government agencies send false signals and messages throughout the market, disrupting other market prices and the decisions consumers need to make. The Federal Reserve System, enacted in 1913, was established by government and was to operate independently of congress. Its main responsibility was to control the supply of money in the country. The activities of the Federal Reserve Bank distort the prices of money resulting in malinvestment or bad investment decisions by companies and individuals in society. These distortions hide the **risk** of various choices; risk is the chance of failure. In other words, what might seem like a responsible and safe choice is actually a high risk choice.

The mortgage crisis of 2008 was the result of new government regulations concerning loan rates and lending practices. The new rules created a moral hazard, a situation where choices do not appear as risky as they actually are, thus motivating people to make choices against their interest and long-term benefit. The new regulations passed through the Clinton and G. W. Bush administrations gave people the ability and motivation to buy a house when they should not have. Price speculation and an economic housing bubble was created by many people obtaining mortgages easily. It was unsustainable and popped in 2008. Many homeowners lost their homes, but the banks that made bad loans were bailed out by the government.[12]

Furthermore, government testing and regulation of many other products for the supposed protection of the consumer are far from effective, efficient, and cheap. Consumers are forced to pay for poor services from

---

12 Tom Woods, *"Meltdown: A Free-Market Look at why the Stock Market Collapsed, the Economy Tanked, and Government Bailouts will Make Things Worse"*, (Regnery Publishing, 2009), pg 12–32. Woods lists several major steps in the build up to the housing crisis. In 1999 Clinton pressured Fannie Mae and Freddie Mac, Federal National Mortgage Association and the Federal Home Loan Mortgage Corporation, to ease lending standards to make loans easier; Clinton brought back a Carter administration act, the Community Reinvestment Act, which further lowered the bar to qualify for a mortgage which triggered widespread speculation in the housing market; the pro-ownership tax code encouraged people to invest in homes through various tax breaks and incentives further driving speculation in the housing industry; FED chairman Alan Greenspan, lowered interest rates from June 2003–June 2004 making cheap money available for even more speculation. The irresponsible and bad business practices encouraged by government regulation was protected later by the government bailout of the banks.

the government. Because the government is not liable for damages and harm when it makes a mistake; there is no incentive for the government to do a better, more efficient, and more cost-effective job. However, the process gives consumers a false sense of security and safety. Moreover, consumers cannot opt out of government services; it is illegal to do so, and there is no choice.

GENERAL INTEREST AND SPECIAL INTEREST

All consumers, collectively, are the general interest. Standing opposed to the general interest is the special interest; the people who make a special interest group are also consumers but they have an agenda that goes against the general interest. As was mentioned in chapter 6, the special interest group is the political expression of a racial project or racialization. Any and every racialization has the potential to become a political special interest group. Many have already become special interest groups and are active in Washington and other places of power to have specific regulations and legislations passed in their favor to the detriment of the general interest. Slowly, over time, the number of special interest groups has grown to a point where much of their activity has been normalized. Organizing as a group (strategic essentialism or self-discrimination) and hiring lobbyists to push their agenda for their own benefit against the interest of everyone else is "race making" and has become big business. It is a slow death for the economy, and the poor are the hardest hit. Elected officials in Washington welcome the attention because it gives them the opportunity to "buy" votes by legislating morality.

Knowledge production to promote special interest causes never ceases and keeps knowledge producers (which are a special interest themselves) busy. Often forgotten in the long list of special interest groups is the most powerful of all special interest groups, the politician. They are the most powerful because they have the ability to write laws and legislation. It is no wonder that government employees or public sector workers are paid at a higher rate and have better benefits than private sector (non-government) workers doing the same job. It is also difficult to fire a government employee no matter how incompetent they are because efficiency is not their goal. Note that in a system where every organization/company must compete with other companies, the government would always lose; this is because the government agencies are designed to run as monopolies, companies ever free from competition and thus, free from the need to improve and maintain quality, service and customer satisfaction. The price of government services are often partially hidden because those services are subsidized making them appear less expensive than they really are. In other words, the price tag at the time of purchase of a government product by the consumer is the price after the consumers were taxed to pay for production and development; consumers are essentially charged for products for which they already paid.

Politicians act in their own self-interest just as any other special interest group. The problem is that the interest of most politicians stands against the general interest; the very group for which they claim to be working. Thus, the politician has to maintain the appearance of working for the people while working for him or herself. The news program *60 Minutes* broke the story of insider trading by elected officials. Members of congress who sit on committees that decide influential regulation know which companies will benefit from various legislations before the public does. Through creative interpretations of the law, they are able to contact their brokers to buy or sell the appropriate stock to reap guaranteed profits.[13] Because congress wrote the laws on insider trading, members of congress are able to exploit ways of getting around the restrictions of insider trading laws. It is in this way that they can avoid arrest and fines that are enforced on the average citizen. The recently passed 2013 STOCK Act (Stop Trading on Congressional Knowledge Act), which was supposed to prevent future congressional insider trading, was revised in a way that preserves much of the insider trading "loopholes." In other words, as with most government regulations, the Act was only cosmetic.[14]

Many regulations passed that were advertised and sold as protection for the general interest are actually protections for special interest groups against competition. Removing competition is against the interest of the consumer, and this type of short-term gain for a business comes at a long-term cost for everyone as the country slowly gets buried under financial obligation after financial obligation; this can also be known as regulatory compliance. These obligations raise the cost of goods and services

---

13 For example, trading on so-called "non-public" information is perfectly legal. (Stephanie Condon, *"Senators introduce "STOCK ACT" to stop "insider trading" in Congress,"* November 15, 2011, www.cbsnews.com.)

14 There are numerous commentaries on the matter that fall under the rules of knowledge production. Though the executive and legislative branches of government and their staff must file financial disclosures, many lobbyists and people who are able to wander the halls of congress are free to continue their practices unimpeded.

throughout the country, which affects the poor more than other racializa-tions. That is, catering to the various special interest groups in the country results in detriment for the poor in the form of higher cost for food and services. Many would argue that the role of government was supposed to be the protection of each individual citizen of the U.S., but has now become the instrument of hegemony to take from the individual, all in the name of helping the poor or protecting the defenseless and ignorant consumer. In the current system, the government often does the opposite of protect-ing the property of the individual against powerful special interests. Some of the worst cases are the various abuses of eminent domain (the right of government to take private property for government or better public use); this includes cases where corporations and individuals use their influence in government to have lands seized below market price and against the wishes of the owners.[15]

Through regulations freedom is denied for business opportunities because startup ventures are squashed under a mountain of red tape and regulation. The price of doing business is distorted to favor those compa-nies that already exist and discourage new companies from forming. The people who suffer most are the poor who are denied lower cost goods so that politicians and their cronies can enrich themselves.

Food trucks, trucks that have been converted to mobile kitchens, are a good example of a relatively cheap business opportunity for lower income families. Families that have few options and no education but are willing to cook and work long, hard hours in all kinds of conditions can take their shot at being entrepreneurs. The primary advantage of the food truck is that the cost of overhead is relatively low. One initially only needs to have enough money to buy the truck and initial supplies. Because successful food trucks are so lucrative and they are mobile, they are an ideal start up business platform. Successful food trucks are successful because of the combina-tion of quality, convenience, and price compared with other food choices. However, food trucks are also competition for more established, expensive and older restaurants in the areas in which they operate. Established busi-nesses exert their influence and political connections to have inspections and licenses required for food trucks, which add to the cost of doing busi-ness. Many cities go a step further and allow restaurants to decide whether or not to issue food truck licenses. Though advertised as protection for the consumer, legislation of this variety is protection of established businesses against new competition, especially low cost competition. The doing away

---

15 Steven M. Greenhut, *"Abuse of Power: How the Government Misuses Eminent Domain,"* (Seven Locks Press), 2004.

of competition through legislation is bad for the consumer, particularly the poor. The opportunity to make money quickly is criminalized, and at the same time, the poor are forced to buy products at a higher price. As has already been discussed, without government regulations, health and safety standards are dictated by the market. If for example, people get sick from eating at a truck, people will stop eating there driving them, either, out of business or to maintain high health standards. Furthermore, reality TV has given people an inside look into the heavily regulated brick and mortar restaurants; they are not as sanitary as many believe them to be.

TOLERANCE: ROOM FOR EVERYONE

It is worthwhile to further note that, within the free market, there is room for almost everyone and almost any ideology. If I want to start a social-ist community where everything is shared, where everyone cooperates for the good of the community and not for the individual, then in the free market, I may. However, I may not force or require others to do the same; participation must be voluntary. This also means that I may not attempt to pass legislation to coerce others to live this way; participation must be voluntary. Attempts to trade with non-socialistic communities must follow the rules of the free market. Further, no one may force another community to trade with that socialist community.

At the same time, in many other societies where socialism or central government planning is dominant, there is no room for the free market as described above. For example, a socialist society would generally not permit citizens to start areas of free trade. That level of freedom, for the average person, would upset the power structure as established and preserved by the state. In a corporatist society, only the approved activities through the approved systems are permitted to exist legally. A free market society has no such bias or agenda and as a result is much more tolerant of difference. This tolerance throughout society establishes a climate that is much more creative and innovative and is directly beneficial to the poor of society.

SUMMARY

The free market prioritizes voluntary cooperation for the consumer; everyone operating within a society is a consumer, so everyone within a society should benefit from the free market. In the free market, the individual, regardless of their racialization, is protected because no special interest is allowed to legislate morality. The voluntary character of the market incentivizes competition among businesses for the patronage of customers. This simple dynamic ensures quality and accountability among sellers to the benefit of the consumer, especially the poor consumer. Protection of any kind through the legislation of morality weakens the position of the individual and is most detrimental to the poor.

QUESTIONS FOR DISCUSSION

1. In the past, if you had a lesson on capitalism, did you learn about the free market? If not, what do you think you learned instead?

2. How is constant change good for the individual and bad for the individual?

3. How might constant change be good for society and bad for society?

4. How might constant change be good for the status quo and bad for the status quo?

THE FREE MARKET
IN CONTEXT

11

GOAL
Present chapter summaries
of Milton and Rose Friedman's *Free to Choose*

THIS CHAPTER WILL ONLY HIGHLIGHT AND SUMMARIZE THE CONTENTS of a video series produced by Public Broadcasting Service (PBS) and Milton Friedman, which can be found at miltonfriedman.blogspot.com. The video series itself is an adaptation of the book, *Free to Choose*, by Milton and Rose Friedman.[1] It is a visual and accessible way to be introduced to the world of the free market and the Chicago School of economics. Though the videos were made in 1980, the relevance of the ideas are just as strong today as they were then.

FROM VOLUME 1: THE POWER OF THE MARKET

SUMMARY

In part one of *Free to Choose*, Friedman explained that economic freedom is a necessary condition for political and human freedom. Allowing individuals to exercise their freedom through voluntary transactions yield a favorable situation for all who live in that society. The role of the government should be limited to protecting the property and freedom of

---

1   Milton Friedman and Rose Friedman, *Free to Choose: A Personal Statement* (Orlando: Harcourt, Inc, 1980).

all individuals in society and not just those of a particular special interest group. It is through the price system that each individual decides what is best for him or herself. The choice each individual makes occurs according to the values and calculations of that individual and so satisfaction is more prevalent throughout society. One may dislike the choices of others, but as long as property has not been damaged, there is no need for government or legal action. Furthermore, because each individual has the freedom to choose voluntarily, transactions are beneficial for all parties involved in that transaction, otherwise, the transaction would not take place. The result of voluntary human action is not achievable through government planning, manipulation or coercion. Rather it is the lack of government intervention that gives people the freedom to generally resolve issues quickly and efficiently. It is the uncoordinated action of the entire population that produces spontaneous order through which life continues.

Friedman illustrated this dynamic with a trip to Hong Kong (1980). At the time, Hong Kong was under British control; however, the government did not interfere with the operation of the economy rather only enforced contracts. Though the government did not impose any standards on the economy, Hong Kong had the highest standard of living in all of Asia. Though people accustomed to the standards of the west could have a hard time seeing the relatively high standard of life, many others in Asia aspired for life in Hong Kong. People continued to flock to Hong Kong, in 1980 because of the opportunity and freedom that existed there. **Sweat shops** are labeled sweatshops subjectively. As long as the transaction of employment is voluntary and there is competition for that labor, then there is nothing technically wrong with a business perceived to have poor working conditions; any perceived wrong is subjective. People who do not want to work there do not apply for a job; people who become dissatisfied with that work strive to obtain a different job. What is important for workers is not **job security** rather it is **job mobility**; the ability to find a different and better job.

Necessary for voluntary employment transactions is the competition for labor. As people become more experienced in the workforce, they become better qualified for higher paying and more productive work. Employers should have to compete for the best workers, which ensures productivity and worker satisfaction. It is the industry and economy that decides what jobs should exist and how much workers should be paid. In the global economy, local government protection through regulation and taxes cannot prevent buyers and producers from doing business in other countries. Businesses respond to changes in the market as they occur; there is no need to wait for a politician to do something first. The ability of individual businesses to respond quickly to changes in the market is way the market creates opportunity.

The desires and calculations of many people can be known by tracking how people **vote with their feet**. People generally move from an undesirable place to a more desirable one. When there is no other way to vote because there is no political or human freedom, people will vote with their feet and migrate to a location with more freedom. This migration behavior continues in spite of government attempts to control this expression of human choice. Even if migration is criminalized by borders and regulations, people will seek to get around those obstacles in pursuit of freedom and opportunity.

Modern trade patterns not only facilitate the creation of wealth, but it also fosters harmony and peace. Friedman used the example of the **wood pencil** to illustrate how thousands of people cooperate to make a pencil, which no individual can make on his or her own. This complex globally produced inexpensive pencil required cooperation between people who may hate each other if they met. In other words, the emotions of racism take second place to the opportunity to create wealth. Trade between countries brings those countries closer together and makes war less likely to occur.

The free market is **impersonal**. It does not signify any racialization over another. Rather it is a system through which people can exercise their personal freedom to live in the way they want. The consumer desires to be free. People should work hard to protect this freedom from the over reach of government.

FROM VOLUME 2: TYRANNY OF CONTROL

SUMMARY

Volume 2 explores what happens when governments interfere with the ebb and flow of the free market. The free market acts in the interest of consumers, generally, by allowing them to buy goods from those who sell at the best or cheapest price. Special interest groups, primarily business people, act in a directly opposite manner by trying to prevent consumers from buying goods from people who are selling those goods at the best price. Friedman explained how governments will act on knowledge produced by businesses to the detriment of the whole society. Governments often and mistakenly try to control the economy to have it perform in a specific way to benefit the cronies of government. This type of government activity is the opposite of the free market and Friedman called this **central economic planning**.

When people are allowed act in their own self-interest to buy and sell goods freely, the whole of society benefits. Sellers in order to sell their products must produce the best quality goods at the best price possible because consumers are trying to buy the best goods at the best price possible. In other words, the unregulated, uncoordinated self-interested pursuit of profit by sellers caters to the self-interest of individual consumers trying to save money (a type of profit), which all results in an ordered society.

Merchant special interest groups always favor markets where there is little to no competition to ensure continued wealth for themselves at the expense of consumers. In other words, merchants and business people do not want consumers to be able to buy from businesses that sell their products for less. Politicians through government regulations are able to legislate coercion according to the desires of the merchants in the name of safety or protection through the knowledge production process. **Protectionist policies** protect business and merchant interests against the interests of consumers. England was burdened by heavy regulation until 1846 when many taxes and duties were lifted on foreign goods. The nation went on to become one of the wealthiest nations in the world at that time. It had since gone back to a nation of regulations.

Friedman then examined and compared the **loom industry** in India and Japan. With modernization, Japan's government did not protect the jobs of the loom industry. Though that may sound like a cruel position to take, the result was an economic boon in Japan through which the vast majority benefitted. People were freed from the handloom and were able to explore employment made possible by increased productivity. Because one person can do the job of hundreds with modern machines, the cost of goods came down as well. Women who were third class citizens in feudal Japan were able to be independent in the free market.

In contrast to this progress was the government protection of the loom industry in India. The protection came in the form of import taxes **(tariffs)** and subsidies for domestic companies. **Subsidies** are tax revenues given to industry to make the cost of doing business cheaper, thus making modernization unnecessary. The intent was to protect the livelihood of many in India. However, the result was very little economic development resulting in widespread poverty. More and more people, including children, were forced to operate hand looms, just to inadequately keep up with demand. Though everyone, including little children, had jobs, everyone was poor. Though everyone was working, the productivity was so low that the costs were still relatively high in spite of the subsidies.

Politicians may claim to have the best **intentions** when they push legislation and policy; they claim to be forward looking and progressive. However, the results of their activities are regressive, they move society backwards and are harmful for society. Having good intentions with carefully crafted knowledge production is not enough bring about positive results; instead there are many detrimental **unintended consequences** that arise for which the government never takes responsibility. In this particular volume the poverty of India would be an example of the unintended consequences of well-intended government action.

The steel industry's request for subsidies to remain competitive with foreign subsidized steel was discussed in the context of **consumer exploitation**. The claim was that competing against government subsidized companies from other countries was unfair and was likened to a crime. To restore the balance and fairness American steel companies deserved to receive subsidies from the U.S. government and tariffs needed to be levied on imports. In this arrangement, the steel business benefited only temporarily while the consumer was disallowed from buying in the way s/he would have likely bought. This is why Friedman called "tariffs" exploitation of the consumer. The perspective of the consumer, rather, is that the more unfair the competition, the better prices will be. Lower prices are always good for the general interest. Though **unfair competition** is bad for certain businesses, those businesses must adapt or close. In the same way the Japanese did not protect their loom industry from foreign competition, the U.S. should not protect domestic industries from competition. The general interest would benefit from the competition and resulting lower prices and increased quality. Protectionist policies only delay the inevitable in the protected country and industry.

Friedman believed that there should therefore be constitutional restraints on the power of the government to influence the free market. Government economic planning only restricts the freedom of consumers in the market place. Central economic planning always uses force to bring about its intended results. This should not be allowed because it reduces choice and competition in the market place. Free trade and free choice are necessary for a free society. Government interference in the economy, or central economic planning, cannot compete with the free expression and creativity of everyone living in the free market.

FROM VOLUME 3: ANATOMY OF A CRISIS

SUMMARY

Volume 3 revisits the beginning of the Great Depression, which started in December of 1930. Though many people believe a failure of capitalism caused the depression, the free market economist sees it as the failure of government. Power had been given to government through the Federal Reserve Bank to control the money supply, or the quantity of cash, primarily to the banks in the U.S. It failed to supply money when it should have done so, which touched off runs on banks all across America; the runs resulted in bank closures and the destruction of money. The inaction occurred partly because of the racism that existed in the Federal Reserve Bank against Jewish people. Friedman pointed to the depression as the event that justified an ever growing wasteful government, which reduces the freedom of the country's citizens.

This failure of government became the failure of capitalism and the excuse to increase the size and power of the government as the only entity able to prevent such a similar crisis in the future. John Maynard Keynes introduced his brand of economics which is now widely accepted by most politicians. His idea was that government can spend money it printed through the Federal Reserve to restart a depressed economy. Today Keynes' idea has become the belief that a country can spend its way out of debt by simply inflating currency. Though many say that the government eased the pain of the depression or that World War II ended the Depression, free market economists generally believe that the government prolonged the depression and that the economy did not really recover until after the world war was over.

The significant effect of the Depression was that government established itself as an all-knowing and all powerful benefactor of society because of the supposed failure of capitalism; it now had a way to increase in size and power through the inflation of currency. Because of the ability to print money, it could now find ways to finance many government programs that act against the consumer and the general interest of society. The belief that private industry cannot provide the kind of economic growth required by the U.S. has become more prevalent. It is the government that must provide safety, security and jobs for the people in the way that benefits the general interest the most. Deficit spending and inflation has come to dominate the monetary and fiscal policy ever since.

This chapter illustrates the dangers of concentrated power in the hands of a powerful opinionated minority. It was the bigotry against Jews and the monopoly on currency that, according to Friedman, touched off the Great Depression. In contrast it is the inability to concentrate power and monopolize money in the free market that should make the market much more attractive to more people. Friedman disagreed with the current understanding that the government can provide the solutions to our social problems. Instead, he believed that the government is the main source of instability in society today. This includes the codification of arbitrary discrimination, what many today call racism and institutional racism.

FROM VOLUME 4: FROM CRADLE TO GRAVE

SUMMARY

As discussed in volume 3, the U.S. federal government has taken on the role of problem solver in the country. The legacy of the Great Depression is the belief that the government can and should protect and provide for people determined to be in financial trouble in society; security from cradle to grave. The government started work programs and social security with good intentions; to help people who were experiencing difficulty in their lives. The expansion of welfare programs to help poor people in general is hard to argue against, for few people could be against helping people in need. Friedman argued that though the programs were meant to be temporary assistance they have become long-term programs. Rather than being beneficial to society, government spending has become a way to **waste** tremendous amounts of tax payer money, reduce personal freedom in society and increase government size and power. Another perspective on this activity sees government taking the power of choice away from individuals by deciding what they should buy, what they should prepare for and how.

Friedman says that the problem of the **wealth redistribution programs** is that people are spending other people's money for another group of people by the rules set up by yet another group of people. No matter how well intentioned a program or organization might be, waste on a large scale cannot be avoided, and Friedman documented a tremendous amount of waste, fraud and abuse. The amount of waste is staggering even in 1980.

At the time, the budget of the Health, Education and Welfare department exceeded the entire national budget of every other country in the world except the former Soviet Union and the entire budget of the U.S.A. In spite of all of that spending, there were still issues of poverty in the country.

This monumental waste cannot be justified as the results of the programs are also unsatisfactory. Public housing projects often fail and leave behind crumbling buildings in crumbling neighborhoods. Government programs are filled with conditions and regulations that often skew incentives and motivate people to make choices they otherwise would not make. Sometimes to qualify for welfare, families must liquidate savings or quit a job or seek a divorce.

Friedman blamed the whole welfare system for creating dependence and destroying independence. This arrangement results in a general moral decay as people are disempowered from making and pursuing their own objectives. The self-interest, incentive, and motivation that are needed to drive the free market are muted and replaced with fear; the fear of losing welfare benefits. The system is established in a way to benefit bureaucrats and the people who oversee those programs are given "godlike" powers. The people participating in those programs are reduced to childlike dependence stripped of their incentive to improve their lives.

Friedman believed that no one spends money as efficiently as people who spend their own money. The slow phasing out and ending of many welfare programs would require people to find work and reverse the trend caused by government programs. Restoration of personal control of life is critical to solving many of the problems wasteful government spending cannot. It is not that helping those in need is bad, rather the current system and process by which people try to help those in need is bad. In the absence of government programs, private citizens and organizations would take on that duty and they would do it in a far more productive and efficient manner.

FROM VOLUME 5: CREATED EQUAL

SUMMARY

Volume 5 deals with the issue of equality. Though it may seem like a straightforward concept, the perception and understanding of equality is subjective; which understanding is the better understanding of equality is the subject of this chapter. The two dominant understandings that are discussed are the **equality of opportunity** and the **equality of result**. Equality of result is the idea that everyone should enjoy a similar standard of life and income no matter one's occupation and ability. In other words, the gap between rich and poor should not be too wide. In contrast to this is the idea of equal opportunity. In this perspective, everyone is free to try to maximize one's resources for the best results to improve one's personal situation. Friedman favored the definition that best preserves the freedom of the individual.

A difficulty for most people with regard to the topic of equality is the belief that the rich are rich at the expense of the poor. It is believed that the wealth of the poor has been taken by the rich to be richer. This creates the **wealth gap** that is seen even and especially today. Though gross inequality in wealth is offensive to many, the question remains whether the free market is to blame for this gap between rich and poor. Friedman argued that it is government policy that magnifies and codifies the gaps seen in wealth among different groups in society. In fact, income inequality and disparity in quality of life is greater in countries that have an authoritarian government and central economic planning. In other words, governments intensify and codify wealth gaps by trying to reduce those very gaps. It is rather the countries that are freer where one may find a higher standard of living among the poor of society. Furthermore, it is the free market that gives the poor a better chance to rise out of poverty and enjoy a comfortable life. Our differences and inequalities give individuals opportunity to take advantage of various market opportunities.

Friedman explained that equality and fairness are signified and measured in inconsistent ways in different areas of life; sometimes extreme inequality is enjoyed and praised while other times they are demonized and penalized. For Friedman personal resources not only include monetary wealth but also wealth of talent and appearance. In other words, one's physical attributes are as much a resource as monetary wealth. However, for many people, it is only the financial aspect of life that is signified and where attempts are made to regulate and redistribute wealth.

The free market gives people the freedom to make the best use of the talents and resources a person has. It is a combination of understanding one's abilities with the opportunity to use those abilities that helps people choose what to do. Choices people make are important because all choices involve some measure of risk. **Risk** is the probability of loss or losing wealth through a choice one makes. Many choices are low risk choices such as climbing a flight of stairs. Other choices are high risk choices such as starting a business; much more is at stake with a much more complicated task. Individuals make the choices they make because they believe they can bear the consequences of that choice. People weigh the potential benefits against the potential loss and then make choices.

Society benefits from the risks taken by people. People who are successful in their ventures create benefit for everyone else in society. Though there are many who fail, they were willing to bear that consequence and try again. In this system the people who make the initial choices are those who must bear the cost of those choices. When government makes choices in research and development, the general interest must bear the cost. Because government does not bear the cost of its choices, there is less care when making those choices no matter the political rhetoric.

This system of taking risks benefits the ordinary or the poor more than the rich of society. This is primarily because the rich are usually already satisfied with what they have; more wealth will not make their lives dramatically better. However, lower income individuals have the potential to gain a great amount and will often decide that a choice is worth the risk. Their willingness to take risks result in various improvements throughout society. So, development and technological innovation have benefitted the poor more than they have benefitted the wealthy. For example, development in farm machinery has relieved the poor of backbreaking work and enabled them to enjoy many of the comforts of the rich. Someone became wealthy through the invention of machinery but lower income people benefited from the innovation, also.

Government attempts to bring about equality of result conflict with the idea of freedom to choose and instead government restricts the use of personal resources by individuals to improve their lives. Government activity for the purpose of creating equality is coercive and causes people to lose independence and the respect for the law in general, eventually leading people to break the law. No matter what the law is, people will continue to act in their own best self-interest. Preserving the freedom of individuals to choose what they believe is best for themselves interestingly results in a more ordered and tolerant society. Government coercion takes away the power of choice, which includes the choice to take risks.

In the free market the equality gap, the gap between rich and poor, is not as important an issue as economic freedom. The priority is to empower everyone in society especially the poor with the opportunity to rise out of poverty. This can happen through the protection of the freedom of choice and the freedom to take risks. Freidman closed the chapter by stating that the society prioritizing **equality over freedom** will have neither; the society prioritizing **freedom over equality** will have a fair measure of both. In order to have equality, freedom is sacrificed; however, if freedom is nurtured, then people are able to make the choices that are best for them at any given moment. This results in a society where, though there are still wealth gaps, the standard of living for the poor in a free society is substantially better than the standards of the poor in countries with planned economies.

FROM VOLUME 6: WHAT'S WRONG WITH OUR SCHOOLS?

SUMMARY

In this volume of the series, Friedman examined the problem of education in the U.S. The problem simply stated is that generally public schools are **government controlled monopolies**. There are other variables which are applicable, but the major issue for many underperforming schools is the lack of choice. There is no choice or alternatives for parents and children; they are required to go to the school of their district no matter the quality of that school. Parents have lost the ability to control where their children go to school and what they learn at that school. Friedman suggested that the freedom of choice be restored to families and introduce a market mentality for education similar in some ways to the way higher education is maintained.

The working poor are often trapped in neighborhoods with schools that do not perform well. They are forced to pay for an educational product that is not very good. The government is continually trying to help and improve performance but schools often only get worse. The poor performance of the government monopoly is often hidden by shifting the focus on the poverty or character of the people who live in that neighborhood. Blame may also be put on the culture of violence in the area. However, when families have the power to choose which school children will attend, one begins to see increase in performance and test results. Friedman gave several examples of education experimentation using non-traditional methods that yielded the desired positive improvement. For example Harlem Prep was a store-front school that opened when large numbers of students dropped out of the public schools in the 1960s. Though these students were the misfits of the public school system, they thrived in the storefront situation where classroom conditions would make educational professionals cringe. These schools were eventually taken over by the education professionals and their success was "strangled."

Friedman suggested that **vouchers** be used to restore choice to families of students. Money that was earmarked for schools are given to parents instead; they would use that money to choose the school for their children. In other words, the monopoly hold of educational bureaucrats is broken through the freedom of choice. It makes sense then that the people who resist the voucher system are the very bureaucrats who benefit from maintaining the underperforming schools. The attitude of many administrators is one of pure arrogance and condescension towards the parents. The feeling is that parents do not know what is best when it comes to the education of their children. This is not to say that all administrators exploit children to maintain employment; it is the system maintained by a few that leads to the issues and the frustration of many teachers, we see today.

The fear of people who are pro-educational monopoly is shown to be unfounded through the example of private higher education. Families can choose which college students will attend. When only the students who enroll in a particular institution must pay for the cost of education, the result is a graduation rate over 95%. The private university system functions like a market where the product is education. Families choose according to their needs and desires.

On the other hand, the state funded schools are shown to be problematic because the lower tuition is made possible by subsidies that come from the taxation of the working poor. Because the working poor generally do not go to college, the situation arises where lower income families are helping to pay for the education of higher income families. The subsidies from the government have created distortions in prices in the market and have incentivized less than ideal behavior. The graduation rate at the University of California, Los Angeles was about 50% in 1980. This is an interesting contrast of public and private universities. Because the price of subsidized universities was lower, more people enrolled; but because fewer students were invested in the enrollment, fewer students graduated.

Friedman's conclusion is that the power of choice must be restored to the families who choose schools for their children. It is the people who are purchasing that education who should have to pay for that education. Vouchers would assist in the transition from the current system to a new market driven system. If this action is implemented, then the quality of schools would begin to improve.

FROM VOLUME 7: WHO PROTECTS THE CONSUMER?

SUMMARY

In this volume the problem of consumer protection is addressed. There is a fear that many consumers are too vulnerable to deception, scams, and misinformation that something must be done to protect them. Particularly the racialization of free market capitalists includes the stereotype of unscrupulous and greedy, which means that capitalists would take advantage of consumers whenever possible. Friedman argued that government agencies fail to perform the role of protector and it is rather the competition for the patronage of consumers that is the best protection people can have, especially as a society. This patronage of consumers must be free from government interference.

One way the government attempts to protect consumers is through the Consumer Product Safety Commission. The well-meaning people who work there attempt to test and regulate safety standards for as many products as possible. This is in spite of the reality that human error causes many more problems and injuries than actual product failure. In the same way one cannot prevent human error, one cannot always produce products that are completely safe. To attempt to do so only reduces choice and variety while enriching the companies that produce approved products.

Instead of arbitrary guidelines, which set **minimum standards**, people should realize that the **freedom to choose** among competing businesses is the best protection for consumers in the market. Minimum standards only serve to impede and misdirect competition and innovation; once standards are set, businesses no longer need to improve that aspect of the product. Generally the minimum standards are standards thath already were prevalent in the market. Freedom of choice acts in the opposite way by incentivizing businesses to compete and continually improve their products and price in order to win more customers. Because low quality, expensive and dangerous goods are unattractive to consumers, companies focus on improving their products to attract away the customers of their competition. The natural "greed" of manufacturers can only be satisfied by producing the best quality product at the best possible price.

The market solution is free but the government option is coerced and extremely expensive. The regulations government arbitrarily declares do not ensure quality and rather act as protections for the existing corporations. The role of government should be to keep the avenues for improvement clear for producers and manufacturers.

How government action destroys consumer choice and protects a handful of businesses is illustrated through the Interstate Commerce Commission (the ICC is no longer in existence) and the Food and Drug Administration (FDA). At one time the U.S. had the most extensive and cheapest rail road system in the world. The protection of the ICC resulted in higher prices, fewer rail companies and lower quality service. With changing technology, trucks began to pose a threat to the obsolete rail industry. The ability of the truckers to serve customers was stifled by the rail industry through the ICC.

The FDA's protection results in limited or no access to effective drugs that are located outside of the U.S. or developed within the country. The process of development and approval of new drugs in the country has become onerous to the point where few new drugs are approved. This is primarily because of the unwillingness of the FDA to take on risk. It is far less risky to approve a safe and ineffective drug than to approve a dangerous and effective one. The monopoly effect of the FDA is often not considered because the people who died because of the inability to access drugs can no longer speak. Furthermore, because the drug industry is focused on volume sales, drugs developed to treat serious diseases that only present in small numbers are rejected. Because many drugs were never approved it is believed that tens of thousands of people have died who could have been helped by unapproved drugs.

In both examples of the FDA and ICC the protection of the consumer was the stated goal; the result was quite the opposite. In the way people are considered not smart enough to make educational choices for their family, people are not smart enough to know what treatment to risk for their own health. People should be given freedom to access information regarding treatment options and be able to decide which treatment to receive. In the way that the government allows activities such as skiing and the drinking of alcohol, the government should stay out of the way and allow people to exercise their own choices. People must stop being deceived by politicians who say the consumer cannot protect him or herself. Consumers should reject the government monopoly control of drugs and reclaim the freedom to choose and be responsible for their own protection. This freedom to choose creates incentive for businesses to compete against each other to produce high quality, low cost and effective products in order to make money.

FROM VOLUME 8: WHO PROTECTS THE WORKER?

SUMMARY

There is fear throughout society that employers will seek to exploit workers by maintaining low wages and poor working conditions. This fear is followed by the belief that the labor union is the organization that will ensure protection and progress for workers against the agenda of greedy employers. To many unfamiliar with free market capitalism it is believed that the market favors the rich employers and places workers at a disadvantage. However, it is the **competition for labor** made possible through the free market which best protects the interests of all workers. In other words, when any organization can establish a **monopoly on labor**, either as the only provider of qualified labor or as the only employer of available labor, there is little protection for the worker in general.

Labor unions are concerned primarily with the interests of their union members. It appears that the interests of everyone else including other workers are secondary. The character of labor unions goes against the interest of the consumer and society as a whole. Unions function as monopolies on skills and labor much like the way guilds functioned many years ago. Certain jobs could only be performed by the correct and legal labor because they were the only people properly trained to do that work. Unions work hard to protect its members from having to compete against lower skilled and cheaper labor. This has the added effect of lowering the incentive for workers to work at peak productivity.

This activity is not only counterproductive but also prevents employers from exercising the freedom to choose who to hire or fire. The justification for disallowing the free choice of employers is usually public safety. In 1980 the controversial idea was the new field of paramedics. Doctors in hospitals opposed the activities of paramedics as unqualified and dangerous because they are not doctors. In other words, the paramedics were intruding on the territory reserved for the doctor's "union." Today it is hard to imagine life without paramedics and the care they provide.

Though often in the past labor disputes included violence, today, unions exert influence in government. The interests of the unions can be coerced and enforced through the regulations of government. One example given is the minimum wage law legislation. In congress people who testify in favor of higher minimum wages in 1980 were not poor people but the labor unions of the U.S. Minimum wage laws serve the interests of the unions by raising the cost of cheap and unskilled labor. In other words, many people will simply not get hired because of their lack of skill. Friedman pointed out that because African Americans are most affected by minimum wage laws, it is the most anti-black law in America; raising minimum wage may not be racist in intent but if judged by its result, it is.

Unions in government are among the most powerful in the country because politicians write the laws everyone else must follow. Not only are government sector jobs higher paid than their private counterparts, but it is extremely difficult to fire government workers. If this were not enough, one of the counties around Washington D.C. was in 1980 the wealthiest county in the country; it is inhabited mostly by government workers. Today there is even more wealth around Washington D.C. as even more power is located there.

Union wages come at the expense of other people in society, the benefits of government unions come at the expense of tax payers. In the free market, however, benefits and wages come at the expense of no one. Rising wages come to workers as a result of higher productivity; each worker can do more work with better quality through modernization and innovation. In other words, unions benefit only their members, while in a free market everyone benefits through the competition among businesses not only for customers but for workers. In order for businesses to compete against other businesses they must have the best labor possible. In order to attract the best labor possible, they will offer more for the labor that people are selling. This in turn incentivizes workers to be more productive and attractive for hire. As long as there are multiple businesses competing for workers,

workers are in general, protected against stagnant wages and poor working conditions.

Spartenburg South Carolina was used as an example of how the market is supposed to work. It was a town with limited opportunity, higher than average unemployment levels and lower than average wage levels. When regulations were bypassed and taxes drastically reduced, companies from all over the world came to build factories and plants in the town; this created competition for the workers who were in town. Workers who once could not find any work were in high demand. Wages increased and unemployment declined. Businesses had to compete with each other to attract skilled labor. If a company did not treat its labor well, workers were able to find another job quickly and easily in the same town. This situation flips the prevalent current situation where cities either lower taxes or use the taxes paid in part by the working poor to build facilities for billion dollar companies with government connections. Instead of businesses competing against each other to build in cities, cities compete against each other to build for businesses using tax payer money.

No one was exploited in the arrangement in Spartenburg as people were able work voluntarily where they wanted. Employers had to consider the happiness of their workers otherwise they would leave and work for other businesses. Because of the increase in productivity there was more wealth for more people. There was more to go around for the worker, employer, consumer, and tax payers. The combination of competition among employers and the freedom to choose where to work is the protection that is needed for workers. Government attempts to achieve the same result are costly, counterproductive, and prone to create monopolistic conditions.

FROM VOLUME 9: HOW TO CURE INFLATION

SUMMARY

Inflation is the depreciation of currency. It is when money loses its value and more money is required to purchase the same goods and services as prices rise. To put it another way, one reason prices may rise is because the value of the money used to purchase goods has declined. Though in some ways this is the most difficult volume to comprehend, it is actually the simplest. Because government has a monopoly on money, it can force people to continue to use a currency in spite of the mismanagement of monetary policy.

Inflation is perceived by people through rising prices. People generally do not like rising prices. Perhaps out of force of habit, people turn to the government for the cure of the inflation problem. Government in turn, blames various phenomena in order to propose legislation that only makes the problems worse. For example one result of high inflation is quickly rising prices and wages; the government response is often price controls or fixing prices so that they cannot change and go higher. Price controls on the cost of certain goods and services affect different people in different ways; some people benefit while other people suffer loss. Inflation and the response together increase ill feeling and animosity among people.

Inflation is a much more common phenomenon today because of fiat currency. Fiat currency is money that has value simply because the government says it has value. The quantity of money is controlled by the government or in the U.S. by the Federal Reserve Bank of America (FED). The FED is charged with the task of controlling the money supply through its printing presses (today much of the quantity of cash is produced electronically). Printing too much money results in inflation; in other words, the quantity of money is too high. Having too much of a commodity reduces the overall value of it; in the case of currency this is inflation. The simple solution is to reduce the printing or production of money. Though the solution is simple, politically it is very difficult to enact. This is because the recovery period to resolve the problems caused by inflation requires about five years; this means five years of a sluggish economy where many people will suffer.

Politicians in general, enjoy inflation in part because it is through the printing of excess currency that the government can pay for all of the programs it had promised to provide in exchange for votes. The unfortunate situation is that though consumers generally dislike inflation, reducing inflation goes against the interest of the government. Because of the government monopoly of money, inflation is a serious issue because political systems based on freedom live or die by economic freedom; political freedom in the U.S. is preserved by controlling inflation.

FROM VOLUME 10: HOW TO STAY FREE

SUMMARY

The greatest danger to freedom, according to Friedman, is the **concentration of power**; too much power in the hands of a few people. One might even frame this as a monopoly of power. Concentration of power means that a small group of people can dictate what and how everyone else must do, with whom and for how much. It is the way subjectivity is codified for everyone. Freedom is maintained in a society by having power **fragmented and diffused throughout society**. The freedom to choose to live in the way that one wants is very important for a free society.

At the height of the Great Depression in 1933, it was believed that capitalism had failed and that government should have more power; Friedman signified this moment in history as the birth of the modern welfare state. Ever since, power in Washington D.C. has grown while the freedom of the people has declined. As power increased in Washington D.C. it attracted people who wished to trade on that power and those who sought to influence that power. These people would be the lobbyists and special interest groups seeking advantages and privileges for their cause and subjectivity. The more they are successful in their endeavors for special privileges, the more people gravitate to Washington. The more privileges are bestowed to special interest groups, the more that is taken from the general interest.

It is easy to simply demonize the entrenched bureaucracy as the main problem; they are, after all, the most powerful special interest group in the country. However, Friedman maintained that it is the responsibility of the people, the general interest, for giving government the power that is now so frequently abused. People must become aware that concentrated power destroys freedom. People must learn that the influence of private wealth pales in comparison to the power of government. Government has grown far larger since 1980.

Friedman pointed out that though there is a staggering amount of power in Washington in 1980, it was fragmented. Opposing goals of competing special interest groups generally may cancel each other out at the end of the day. But this is the other problem of big government; all of the conflicting government activity was paid for by the general interest. This means that there is a tremendous amount of waste for the activities that result in the reduction of individual freedom. For example, some groups lobby to try to curb smoking tobacco products while other groups lobby to try to increase production of tobacco. This activity is not good for the general interest of society as both groups are engaged in increasing the amount of regulation in our lives. The practical problem of increased regulation is the criminalization of otherwise peaceful, law abiding citizens.

All of the political and regulatory activity diverts talent and resources away from productive endeavors towards subjective endeavors through the special interest groups in Washington D.C. The good intentions of those who seek to influence and possess this power are not enough to offset the great amount of harm imposed by the restriction of freedom. The fanatical and legislated restriction of freedom results in resentment of law, evasion of law, and finally declining respect for law by individuals living in society.

The free market preserves freedom for everyone. With this freedom society as a whole benefits from the self-interested free choices of individuals. Preservation and respect for freedom not only for oneself but for everyone in society would unleash human creativity and productivity in a way that would benefit the poor the most. The type of society that would exist would be very much like the kind of society many people desire. This type of society would be tolerant, free, and prosperous.

PAPER OPTION #1
RACE AND POVERTY:
VOTING WITH YOUR FEET

WHAT: Do a geographical family history; that is, trace the movement of a *single line* of your family over time.

WHY: This assignment will help you to understand that not only are we a country of mostly immigrants, but voluntarily moving is critical for the well-being of people in general; that is, the ability to move freely, to vote with one's feet helps people rise out of and/or stay out of poverty.

THE ASSIGNMENT: Talk to your family and trace a single line of your family's movements as far back as you can while remaining within the page limitation of this assignment (4).

- "Single line" means: choose *one* of your parents only; then choose *one* of that person's parents; and then *one* of that person's parents, and so on.
  - » Example: First you choose your father, then your father's father (your grandfather), and then your grandfather's mother, etc.
  - » Doing multiple lines is a good lifelong activity but should not be done for this project.
- *Focus* on where they lived and why they moved to another place. Try to get the name and address of the area that they lived, when they lived there, and why they moved.
  - » You may present this information as a list or as a narrated story.
- Including personal details or "family drama" is NOT necessary; listing a simple reason for moving is enough.

- Then answer the questions below and make some observations about moving in general. For example, explain how it has affected your family, positively or negatively.

ALTERNATE ASSIGNMENT: There are some legitimate reasons for preferring not to do this assignment. Students who are adopted, whose grandparents are/were part of a political group like the IRA (Irish Republican Army), or who have no living relatives may want to do an alternative assignment. If so, complete the alternate assignment listed on the sheet entitled "Alternate Final Project." If you are daring you may try the third option, "Innovate not regulate," which tests to see if you can see the box and think outside of it.

THE CONTEXT: This class has deconstructed race and poverty; thus, the stereotypical understanding of the relationship between these two constructs should have, by now, been challenged, if not obliterated. As you begin your journey with Milton Friedman, you will know that people *vote with their feet* when there is no other way to vote. Everyone's family has, at one time or another moved; try to track that movement through oral interview(s).

PROCESS: Interview your family and choose a single person, as stated above. They may not remember everything, and what they remember might be fuzzy. Do your best; this is just an introductory assignment for what I hope you do in your spare time for the rest of your lives. Sometimes students want to choose the line that has the most number of moves; some choose the line with the fewest. Sometimes families have not moved in 300 years; some families move every year. No matter the situation, *why they moved or why they did not* move is what is key and always so very interesting.

ANALYSIS: Note that I need you to simply show me that you have thought about these questions and have considered how they relate to your personal history. Some questions may not actually apply to your particular situation, but it is good to consider that these issues may apply to the situation of others.

- What is the generalized reason for your family's migrations or lack of migration?

- How important do you think it is to be able to migrate when you think you need to?
  - » Looking at the reasons for moving (or not moving), what does this say about the likelihood of moving for any family?
  - » How important do you think it is to keep everything the same?
- What might have happened if the ability to move was prevented or delayed indefinitely by law or otherwise?
- **Identity questions:** How might this have shaped how you understand yourself? In other words:
  - » How "native" are you? That is, how "American" do you feel?
  - » How might this explain how (un)patriotic your family is; in other words how "traditional" is your family to the "old world" of the family?
    - » e.g., Many German immigrants tried to hide the fact they were from Germany by changing the spelling of their last name, {Moller to Miller} or ceased speaking and teaching German to their children, etc.
  - » Remember that intense racialization or conflict in society may cause people to preserve old family values more than they would in a welcoming environment or community.

GUIDELINES:

- **Do not exceed 4 pages.** Pages should be double spaced and typed.
- Due as indicated in the syllabus.

PAPER OPTION #2
RACIALIZE YOURSELF

It is strongly encouraged that you do the Family Genealogy final project when you have a chance sometime in your life. However, for whatever reason you are doing the alternate project, the goal will essentially be the same: write your own racialization.

WHAT: Racialize yourself: For this paper, you must racialize yourself as you see yourself, how you think others see you and as you would like others to racialize you.

WHY: An important aspect of making race is identity construction. When we otherize people we are essentially comparing ourselves with those others and finding difference. The details or characteristics we signify in others are those details which are important to us. How and why we make adjustments in our own conscious efforts to shape or reshape our identity is very subjective. The sum total of *all* of your racializations is your *identity*. This identity will constantly change throughout your life as your interests change, as your knowledge changes, and as your understanding and view of the world changes.

HOW: Try to make racializations on your own first, and then ask people around you to describe you. Be prepared, if they are honest, you might be surprised by what they say.

DETAILS:

- Think of all the categories into which you think you can be put and list them; you may stop if you get to 100.

» Because of space you need not put the list in columns but simply use commas; e.g. smart, energetic, geek, sports fan, brother, son, gamer, procrastinator, etc.

» The categories should include those you like and dislike; those you accept and reject; racializations from your past and present.

- List the categories you would like others to see when they see you. In other words, what is the impression or image you want to convey to others?

  » Once you have your list, explain why you might want people to racialize you in this way.

- Some questions to answer to conclude your paper:

  » How much of what you want to project or have others see is the result of what you think people see when they look at you? E.g. because people see you as clueless, you want to be seen as not-clueless.

  » How much of your self-racialization is based on things you have seen on TV or in others?

  » Do you think there is an "original" racialization in your identity? That is, do you have a racialization that is *not* based on something you have seen elsewhere?

- Length: 4 pages.
- Due: See syllabus.

PAPER OPTION #3
INNOVATE NOT REGULATE

Early in the class I challenged people to try to see the "box" and in that way try to think outside of it. Now is your chance to test whether you can see the box and think outside of it. The premise of this assignment (and it will not be an option for many of you) is that one type of box is created and maintained through legislation. Legislation will destroy creative innovation for many, but for some, it is the inspiration to invent and develop. Thinking out of the box means breaking free from government coercion and socialization through innovation and the exploitation of loopholes.

WHAT: Improvement of goods and services is inevitable wherever there is freedom; there are two ways this can be achieved in the current social situation: it is either through innovation or the exploitation of loopholes.

- Innovation: You must describe how to improve or revolutionize a job, product, method, or service by suggesting an alternative process to accomplish the same task. The alternative you suggest or propose must result in cheaper goods or services that maintain high quality without the legislation of morality and government subsidy. Adaptation of existing technology for alternative applications is an example.
- Exploitation of loopholes: It is assumed that any regulation necessarily creates loopholes; the trick is to find them. By finding and exploiting loopholes, one may undermine the status quo and keep people free. For example, FedEx's and UPS's exploitation of terminology enabled them to get around the monopoly of the United States Postal Service.

WHY: This class suggests that issues of poverty can be better addressed by making products and services more affordable in society through voluntary cooperation with competition. Making products more affordable is usually the result of higher productivity; fewer people are required to do the same job while maintaining or improving quality. By making products and services cheaper, people will have more resources to develop other yet-to-be-realized areas of life, resulting in a variety of new jobs for people to work. In Friedman's Volume 2, it was seen that increased productivity results in wealth throughout society, but the poor and disempowered benefit most.

HOW: Propose an alternative use of existing technology OR discuss how some people are already adapting new technology to revolutionize a product or industry. Another way is by proposing or discussing ways to get around regressive regulatory restrictions. Exploitation of loopholes demands creativity and intimate knowledge of the field. Some students, who are already involved in their future field and are familiar with how things work, can identify sources of inefficiency or may be inspired to use technology developed in another field to promote productivity.

DETAILS: Though many people are uncomfortable with continuous innovation and development, the poor benefit most when the costs of goods and services are reduced while society develops more jobs to keep pace with the increased productivity. Politically connected, old, and established companies tend to get bloated and inefficient, which slows down innovation. Change works against the interests of large corporations, which is why many powerful companies often favor more regulations while pretending to be opposed to them. Keeping the fires of innovation and competition burning will create opportunity that will benefit the poor without increased regulation.

- Clearly state the innovation or loophole.
  - » Explain what the innovation resolves or addresses (like less land usage, less water usage, etc.), which should result in lower costs for everyone.
  - » In the case of the loophole, explain what regulation seems to be holding everything back in the interest of existing industries and their business models.

- Explain how this will benefit the general interest in cost or quality or by undermining the status quo.
- Remember this must be achieved without subsidies or more regulations.

NOTE: This is fundamentally a subversive THOUGHT EXERCISE; just think about it. Acting on these ideas is always a high-risk choice. However, this is how one becomes a productive rebel; a rebel with a cause, if you will. The instructor is NOT liable for any potential legal issues that may arise if students try to actualize the theories generated by this assignment.

YOU MUST HAVE YOUR TOPIC APPROVED BY ME. A simple email will suffice. This is to ensure you are on the right track. Some topics are harder than others, and some topics do not apply to this assignment. This is an advanced-level assignment.

IN ORDER TO COMPLETE THIS AS ASSIGNED, YOU MUST:

- Assume regulations in general are regressive
- Assume regulations will usually create loopholes
- Assume innovation renders regulations irrelevant
- Assume that it's ok for everyone to have an opportunity to be wealthy
- Present your ideas within four (4) pages
- Turn this in when it's due, as indicated on the syllabus

SOME EXAMPLES:

- Crypto currency to get around the government monopoly on money
- Hemp as replacement for many currently used products
- The artificial leaf (mentioned earlier)
- Bladeless turbines (windmills) for bird safety
- Generate electricity and safe drinking water by cleaning contaminated water (as a 17-year-old Australian student suggested in 2015); or generate electricity by processing CO_2, as discussed earlier in the text
- Figure out a way to use a hated material AND save whales at the same time (John D. Rockefeller and skunk oil)

- Lab-grown beef and milk to end the need for millions of acres of grazing land
- 3D printing for everything from cars to human organs
- New medical treatments: disease treatment at the DNA level; designer drugs to avoid many risk factors
- The internet for alternative and/or home school; e.g., Kahn Academy
- Uber and Lyft to get around the taxi cartels
- Research the difference between dumb systems and smart systems

WHITE PRIVILEGE 12

GOAL
For students to understand white privilege
and how the free market deals with privilege

I T IS SAID THAT **WHITE PRIVILEGE** is the construct that points out the fact that white people have unearned advantages over others simply by having white skin. Being white in the U.S. gives white people perks and advantages that make life easier to live than if one were a person of color. Some examples of white privilege would be that one can go shopping without being harassed by store security; one can see positive images of whites on TV, news outlets, and textbooks; and one does not have to educate one's children about racism for their own physical protection. The existence of privilege means that society is unfairly biased so that some people will tend to be rich and others will tend to be poor.

The existence of white privilege is a cause for concern because of the effect on the construct of **meritocracy**. Meritocracy is the idea that success in a society is based on the principle that people are rewarded based on ability, talent, and how hard one works, rather than class, wealth, or in this case, skin color. If one works hard, then one should be able to receive compensation for that work equal to what others who do the same work at the same level of intensity receive. White privilege undermines the idea of meritocracy because some people do not have to work as hard to get more than others. Privilege is often unrecognized by those who have and enjoy that privilege because it benefits them to believe that what they have is earned and not unearned.

Privilege also means power over others. Being white means that it is easier to rise to the upper levels of social structure; this includes the power to "govern" or be in charge of others. Having the power to rule does not mean that one will do what is best for society as a whole; having power does not mean that one automatically has the moral code to use that power justly. This means that people without privilege will be at a severe disadvantage in life. The selection below is a conversation about whiteness which took place on NPR (National Public Radio) and includes Peggy McIntosh and David Roediger.

MEMBERSHIP HAS ITS PRIVILEGES

by Michael Eric Dyson

In July 1998, I participated in a wonderful conversation about the field of whiteness studies on NPR's *Talk of the Nation,* hosted by distinguished journalist Ray Suarez, now a correspondent with *The NewsHour with Jim Lehrer.* My partners in dialogue that day included David Roediger, a gifted intellectual who has helped to establish the scholarly legitimacy of the field, and Peggy McIntosh, a pioneering thinker in exploring the often unconscious privileges of whiteness. Since our discussion, many colleges and universities have explored the varied and conflicted meanings of whiteness in courses, conferences, and curricula.

Ray Suarez: Whiteness is a funny thing in the lives of white people, certainly in this country. People have gotten into a habit in the twentieth century of making being white the normal state of affairs, the condition of a regular person. Race, then, is used as a marker to describe people who are set apart from that normality. We use race as a label of non-whiteness. But whiteness itself? It's transparent. White life in America is just life in America. White history is history. Even for those who complain about race designation as social constructs, that is, something we impose as an organizing tool on society in the absence of any real biological difference, whiteness is transparent. People hostile to racial designations see those labels as something that white people lay on blacks and others, and white people are left out of the equation, sort of by elimination. Is there a construction of identity around whiteness that is not the kind found at white Aryan resistance meetings?

Is there a history of whiteness in America, the ideas around it, its uses, its definition that is a worthwhile field for academic study?

The scholars who are taking those first pioneering steps into this lightly charted territory answer: yes, you bet. But what is there to study? What is there to write about that doesn't end up treading well-worn territory? What is there to say that isn't a prisoner of the repetitious and sometimes kind of boring arguments we've gotten so good at having in America? Peggy McIntosh, is whiteness studies a fully fleshed-out area of academic inquiry yet?

Peggy McIntosh: Not yet fully fleshed out, but well worth working on. It's the complement to the development of black studies and ethnic studies in the last couple of decades.

Suarez: Do you have a sort of definition-of-terms problem up at the top, where you have to tell people what it is and what it ain't?

McIntosh: Well for me, it was best to start autobiographically, in realizing that though I had been taught I didn't have race, other people did, I came to realize that having skin of the color I have opened many doors for me and gave me conditions of existence which I had been taught never to see. These conditions of unearned advantage that I saw that I had were transparent to me, and to the people of my race, place, and class that I grew up with.

Suarez: Does it undermine the attempt to build this as an academic field, that so much of what we say about race either starts with autobiography or personal narrative?

McIntosh: Well, of course, by the academic standards I was taught in three degrees from Harvard, for example, yes, any personal testimony undercuts the objectivity of scholarship. I now believe that, for me anyway, it was best to start testimonially. And in fact, the power of my analysis rests in the fact I don't claim it applies to all white people. I claimed only to mine my own experience, for what turned out to be a list of forty-six ways in which I daily experience, and know that I experience, unearned advantage based on my skin color, relative to just one tiny sample, which is, African American women in my building in my line of work.

Suarez: Well Michael Eric Dyson, you're right now a professor of African American studies, do you go along with Peggy McIntosh's assertion that white studies is implied by the existence of black studies?

Michael Eric Dyson: No question. I think that the development of white studies is itself in response to—similar to whiteness—the existence of blackness, of black studies, of African American studies throughout the Diaspora. So that in one sense, blackness and whiteness are called into existence mutually by one another, not always in equal fashion or form, and not, certainly, on an equal playing field. But nonetheless, they exist in a symbiotic relationship to one another. So when we think about whiteness studies in the academy, as Professor McIntosh has indicated, not only does it have to do with one's own autobiography—"Who I am as a white person and thinking about the psychology that structures my consciousness; unearned advantage; the ways in which those advantages work for me that don't work for other people"—but also about coming into an awareness of how, in relationship to African Americans or Native Americans or Latinos and so on, that whiteness is reinforced in very powerful ways. It stigmatizes the things that fall outside of its circumference.

So what we have to do is to begin to break down the transparency and the invisibility of whiteness—the way in which it is silenced—and name it for what it is, to allow it to speak in its very powerful vocabularies. Because as Professor McIntosh has indicated, whiteness is a very huge, multivariegated thing. It's a very differentiated thing; it has a lot of different components. We talk about so-called white trash on the one hand; we talk about elite whites on the other hand; we talk about the white working class, about which Professor David Roediger has written brilliantly. So, I think when we think about whiteness studies vis-à-vis African-American studies or other so-called ethnic or area studies, it is good, because it forces white Americans, and those of us who write about race and ethnicity in this country, to understand that not only do whites possess a race, but the invisibility of thinking about that race has really led us down some very treacherous paths that we need to really make up for.

Suarez: But, it's easy to see, I think, where the lines of inquiry are, if you're writing about oh, black freedmen in Charleston or Norfolk in the nineteenth century. It's easy to see what it is you're talking about because you're talking about the survival of a minority within the bounds created by a majority. But if you go to do studies at a county in Indiana where 97 percent of the population is white, what you're writing about is the state of circumstances of life. Where does whiteness come into it?

Dyson: Well, that's a very good question. And I think that even taking that example of Indiana—for instance, Indiana is not unfamiliar with, say, the rise of the Ku Klux Klan. So when we think about Indiana, that specific example, we think about one of the birthplaces of a very virulent strain of whiteness that has existed, and to a certain degree, has been allowed to survive, precisely because it has remained untheorized. That is, people don't ask questions about how whiteness exists, what it exists against. Implicit in your question is the presumption that because it's normal, or because it becomes normalized, it doesn't have anything against which it pitches itself—that is, the background against which we understand whiteness. Whiteness looks like the universal, therefore it never gets talked about in any particular fashion.

So I think in that example alone, the difficulty—but also the reward of thinking about and interrogating whiteness—is that you begin to say, "Hey, how did something that's very specific and particular, growing up in Indiana as a white person where 90 percent, or 95 percent, of the population is white" [which] only begs the question, how can we get beneath the surface, as it were, to find out what makes us white? Why do we think about ourselves as not having a race? Why, when we think about race, do we think about those folk across the river, say a few miles down the road in Chicago or over in St. Louis?

Why don't we think about ourselves as possessing a race? And what difference does that make? And how has that made it painful for other people to exist? And also, how has it really deprived us of some intellectual resources to think about our own lives? So, I think in that sense, even though it is more invisible, it well repays the effort of thinking about it, because white people then, and people who think about whiteness, have to come to grips with the complexity, and the variety of whiteness, and that's often masked by assuming that all white folk are the same.

Suarez: Well David Roediger, a lot of the twentieth century has been spent by left-of-center academics trying to explode the use of race, and using class analysis and the styles of economic relationships between groups, between people, between professional groups, between people who live in different countries. Using that way of unlocking; unbundling what it is that human beings bring to life. What's tough about bringing race into the equation, especially with whites?

David Roediger: Well, my work actually grows out, very much, of that tradition, and my interest is in whites for whom whiteness doesn't pay off. And I think it's kind of easy to understand why, for example, a plantation owner would identify with white supremacy. My interest is in trying to figure out why white working people—whose wages, whose benefits, whose privilege don't really measure to a lot—also identify with whiteness. I'm a labor historian. It's really out of those kinds of class questions that I felt the need to bring in white racial identity, and to begin to ask the question: why do people call themselves white workers, and within that, why do they accent the white more often than they accent the workers?

Suarez: And is this kind of inquiry going on basically in the research, in the publication, or does it exist as a practical matter, in the course catalog, for university students? If I want to take white studies at your own University of Minnesota, what would I sign up for? What would greet me on the first day of class?

Roediger: Well, I don't think there are any such courses at Minnesota. I know that I teach classes on race in the United States, and race and class in the United States. And although I identify with what Peggy said at the start, sometimes I think that the way to study whiteness is in a constellation of racial relationships, and I'd be a little bit hesitant to teach a course that's just on whiteness studies, and I certainly wouldn't envision departments, programs, et cetera, of white studies. In that sense, I think it's not symmetrical to black studies.

Suarez: Peggy McIntosh, do you agree?

McIntosh: Well, picking up on what David said, a very good course on whiteness studies taught by Arlene Avakian at University of Massachusetts in Amherst differentiates between many kinds of white people's experience. And I think it, therefore, does both recognize and avoid that pitfall David is talking about—the pitfall of assuming that white skin privilege works equally for all whites in all circumstances. However, to go back to both the Indiana question and the working-class whites question, here, I'm gonna read three things from my list which, indeed, I would say working-class people do benefit [from], and white Indianans do benefit [from], in ways they may not know about.

I wrote in one of my forty-six points: "I can turn on the TV or open to the front page of the paper and see people of my race widely and positively represented." I should add, that's in cases where the front page has anything positive on it at all. Next: "When I'm told about our national heritage or about so-called civilization, I'm shown that people of my skin color made it what it is, or gave it its best qualities." And a third: "I can be sure that our children will be given curricular materials that testify to the existence of our race, in every single course at every single grade level and every single subject area." Now, whether or not you're a laborer or a white Indianan, those things are working for you to put some sort of floor under your sense of identity.

Suarez: And if you're living in Indianapolis and heading for the phone, I mean, I just picked Indiana out of the basket folks. [*Laughter*] There's no prep that went into singling out Indiana. Petaluma, California, is our first stop this hour. Hi ya, Rick.

Caller: Hi, I'm really excited to be on the air here today. And I wonder, with each of your panelists, if there is any consistency in how many races each believes there are. And I wonder if they could each go around and comment on that, and delineate them for us?

Suarez: Notice how they're all jumping in here, Rick. [*Laughter*] It's not a question for which there is an easy answer, I'm sure.

Caller: I think that astrologers might actually have more coherence in their comments about their schemes of categorizing people, than people who think long and hard about race.

Suarez: But Rick, isn't self-identification almost as important as sort of hard-and-fast rules that we might set up about racial categorization?

Caller: I think that internal definitions really *are* important and that's how we *should* judge people and think about people, in their own terms, and not apply our classifications upon them, but I—

Dyson: Well—

Caller: —would like to do this experiment and have them each say how many and what they are.

Suarez: Michael Eric Dyson.

Dyson: Yeah, I think, in response to that—and I won't dodge the bullet, I'll answer finally. I was just having lunch with my wife at a restaurant here in New York, and I was among the only black patrons with my wife in the restaurant, and noticed that I was getting short shrift in regard to the waitress. And the burden of race, it seems to me, is that one is forever fixed by external categories that people impose *on* you. So that I have to think: "Is she treating me this way because A) I'm black or B) she doesn't like the Chicago Bulls shirt I have on, because she voted for the New York Knicks, or is it that she's having a terrible day? But she's speaking so kindly and so fluidly to the other white patrons." So that the atmosphere that is poisoned by the presumption I have about who she is, and perhaps about who she thinks I am, is something that's beyond my control.

So, when I think about race, and I think about racial identity, it's not something that people control, or they can merely categorize. I can answer by saying I think that there are as many races as people need there to be. You know, if we talk about Tiger Woods, who as a youth called himself Cablinasian, trying to fix on the map of identity the coordinates that constituted who he was. Well, all of us have that problem in the final analysis, but I'll tell you what: I can go out here in New York and tell the person that I want to pick me up in a cab, "Hey, listen, race is a metaphor; it doesn't exist; it's a social convention. We're all just part of the *human* race, and so let's not categorize each other." But you know what? That cab driver constantly refuses to stop for me at certain times in New York. So, it's not about a simplistic way of me saying, "Hey, I want to get beyond race and racial categories." The real question is how does race function, in a very serious way, to deny me social benefit, to make me uncomfortable, to reinforce my disadvantage, and to remind me of my place in the hierarchy of American priorities. So, to me—

Suarez: But, I think Rick was also trying to get at the arbitrariness of it all, which is, I think, an important thing to remember too.

Dyson: There's no doubt that it's exactly arbitrary, except it's arbitrary in consistent patterns, right? That sounds like a contradiction. It's arbitrary all right, because it can show up at any point. It can blow up in your face at any point. It can name you or deny you at any point. But there's a consistency. The cab metaphor I used, for instance: there are a lot of black men, and black people in New York, who can't get a cab. And so it's arbitrary on the one hand because

I never know when it's gonna happen and when it's not gonna happen. But there are some consistent patterns of treatment, and that's just one of them. And I'm sure David and Peggy would have many more to add to that, but I'm indicating that the arbitrariness of race has to do with the inability to name and predict when it's gonna show up in our faces and hurt us and harm us, or give us advantage. But what's not arbitrary is the kind of hierarchy where race is assigned a certain privilege—whiteness and blackness exist, Latino identity and Native American identity exist, in very specific ways, that I think are not quite as arbitrary as we'd like to make them to be.

Suarez: Peggy McIntosh.

McIntosh: Both biologists and anthropologists agree that there is very little basis for clear distinctions between races, but what Michael Eric Dyson says is absolutely true in my experience, that race functions as social categorization, politically constructed categorization. And I have stood on the curb in New York City in order to hail a cab for an African American man who could not get one to stop for him. So, we have different kinds of melanin, and they do play out in what gets projected on to us in the way [we are considered] trustworthy citizens, or rich citizens, or people able to pay a cab fare, or safe citizens. And that's the part of this whole matter that makes me not want to simply abolish a term like race. And it's a little bit like male and female in that there are tremendously verifiable differences between male and female. On the other hand, there's lots that men and women share in common. Yes, because of projections on to us, we were raised to think of ourselves, at least in my subculture, as opposite sexes. So we were made to seem more different than we actually are. If you do cognitive studies on men and women, our thought processes are much more similar than they are different. We are not opposite in the ways we think. But, the language has the social and political force of making us seem very different, and therefore justifying quite different treatment of the two sexes.

Suarez: David Roediger.

Roediger: I think it's clear that there's one human race biologically. Beyond that, though, we speak of the social construction of races, and Michael and Peggy both emphasized that this has consequences. And one of the things that I like to tell my students is that, when we talk about socially constructed races, the buildings that we work in, live in, are also social constructions. They're the product of groups of people getting together and making them over time. Now realizing that, we can't jump through the walls of the buildings. We can't ignore the realities of those constructions. I spent a great deal of time in South Africa in 1990 during the liberation period, and one of the favorite sayings of freedom fighters in South Africa was, "The way to nonracialism"—which was the goal of the freedom movement—"is through race." And I think that that's still a reality here in the United States—that we need to think about racial privilege if we're going to get to this ideal of nonracialism.

Suarez: South Bend, Indiana, is next. Hi ya, Lisa.

Caller: Thank you for taking my call. I'd like to make a point about the idea of whiteness as property, or whiteness as a social wage, and what that can add to President [Bill Clinton's] "dialogue on race." The idea of whiteness as a social wage comes from W. E. B. Dubois, and what he meant was that whiteness is a form of symbolic compensation for those of us who don't control Wall Street or Washington that are white. And the idea is that even if we're not in charge, at least we've got something to keep us off the bottom, which is that black folks are down there looking up at us. I think that the conservative whites showed us that people can be mobilized politically by their property in whiteness, and that the message of the right has been: pay attention, you're losing that property in whiteness.

My point is that I don't think the president's dialogue on race is going to get very far if it continues to be a conversation about how to achieve equality for black people and brown people, because where white people are invested in whiteness as property, equality is very difficult to achieve. And politically, what we need to recognize is that white privilege is something that we need to resist and transform politically, by dismantling the laws that support it. So, for example, we could start by changing the practice of funding schools through property taxes, 'cause that just encourages white flight to the suburbs where you can tax yourself to pay for good public schools and leave the urban schools to crumble. I'd like to ask the panel, as scholars who study whiteness, what would they recommend to the president to dismantle the privileges of whiteness that you've been talking about?

McIntosh: That's a great question. I'll answer briefly and give it to the other two. But I think until those dialogues themselves address the fact that white unearned advantage does exist, then they can't get anywhere at all on all of this.

Suarez: But, I'm sure you realize that that is a very, very hard nut. I mean, a lot of people just will not stand for that argument. Their first—

McIntosh: No, I think it's—

Suarez: —answer is, "What are you talking about white skin privilege?"

McIntosh: Well, I know. I was taught to see racism only in individual acts of meanness, and not in invisible systems that confer dominance on my group. Therefore it's a matter, I think, of conceptualizing differently the consequences of having lighter skin for people. You say they will be resistant, but I say, Ray, that this idea isn't yet even in the public world. It's in the universities, without question.

Dyson: I think that whiteness functions—and that was a great question from Indiana—in a variety of ways. It functions as an identity; it functions as an institutional expression of supremacy, or deference to that supremacy; and it functions as an ideology of superiority in a culture where, as David Roediger has indicated, and Peggy McIntosh [as well], this constellation of relations makes sure that brown and black are rendered inferior to white and so on. Ray, you're absolutely right, it's very difficult to ask the president himself to unmask some of the ways in which whiteness has been deployed by his own administration to protect him. And I'll give you a couple of quick examples and be quiet. First of all, when he was running for president the first time, he played the race card, if we can use that metaphor, in a very violent, and I think vicious, way that appealed to whiteness. That is, when he indicated that he would be running for suburban issues and not the cities, that was a real play toward whiteness, and I think that that's crucial. And then also with the Sister Souljah incident, where he refused to acknowledge that he was playing the race card.

Suarez: Today, we're talking about the emerging academic field often called whiteness studies. Joining us now is Anna Meigs. Welcome to the program.

Anna Meigs: I'm happy to be here.

Suarez: So, what do you study about, and what do your students write about?

Meigs: Well, this is a course, basically, in what I like to consider a "racial literacy," where the students learn to see race and to talk race. And given that the vast majority of the students in my classes are white, we spend a considerable amount of time in the class on these issues that your panelists have been discussing—you know, whiteness and race privilege—that people of color in the class, and whites, can see whiteness, name it, talk about it. And talk about it not just in general and in theoretical terms, but in terms of their own life. What happened today, what they saw today on the TV, or heard on the radio, or talked about at lunch.

Suarez: A lot of the places this conversation has been going so far, frankly, concentrate on the negative content of that vessel we'll call whiteness for the purposes of this conversation. Is there a disinterested critique in the functioning of whiteness, or does it inevitably get to the bad things white people do or have done, or the malign systems that they've put up for other people to negotiate? I mean, does this all end up, somehow, being an attack on the actions of white people through history?

Meigs: From my perspective, whiteness is about domination, and that's inescapable. It is about nothing else but that. But the good news is that in facing that, and dealing with that as a white person, you can come to stand in a place which is more positive, more helpful, more productive. I can't think of good things to say about whiteness. So I suppose from that perspective, there is a downer aspect to it, yes.

Suarez: And can you give me an example of some of the term projects or papers that some of your students have written? The kind of places they've been going to look for fresh questions to ask?

Meigs: The project that they do that I think they like the best is a thing called "race discourse analyses," where about ten times in the semester, they're required to turn in a paragraph or two which describes a racial incident. Well, the assumption of the course is that all incidents in the United States are racial, and that what they're looking for is to try to unpack, discover, what is racial about the interaction they had at lunch; the course that they are taking which isn't apparently about race; what someone said. The ideas we have about race are ideas that our culture gave us. We didn't generate them ourselves. We don't have the burden of that particular responsibility, but we do have the burden of carrying the ideas that the culture has given us. And now we try to discover where we are using them and where other people are using them. And let's look at them; let's look at what's going on here racially. So that's the literacy aspect that I'm looking to teach them so they can decode the events of their environment, the things they see on TV, from a racial perspective. And of course, whiteness is an important part of that. If they're only thinking it's racial if they see a person of color, well, they're missing an awful lot.

Suarez: And are these heavily signed up, these courses?

Meigs: Yeah, this course of mine is—well, I haven't been teaching it for very long, but it was one of the first to close. It enrolled very rapidly this past semester. And students are very enthusiastic about it. White students are eager to understand what it means to be white so that they can take responsibility for it. That's something that students here, at least at Macalester, are seeking—not all of them, but certainly the students in my course and beyond as well.

Suarez: Professor Meigs, thanks for being with us this hour.

Meigs: You're welcome.

Suarez: Did anything that Anna Meigs just say give anybody pause?

McIntosh: I think white privilege has positive aspects which are conditions of life that I would want to have available to everybody. So, though I respect her work and I'm delighted to hear that the students do too, with regard to the list I wrote, this kind of thing I'd like to be true for everybody, not just for whites. It's not negative; it's positive. "The day I move into new housing that I have chosen, I can be pretty sure that my new neighbors will be either neutral to me or pleasant to me." Or, "I can go shopping in the department stores of my area without being tailed by the store detective on grounds that I might be shoplifting or soliciting men." Or, "Whether I use checks or credit cards or cash, I can count on my skin color not working against the appearance that I'm financially reliable." Now these are things that make my life easy and I would like such ease to be there for all people. So to answer Anna Meigs on the fact that she can't find much positive to say about whiteness, I just want to say that the freedom from anger that these privileges allow me is a freedom I would want for everybody.

Suarez: But denying any positive value to the content of an entire culture, for want of a better term, I think starts from a proposition that we do not extend to any other field of ethnic studies.

McIntosh: Yeah, well that's interesting and I am sure the other two panelists have something to say about this. I've been trying to study what it is that the habit of being a colonial ruler developed in people of my skin color that is, in the lineup of human attributes, useful. I mean, I think among other things that this business of organizing everybody, though it was too concentrated in just a few—but that's a highly useful habit. Or categorizing; or making encyclopedias. They may have stemmed from an urge to get control of *everything*, on behalf of *everybody*. On the other hand, they did develop skills in some of white male culture, or colonial culture, that, I think, are part of the array of what the human brain is capable of. So, I wouldn't want to write it off.

Dyson: I'm torn in this regard because I think that I'm highly sympathetic to, and deeply, deeply committed to, the project of understanding whiteness, and how whiteness functions—and have learned, especially from David Roediger and from Peggy McIntosh, in the abolition of whiteness movement, about really abolishing those very fundamentally scurrilous expressions of whiteness that have undermined the very civility that all of us want to enjoy. And that Peggy McIntosh has written about and talked about here, and certainly David Roediger. But I'm suspicious also—or skeptical may be the more correct term—about labeling whiteness itself as impervious to any redemptive or uplifting or edifying term. Now, if we understand whiteness to be the same as dysfunction or colonizing, or if we understand it as undermining and subverting, then of course whiteness has got to go. But if we understand whiteness as a much more complex phenomenon, that is both good and bad, if you will, both edifying and degrading, then we've got to figure out ways in which whiteness has functioned in our culture.

I'm reminded of Martin Luther King, Jr., who argued with those foes of his within African American communities about whiteness—and these were some of the most brilliant interpreters, if you will, of whiteness—when he said, "Listen, whiteness is not just one thing; it's a whole bunch of things at the same time." And the simultaneity of whiteness means that we've got to learn to differentiate it. We have to have a kind of grassroots ethnography where we begin to interrogate the forms and function of whiteness on the ground as it were—and where it has cohabited with blackness, with Latinoness, with redness, with yellowness. Where it's been made, and remade, in conjunction with, and in cooperation with, blackness. I mean, there are tremendous degrees of complexity within whiteness. At the same time I am skeptical, [I am also] embracing of the abolition of whiteness movement because I think that it's a very powerful movement to at least force white Americans, and the rest of us, to see that whiteness is not given. It's not natural. It's not something that we have to be stuck with our entire lives. But we've got to figure out ways in which we can allow white people to exist, while destroying the very meanings that they have created around whiteness itself. So, I'm quite frankly torn about that.

Roediger: I think that clearly there are anti-racists who are white—I'm involved in part of an effort to re-celebrate John Brown Day for example—and I think that that kind of highlighting of variety of white perspectives is useful. But I wonder if there is a white culture outside of domination. On that point I agree with Anna. And Peggy moves the discussion to: what do colonial officials do? And that's still around the issue of domination. I once asked a class at the University of Missouri what they'd put in a white cultural center—there was a debate about a black cultural center. Some conservative white kids said, "We need a white cultural center if we have a black cultural center." And I said, "Well, what then would go in a white cultural center?" And there was the longest silence that I have ever experienced in a classroom after that. And the silence was broken by a hand going up, and a shout: "Elvis!" And then laughter, that Elvis would somehow be considered unambiguously white. [*Laughter*]

Suarez: Let's go to Burbank, California. Tom is with us now. Hi, Tom.

Caller: Hi. I would bring the point that I'm an Irish-American, and I am a Catholic. And some of us, when we filled out our 1990 census, put "other" and put "Irish," because to me, white in this country means White Anglo-Saxon Protestant. And not only is there no Anglo-Saxon Protestant bone in my body, my sense of American history is the Know Nothing Party against the Catholic immigrants from different countries, the Molly Maguires, the IWW and the organizing of working people. When my grandmother Annie Gleason came into New Orleans, the French side of my family called us "Shanty Irish," and it took me a few years to understand that that was not a compliment. So, I think that there is a white European ethnic Catholicism which is not part of any colonialism. The Irish didn't colonize anybody; we were colonized. We were subjected to the last bigotry besides racism, which is anti-Catholicism.

Dyson: I'm sure all of our panelists are thinking about Noel Ignatiev's book, *How the Irish Became White,* and I'll defer to my colleagues here to explain the complexities of that text in the next five minutes. But I think that Irishness itself is a very specific ethnic grouping. And you're absolutely right—there have been contests over Irish identity in this culture. And as a result, we think about schools that were prejudiced against the Irish in the early part of this century, and I went to school with Irish people. So, there's no question that there's a whole range of differences between, say, white Anglo-Saxon Protestants and the Irish, about notions of who is white and who is not. But the perverse ingenuity of whiteness is that it absorbs people by virtue of skin color. So that many people who are unable to tell the difference between Irish or Scottish or British, or white Anglo Saxon Protestant for that matter, are the same people who understand that whiteness functions beyond ethnic groups to unite different ethnicities within white European countries, for example, around the issue that, when they come to America, they're made the same. [Whiteness] has a kind of pulverizing homogeneity; it makes people of similar skin the same despite those internal differences. And I'll add this one further point: the restaurant I was speaking about, in which I had the enormous problem in regard to the waitress, indeed was an Irish restaurant.

Suarez: Well Tom, if you're gonna drop out and no longer be white, I guess you're gonna have a lot of company if you're gonna use that fairly restrictive de-finition of whiteness. Was Michael Dukakis white?

Caller: No, I considered him an ethnic American.

Suarez: Okay. And—Telly Savalas?

Caller: Well, I consider white to be an anomaly that should actually be extricated. I'm much more in favor of hyphenated Americanism, because I think it shows a pride in one's own culture, one's own addition to the melting pot. I mean, I came to understand, to the extent I can understand, the black experience in America when I spend time as I do every year in the ghettos of Northern Ireland. And I was explained to by my Irish brothers and sisters in the North that they followed and modeled their civil rights movement, before Bloody Sunday in Derry, on Martin Luther King. And they understood immediately what happens when there is tumult and there are problems in the urban centers of this country. And I visualize Belfast and Derry and Armagh and the rest, and that is where I started to get some sort of wisdom about being a subjected people.

Suarez: Sorry. Before we close for the hour, thanks for your call, Peter in Saint Paul. We have a couple of interesting letters. Herbert Lewis, who is a professor of anthropology in the Wisconsin University system, writes: "Whiteness does not refer to any group of people that shares a history, a music, a culture despite the obfuscations of the advocates of this view. Most of what we're hearing about whiteness consists either of resentment against whites, or of simple-minded stereotypes of so-called 'white people.' This is no way to understand the complexity of our lives. It can only result in confusion at best, in unpleasantness and division at worst. We will not understand ourselves, our culture or history better. We will only be more angry at each other."

And Amy writes from Seattle, Washington: "Chatting about this in the classroom is OK, but doesn't mean much until it enters the everyday. And since

that's where racism destroys and degrades actual lives, I think most of us want to see how this work is going to help change society for the average Juan y Juana. Cheers to your panel for addressing practical applications."

That's all the time we have for this hour. Thanks to everyone who called. And thanks especially to my guests.

COMMENT

The following critique does not question the validity of the subjective knowledge production of white privilege and does not deny that there is such a thing as white privilege. However, because it is based on a particular racial project, it suffers from the same limitations as most racial projects, including the color-based racializations. The white privilege argument assumes some measure of universality and arises from the subjective view of life as being static; the view assumes that society will always be skewed to favor whites unless awareness is raised and government intervenes through regulation and law. The people who share the perspective of white privilege should recognize that the underlying legal and legislative system protects and maintains those fields which are skewed through the favoring of certain racial practices. This seems to give evidence for white privilege as a problem.

Throughout the conversation the scholars express difficulty describing whiteness and what exactly white culture is and represents. Further, the scholars are reluctant to say how many different racializations there are in addition to the well-known white and black racializations. This difficulty arises because the only shared aspect of whites is their designation as white. It has been noted already that any attempt to understand a large and diverse group of people through a single racialization can only result in a caricature of those people. In other words, all other aspects of individual identity, cultural value, religious belief, and other possible racialization are suppressed and ignored in order to say something about whiteness. For example, not all whites are European, as many people from Russia and the former satellite southern states of Russia self-identify as Asian.

The concept of white privilege cannot account for the failures and difficulties of many whites and the success of many blacks which could also become the source of a discourse within a discourse. White privilege ignores the success and failures of racializations other than white and black; attempted interpretations of non-white success and failure become unnecessarily complicated in a subjective way. Many Asians, for example, enjoy success and suffer failure in many areas of life. These successes and failures are framed within white privilege in order to support or challenge that framework of white privilege. In other words, alternative interpretations or responses by thinking human beings are not prominent as an explanation of social dynamics. Even what is measured as success and failure seem to prefer a system of value which might be identified as stereotypically white.

The idea of white privilege is too general and too narrow at the same time. The argument of white privilege fails to recognize the power of innovation against the established status quo, which is dominated by white people in the U.S. The idea of white privilege is too general because it generalizes large groups of people to make knowledge to explain what is observed. To make the argument, the individual and the exception to the theory are sacrificed and ignored. This becomes a problem when individuals seek to construct self-identity according to the knowledge production already available. In other words, the prescriptive declarations of white privilege give people an explanation for their lives that may or may not actually be relevant. Does a poor, white, moderately intelligent person succeed in life because s/he is white and the pathway to success was easier, or was it because that white person overcame adversity to be successful through his or her own creativity? When a colored person is successful is it because that person adopted the ways of whiteness and betrayed his/her race? How does the hip hop industry (so-called "black music") fit within the framework of white privilege, or is hip hop just white music? If a white person gets a lucrative contract or job, was it because of his/her white privilege? What does one do with all of the whites who do not succeed according to the implied standards of the scholars in the conversation above? It should be remembered that even if white privilege is a serious issue for those without white privilege, there are many whites who do not enjoy the success that seem to be available to all whites. Even in the southern states during the time of the racist Jim Crow laws, not all whites enjoyed the kind of social clout which the color of their skin should have given them. It is not unknown that poor whites were mistreated by black people even in the south.[1]

The subjective view of white privilege is also too narrow, as it ignores the many other kinds of privilege that exist in society. It does not seem to occur to those in the NPR transcript that one could possess multiple sets of privilege which have nothing to do with skin color; e.g. intelligence, creativity, memory, dexterity, artistic ability, musical ability, health, longevity, physical strength, etc., just to name a few. In fact, sometimes privilege through another racial project is enough to overcome privilege dictated by color; e.g. Jackie Robinson became the first African American to play professional baseball because he was just that good. In other words, privilege from a different racial project may be used to overcome the privilege of other racial projects to create new systems of privilege where there are winners and losers. It is not necessarily a perfect system nor is it necessarily faster or slower than legislating morality. This analysis does bring into focus the explanation of how certain types of privilege persist longer than they logically should.

Every racialization has its privileged and under-privileged class of people. With each signified characteristic, often there is an area of life which relies on that characteristic; in this particular area or field of life, people who possess and use that characteristic better than others tend to be more successful in that field. Some people may refer to this as cultural capital, or assets which are not necessarily material and easily transferable from one person to another. The early jazz era of America was dominated by African Americans because of its African origin and the so-called lack of ability among white Americans. Today, most children in school are not categorized by color but by ability; often so-called "gifted" students are signified to be given a different program of study. Medical school admissions tend to favor students who are privileged in memorization skills. Engineering schools favor those who are privileged in mathematical ability. Various sports privilege different physical abilities over others to determine employability and success.

1   Eric Lincoln, *Coming through the Fire: Surviving Race and Place in America*, (Durham: Duke University Press, 1996), pg 19.

Any given privilege is not necessarily global, nor is it the only kind of privilege useful to explain life as it is lived every day all over the world. For example, the privilege of whiteness does not figure heavily in everyday life in South Korea. One cannot get a coveted job in South Korea simply because one is white. If one objects and says that the context of white privilege discourse is restricted to areas of life in America, then one simply verifies the existence of localized subjective thinking. Because of globalization, privilege is not necessarily an absolute privilege if it cannot ensure success on a global scale. In other words, simply being white may make it easier for a person to get a job at a particular business, but there are no guarantees that the business will remain operational in the face of global competition. In fact, in light of our earlier discussion on the cost and price of racism in chapter 10, as long as a company prioritizes unrelated and arbitrary characteristics as a part of doing business, that business will always lose against one which focuses on valued characteristics such as skill, efficiency and diligence. In other words, the persistence of the subjective view of white privilege can only exist within a protectionist environment; this is an environment where competition is limited to ensure that underperforming businesses remain open by competing against other underperforming businesses. In the case of white privilege, protectionist regulations protect the businesses which favor white skin over ability and productivity. These businesses do not fail rather their continued national dominance affirms the impression that white privilege is the fundamental problem and not the phenomenon of the legislation of morality (chapter 5). One should note that the fewer the regulations in a field of life the more choices there are and the cost of participating in that field is lower; e.g. successful cell phone manufacturing companies are not white dominated companies and the price of quality phones is always falling.

Another example would be the car industry; when Japanese car companies outperform U.S. car companies, is it because the Japanese are doing things the white way, only better? Are the Japanese auto workers working whiter than Americans? Are those Japanese car companies run by white people? Is yellow privilege superior to white privilege? Rather than making arguments and statements narrowly focused on white privilege, perhaps it would be better to realize that there are an infinite number of possible privileges in society, and most, if not all, people have more than one set of privilege. Perhaps the Japanese value and privilege the ability to innovate or to increase efficiency or the desire to work harder than one is required to work resulting in increased productivity which would normally lower costs. This results in cheaper and higher quality products against which American companies cannot successfully compete. Rather than fail, knowledge is produced to shift the attention away from bad business practices to cries of unfair competition or perhaps a xenophobic position against foreign goods in favor of domestic goods. The result is the perpetuation of companies which maintain poor business practices which include the favoring of white skin over productivity.

To reiterate, there are many areas of life where whiteness does not contribute to the success of the individual. In many fields of life, privilege is determined along different sets of racializations which do not involve color. There are many examples and situations in society where this can be observed. Height, for example, is a type of privilege. There are some fields where being tall is an advantage over shorter people; e.g. basketball. However, there are professions in which being tall is a disadvantage; e.g. horse jockey. Physical appearance or beauty is also a type of privilege. Sometimes one's appearance is an advantage, and in other situations, it is a disadvantage. The modeling industry often goes through trends in regard to appearance; currently the racially ambiguous appearance is popular. Racially ambiguous would be the appearance where most people cannot easily identify the ethnicity of a person. In this modeling example being white would be a disadvantage and not a privilege.

In fact there are areas of life where whiteness is a disadvantage. In the hip hop industry, being white is not a privilege. Also, assuming white privilege can mean that people will expect more, and therefore, demand more from white people. Thus, though it has been shown by many studies that white people on average earn more than other kinds of colored people, it also means that the expected output of those employees must justify the higher pay. In other words, standards may be higher for whites than for others because of their privilege. In this way, some or many white people will be excluded from the perks of being white.

Roediger, in the transcripts, wonders why white workers identify with the racialization of "whiteness" more than with the racialization of "worker." Perhaps he imagines a society where white and black workers will only signify one racial project and recognize their common situation and unite against the privileged white and blacks of society. Winant would surely point out that racialization forms partly as an expression of conflicts in society. The underlying differentiation between white and black workers is because both groups often compete for the same jobs as separate groups of potential workers with potentially different wage scales. As Walter Williams points out, when there were no price controls in the labor market, black unemployment was lower than white unemployment.[2] This competition can only lead to the social conflict to which Winant refers, which leads to self-identification along the lines of color, as opposed to self-identification as "worker." To put it in another way, the "worker" label can only hide the persistent, adversarial and competitive conflict between white and black workers. So, systems of privilege are not overcome, rather the system of privilege is only superficially hidden because the underlying competition and conflict remain. The actual result of the creation of the "worker" label and discarding color references is that the price and cost of catering to a certain kind of privilege has been mitigated enabling under-performing businesses to continue to exist in a protected market.

Without regulation and legislation, the system of white privilege would be difficult to maintain in a dynamic society, because, as previously stated, racism is expensive and new competition is always waiting to unseat the current leader in the field. Many of the white-dominated structures in society today have become bloated and inefficient (e.g., Hollywood and the auto industry), becoming a drain on the public and society in general. If whites generally benefit from those systems, then allowing competition through the free market will do more to undermine the supposed structures of white privilege than any amount of legislation. In this example of the white and black workers, rather than focusing on the color of the skin of workers, a new and more successful company may focus on skill and productivity. The result would be the failure of the discriminatory company and real opportunity for workers who are the most productive with no regard to their skin color.

Placing importance on issues of color which serves to prop up inefficient and non-competitive companies ignores the power of innovation to undermine the status quo of white privilege. Change in technology often disempowers the hold that certain companies have over the marketplace. A new company may introduce new popular technology which would render existing companies and their now obsolete undesirable technology at a disadvantage. Companies which are faced with matching the new technology will often be forced to streamline their workforce. The new challenge presented through innovation would require businesses to remember that arbitrary prioritization of various privileges unrelated to productivity will result in failure. In other words, businesses which focus on white privilege have a higher risk of failing than businesses which focused more on productivity and innovation. Airbnb, Uber, Lyft, and 3D printing are examples

---

2   Walter Williams, *Race and Economics: How much can be blamed on discrimination?* (Standford: Hoover Institution Press, 2011), pg 31.

of establishment threatening opportunities made possible through techno-logical innovation. Uber and Lyft are taxi type services which can make anyone a part-time taxi driver to make extra money. Airbnb is a way for people to offer their own home as a cheap alternative to a hotel room. 3D printing technology has many applications including printing $80,000 prosthetic limbs for $10. 3D printing can also reduce the need for health insurance to cover the cost of expensive devices. Robert Graboyes discusses the potential of having artificial organs printed using a person own cells reducing or eliminating the dangers of rejection and problems of supply. Companies which profit through the traditional methods of treatment through traditional modes of payment would be at risk.[3] Innovation enables anyone to have access to and be able to produce products previously only available through specialists. In other words, innovation makes it difficult for any system of privilege to last a long time.

One might reject innovation because of the instability it creates; how-ever, it is a productive instability and the issue of white privilege loses its urgency. In order to take advantage of the productive destabilization of innovation, there must be freedom for people to take advantage of the privileges/talents/abilities they have. In light of the discussion of the power of innovation and the existence of a variety of privileges, many of which are yet to be realized, the need to continue to focus only on white privilege is decreased.

SUMMARY

The existence of white privilege is not denied, but it is wrong to assume that white privilege is the only kind of privilege in society. There are as many different kinds of privilege as there are racializations. Within each racialization, there are those who have an advantage or privilege over oth-ers. Rather than focusing on one type of privilege, society should maintain freedom so that the various racializations may be able to take advantage of their privilege and succeed in society and life in ever more creative and unexpected ways.

---

3   Robert Graboyes in an interview with reason.tv, July 1, 2014; *How to Grow the Supply of Healthcare.*

QUESTIONS FOR DISCUSSION

1. As a horse jockey, how important is the color of one's skin?

2. Can you think of other situations or areas of life where blacks do not seem to be hindered by the color of their skin or the lack of white privilege?

3. What are some other privileges that seem unfair to those who do not have them?

INSTITUTIONAL RACISM EXPLAINED THROUGH WHITE SUPREMACY 13

GOAL

For students to understand what institutional racism is and how the free market would deal with the issues signified by it

U P TO THIS POINT, the broad and inclusive perspective of race and racism in this book maintains that any identifiable characteristic of a person can be used to construct and define racism. One popular way of describing racism in a narrow or subjective way is through **institutional racism**. Institutional racism is the construct which represents racism not as the expression and practice of racist individuals, but as a fundamental part of the entire social system in which we live. It must be noted that the kind of racism that is usually the focus of institutional racism is white racism or the racism expressed by white people; white racism particularly against black people in and through the various institutions of society.

Most people are familiar with an individual who has hatred for a particular kind of person (e.g. whites who hate blacks). Institutional racism goes beyond the individual and maintains that the structure and rules of society are governed by the racism of white supremacy. If racism was simply a matter of individual racists, society could simply find those people and re-educate them or re-socialize them to make them no longer racist. Many in society already try to prevent people from ever becoming racist by influencing children's programing to include themes of inclusivity and racial harmony. It is also not unusual for a TV show to be criticized for not having enough color diversity in its cast.

Institutional racism maintains that racism is part of the very fabric of society; there is no way to escape it even if one moves to a different city. Institutional racism is commonly understood as having three characteristics; first, it is systemic. This means that people and society in general prefer whites and function with white values, preferences, biases, and prejudices. There is no space in society that is free from white preferences, as people have also been socialized to function and work within the racist system. Second, institutional racism is said to shape everyday social relations. This means that, because the biases of racism are in the system, people censor and monitor their behavior to be context-appropriate in order to avoid offending others or being accused of being a white racist. People will change how they speak and what they say if people of color are in the room. Finally, the definition, form, and expression of race change over time. Because overt racism is illegal in the U.S., racial prejudice continues in other ways, such as dress codes and patterns of speech. In the excerpt below, author bell hooks explains institutional racism through the black perspective, which sees white supremacy pervading society to the detriment of black people in the U.S.

TALKING RACE AND RACISM

by bell hooks

Teachers are often among that group most reluctant to acknowledge the extent to which white-supremacist thinking informs every aspect of our culture including the way we learn, the content of what we learn, and the manner in which we are taught. Much of the consciousness-raising around the issue of white supremacy and racism has focused attention on teaching what racism is and how it manifests itself in the daily workings of our lives. In anti-racist workshops and seminars, much of the time is often spent simply breaking through the denial that leads many unenlightened white people, as well as people of color, to pretend that racist and white-supremacist thought and action are no longer pervasive in our culture.

In classroom settings I have often listened to groups of students tell me that racism really no longer shapes the contours of our lives, that there is just no such thing as racial difference, that "we are all just people." Then a few minutes later I give them an exercise. I ask if they were about to die and could choose to come back as a white male, a white female, a black female, or black male, which identity would they choose. Each time I do this exercise, most individuals, irrespective of gender or race invariably choose whiteness, and most often white maleness.

Black females are the least chosen. When I ask students to explain their choice they proceed to do a sophisticated analysis of privilege based on race (with perspectives that take gender and class into consideration). This disconnect between their conscious repudiation of race as a marker of privilege and their unconscious understanding is a gap we have to bridge, an illusion that must be shattered before a meaningful discussion of race and racism can take place. This exercise helps them to move past their denial of the existence of racism. It lets us begin to work together toward a more unbiased approach to knowledge.

Teaching, lecturing, and facilitating workshops and writing about ending racism and other forms of domination, I have found that confronting racial biases, and more important, white-supremacist thinking, usually requires that all of us take a critical look at what we learned early in life about the nature of race. Those initial imprints seem to overdetermine attitudes about race. In writing groups we often begin simply with our first remembered awareness of race. Exploring our earliest ways of knowing about race, we find it easier to think about the question of standpoint. Individual white people, moving from denial of race to awareness, suddenly realize that white-supremacist culture encourages white folks to deny their understanding of race, to claim, as part of their superiority that they are *beyond* thinking about race. Yet when the denial stops, it becomes clear that underneath their skin most white folks have an intimate awareness of the politics of race and racism. They have learned to pretend that it is not so, to take on the posture of learned helplessness.

It has become more fashionable, and at times profitable, for white folks in academic environments to think and write about race. It is as though the very act of thinking about the nature of race and racism is still seen as "dirty" work best suited for black folks and other people of color or a form of privileged "acting out" for anti-racist white folks. Black folks/people of color who talk too much about race are often represented by the racist mindset as "playing the race card" (note how this very expression trivializes discussions of racism, implying it's all just a game), or as simply insane. White folks who talk race, however, are often represented as patrons, as superior civilized beings. Yet their actions are just another indication of white-supremacist power, as in "we are so much more civilized and intelligent than black folks/people of color that we know better than they do all that can be understood about race."

Simply talking about race, white supremacy, and racism can lead one to be typecast, excluded, placed lower on the food chain in the existing white-supremacist system. No wonder then that such talk can become an exercise in powerlessness because of the way it is filtered and mediated by those who hold the power to both control public speech (via editing, censorship, modes of representation, and interpretation). While more individuals in contemporary culture talk about race and racism, the power of that talk has been diminished by racist backlash that trivializes it, more often than not representing it as mere hysteria.

Individual black people/people of color often describe moments where they challenge racist speech at meetings or in other formal settings only to witness a majority of folks rush to comfort the racist individual they have challenged, as though that person is the victim and the person who raised questions a persecutor. No wonder then that while discussions of white supremacy and racism have become rather commonplace in individual scholarly writing and journalistic work, most people are wary, if not downright fearful, of discussing these issues in group settings, especially when among strangers. People often tell me that they do not share openly and candidly their thoughts about white-supremacist thought and racism for fear that they will say the wrong thing. And yet when this reason is interrogated it usually is shown to cover up the fear of conflict, the belief that saying the wrong thing will generate conflict, bad feeling, or lead to counterattack. Groups where white folks are in the majority often insist that race and racism does not really have much meaning in today's world because we are all so beyond caring about it. I ask them why they then have so much fear about speaking their minds. Their fear, their censoring silence, is indicative of the loaded meaning race and racism have in our society.

One of the bitter ironies anti-racists face when working to end white-supremacist thinking and action is that the folks who most perpetuate it are the individuals who are usually the least willing to acknowledge that race matters. In almost all the writing I have done on the topics of race, I state my preference for using the word white supremacy to describe the system of race-based biases we live within because this term, more than racism, is inclusive of everyone. It encompasses black people/people of color who have a racist mindset, even though they may organize their thinking and act differently from racist whites. For example: a black female who has internalized racism may straighten her hair to appear more like white females. And yet this same individual might become irate if any white person were to praise her for wanting to be white. She might confront them about being racist while remaining in complete denial about her allegiance to white-supremacist thinking about the nature of beauty. It may be just as difficult to break through this person's denial about her collusion with white-supremacist thinking as to try to create awareness in a racist white person. Most people in our nation oppose overt acts of racist terror or violence. We are a nation of citizens who claim that they want to see an end to racism, to racial discrimination. Yet there is clearly a fundamental gap between theory and practice. No wonder, then, that it has been easier for everyone in our nation to accept a critical written discourse about racism that is usually read only by those who have some degree of educational privilege than it is for us to create constructive ways to talk about white supremacy and racism, to find constructive actions that go beyond talk.

In more recent years, as discourses about race and racism have been accepted in academic settings, individual black people/people of color have been to some extent psychologically terrorized by the bizarre gaps between theory and practice. For example: a well-meaning liberal white female professor might write a useful book on the intersections of race and gender yet continue to allow racist biases to shape the manner in which she responds personally to women of color..... She may have a "grandiose" sense of herself, that is, a confidence that she is anti-racist and not all vigilant about making the connections that would transform her behavior and not just her thinking. When it comes to the subject of race and racism, many folks once naively believed that if we could change the way people thought we would change their behavior. Move often than not, this has not been the case. Yet we should not be profoundly dismayed by this. In a culture of domination almost everyone engages in behaviors that contradict their beliefs and values. This is why some sociologists and psychologists are writing about the reality that in our nation individuals lie more and more about all manner of things large and small. This lying often leads to forms of denial wherein individuals are unable to distinguish between fantasy and fact, between wishful dreaming and reality.

While it is a positive aspect of our culture that folks want to see racism end; paradoxically it is this heartfelt longing that underlies the persistence of the false assumption that racism has ended, that this in not a white-supremacist nation. In our culture almost everyone, irrespective of skin color, associates white supremacy with extreme conservative fanaticism, with Nazi skinheads who preach all the old stereotypes about racist purity. Yet these extreme groups rarely threaten the day-to-day workings of our lives. It is the less extreme white supremacists' beliefs and assumptions, easier to cover up and mask, that maintain and perpetuate everyday racism as a form of group oppression.

Once we can face all the myriad ways white-supremacist thinking shapes our daily perceptions, we can understand the reasons liberal whites who are concerned with ending racism may simultaneously hold on to beliefs and assumptions that have their roots in white supremacy. We can also face the way black people/people of color knowingly and unknowingly internalize white-supremacist thinking. In a class I was teaching recently, we discussed a talk I had given where many white students expressed their disdain for the ideas I expressed, and for my presence, by booing. I challenged the group to consider that what I was saying was not as disturbing to the group as was my embodied young-looking presence, a black female with natural hair in braids. I had barely finished this comment before a liberal white male in the group attacked claiming "you are playing the race card here." His immediate defensive response is often the feedback that comes when black people/people of color make an observation about the everyday dynamics of race and racism, sex and sexism that does not conform to privileged white perceptions.

Understanding the degree to which class privilege mediates and shapes perceptions about race is vital to any public discourse on the subject because the most privileged people in our nation (especially those with class power) are often the most unwilling to speak honestly about racist biases. Working-class whites in our nation will often speak quite eloquently about the way racist assumptions fuel our perceptions and our actions daily, while white folks from privileged class backgrounds continue to do the dance of denial, pretending that shared class privileges mediate or transform racism. I explained to the group that one of the manifestations of daily life in an imperialist white-supremacist capitalist patriarchy is that the vast majority of white folks have little intimacy with black people and are rarely in situations where they must listen to a black person (particularly a black woman) speak to them for thirty minutes. Certainly, there were no black teachers when I was an undergraduate English major and graduate student. It would not have occurred to me to look for black female teachers in other disciplines. I accepted this absence.

I shared with the class that in my daily life as a member of the upper classes, living alone in a predominantly white neighborhood and working in predominantly white settings, I have little organic contact with black females. If I wanted to talk with or listen to black women, I have to make an effort. Yet here was an upper-class white man living in a predominantly white world, working in a predominantly white setting, telling me that white folks have no trouble listening to black females teach them, listening to black females express beliefs and values that run counter to their own. I asked the group to consider why the response to my initial ideas about the rarity of white folks having to listen to black women talk and/teach was not: "Gee. I have never thought about how race determines who we listen to, who we accept as authorities." It would have been interesting had the white male colleague who vehemently disagreed withheld his comments until he had given the matter serious thought, until he was able to present cogent reasons why he disagreed with my statement. By evaluating me (i.e., suggesting I was being false and "playing the race card") he avoided having to present the fact-based and/or experiential reasons he thought differently from me. His response personalized an observation that I do not consider personal.

Given the nature of imperialist white-supremacist capitalist patriarchy as a system shaping culture and beliefs it is simply a fact that most white folks are rarely, if ever, in situations where they must listen to black women lecture to them. Even the white folks who have black maids and housekeepers working in their homes daily do not listen to these women when they talk. This reality was graphically depicted years ago in the 1950s' box office hit, *Imitation of Life,* when Laura, the rich white woman comes to her black housekeeper/maid Annie's funeral and is awed that Annie had friends, was a highly regarded church woman, and so on. Certainly the biographies and autobiographies of white women who were raised by black female servants abound with testimony that they did not dialogue with these women, or listen to them tell their stories, or share information they did not want to hear.

We operate in a world of class privilege that remains undemocratic and discriminatory so that most upper-class black folks in white settings are isolated and must make an effort to hear black females talk and/or lecture for thirty minutes. My honest testimony to this fact was a critical intervention that created a moment of pause in the minds of those students who were not operating with closed minds. They could ponder my comments and relate them to their lives. They could ask themselves "who do I listen to?" or "whose words do I value?" I offered Oprah Winfrey as an example of a black female who daily commands the attention of masses of white folks, and yet her role is usually that of commentator. She listens and interprets the speech of others. Rarely does she express her particular views on a subject for more than a few minutes, if at all. In many ways she is seen in the racist imagination as "housekeeper/mammy," not unlike that of Annie in *Imitation of Life* whose primary goal in life is to make sure white folks can live the best possible life. Remember that for fifteen years Annie sent the old milkman her hard-earned money every Christmas pretending that it came from the selfish, rich, white woman. This was Annie's way of teaching by example. Her motivation is to make Laura a better person and, of course, by doing so she reveals what a good person she herself is.

Annie is the black woman who knows that her place is to be subordinate and to serve; she serves with acceptance, dignity, and grace. She does not confront the white mistress with ideas and critical perspectives that white females do not want to hear. This is the model offered black females by the racist, sexist imagination. That model is represented currently in almost every Hollywood representation of black womanhood. No wonder then that so many white folks find it hard to "listen" to a black woman critic speaking ideas and opinions that threaten their belief systems. In our class discussion someone pointed out that a powerful white male had given a similar talk but he was not given negative, disdainful, verbal feedback. It was not that listeners agreed with what he said; it was that they believed he had a right to state his viewpoint.

Often individual black people and/or people of color are in settings where we are the only colored person present. In such settings unenlightened white folks often behave toward us as though we are the guests and they the hosts. They act as though our presence is less a function of our skill, aptitude, genius, and more the outcome of philanthropic charity. Thinking this way, they see our presence as functioning primarily as a testament to their largesse; it tells the world they are not racist. Yet the very notion that we are there to serve them is itself an expression of white-supremacist thinking. At the core of white-supremacist thinking in the United States and elsewhere is the assumption that it is natural for the inferior races (darker people) to serve the superior races (in societies where there is no white presence, lighter-skinned people should be served by darker-skinned people). Embedded in this notion of service is that no matter what the status of the person of color, that position must be reconfigured to the greater good of whiteness.

This was an aspect of white-supremacist thinking that made the call for racial integration and diversity acceptable to many white folks. To them, integration meant having access to people of color who would either spice up their lives (the form of service we might call the performance of exotica) or provide them with the necessary tools to continue their race-based dominance (for example: the college students from privileged white homes who go to the third world to learn Spanish or Swahili for "fun," except that it neatly fits later that this skill helps them when they are seeking employment). Time and time again in classes, white students who were preparing to study or live briefly in a non-white country talk about the people in these countries as though they existed merely to enhance white adventure. Truly, their vision was not unlike that of the message white kids received from watching the racist television show *Tarzan* ("go native and enhance your life"). The beat poet Jack Kerouac expressed his sentiments in the language of cool "the best the white world had offered was not enough ecstasy for me." Just as many unaware whites, often liberal, saw and see their interactions with people of color via affirmative action as an investment that will improve their lives, even enhance their organic superiority. Many people of color, schooled in the art of internalized white-supremacist thinking, shared this assumption.

Chinese writer Anchee Min captures the essence of this worship of whiteness beautifully in *Katherine*, a novel about a young white teacher coming to China, armed with seductive cultural imperialism. Describing to one of her pupils her perception that the Chinese are a cruel people (certainly this was a popular racist stereotype in pre-twentieth century America) she incites admiration in her Chinese pupil who confesses: "Her way of thinking touched me. It was something I had forgotten or maybe had never known. She unfolded the petals of my dry heart. A flower I did not know existed began to bloom inside me.... Katherine stretched my life beyond its own circumstance. It was the kind of purity she preserved that moved me." The white woman as symbol of purity continues to dominate racist imaginations globally. In the United States, Hollywood continues to project this image, using it to affirm and reaffirm the power of white supremacy.

When people of color attempt to critically intervene and oppose white supremacy, particularly around the issue of representation, we are often dismissed as pushing narrow political correctness, or simply characterized as being no fun. Writing about cultural appropriation in *English is Broken Here* Coco Fusco explains: "The socialization I and many other affirmative action babies received to identify racism as the property only of ignorant, reactionary people, preferably from the past, functioned to deflect our attention from how whiteness operated in the present … To raise the specter of racism in the here and now, to suggest that despite their political beliefs and sexual preferences, white people operate within, and benefit from, white supremacist social structures is still tantamount to a declaration of war." When white supremacy is challenged and resisted, people of color and our allies in struggle risk the censorship that emerges when those who hold the power to dominate simply say to us, "You are extremist, you are the real racist, you are playing the race card." Of course the irony is that we are not actually allowed to play at the game of race, we are merely pawns in the hands of those who invent the games and determine the rules.

Every black person and person of color colludes with the existing system in small ways every day, even those among us who see ourselves as anti-racist radicals. This collusion happens simply because we are all products of the culture we live within and have all been subjected to the forms of socialization and acculturation that are deemed normal in our society. Through the cultivation of awareness, through the decolonization of our minds, we have the tools to break with the dominator model of human social engagement and the will to imagine new and different ways that people might come together. Martin Luther King, Jr. imagined a "beloved community," conceptualizing a world where people would bond on the basis of shared humanness. His vision remains. King taught that the simple act of coming together would strengthen community. Yet before he was assassinated he was beginning to see that unlearning racism would require a change in both thinking and action, and that people could agree to come together across race but they would not make community.

To build community requires vigilant awareness of the work we must continually do to undermine all the socialization that leads us to behave in ways that perpetuate domination. A body of critical theory is now available that explains all the workings of white-supremacist thought and racism. But explanations alone do not bring us to the practice of beloved community. When we take the theory, the explanations, and apply them concretely to our daily lives, to our experiences, we further and deepen the practice of anti-racist transformation. Rather than simply accept that class power often situates me in a world where I have little or no contact with other black people, especially individuals from underprivileged classes, I as a black person with class privilege can actively seek out these relationships.

More often than not to do this work I must make an effort to expand my social world. In recent years, individual white peers who have always seen themselves as anti-racist have adopted children of color, only to realize (what should have been apparent) that they did not really have intimate friendships with people of color. They need to do their active unlearning of white-supremacist thinking (which says you are superior because of whiteness and therefore better able to raise a non-white child than any colored person) by seeking to forge relationships with people of color.

Time and time again I have observed white peers working to unlearn white supremacy as they become aware of the reality that they have little contact with non-white people. They open their "eyes" and see that there were always non-white folks around them that they did not "see" when they were blinded by white privilege stemming from racist foundations. Time and time again I come to do anti-racist work at liberal arts colleges that I am told are "all white" only to find that the majority of support staff and service workers are non-white. The presence of black people and/or people of color who are not seen as class peers is easily ignored in a context where the privileged identity is white. When we stop thinking and evaluating along the lines of hierarchy and can value rightly all members of a community we are breaking a culture of domination. White supremacy is easily reinscribed when individuals describe communities of students and faculty as "all white" rather than affirming diversity, even if it's evident only by the presence of a few individuals. Anti-racist work requires of all of us vigilance about the ways we use language. Either/or thinking is crucial to the maintenance of racism and other forms of group oppression. Whenever we think in terms of both/and we are better situated to do the work of community building.

Imagine the difference: on one campus I hear that white people remain the larger group but are made diverse by the presence of non-white individuals and that the majority wants to become diverse. On another campus, I hear that "we are all white," which negates the value of the presence of people of color, however few in number they may be. The language we use to express these ideas is usually awkward at first, but as we change to more inclusive language and normalize its use that awkwardness becomes less. Much of the white-supremacist thought and action we have all unconsciously learned surfaces in habitual behavior. Therefore it is that behavior we must become aware of and work to change. For example: black mothers frequently come to me to ask what they can do when their children come home from school saying they want to be "made white." Often these women will share that they have done everything to instill love of blackness. However, in every case the woman seeks to change her appearance to look lighter or to make her hair straighten.

In every case the individual resists the notion that the child "reads" her hypocrisy, that the child assumes that "if I cannot even be seen as beautiful, acceptable, worthy by my mother then that larger world that is telling me white is better every day must be right." This is a direct quote from a beautiful black female student in her early twenties who shared that this is what she used to tell herself. And as an adult when individuals would tell her how beautiful she is this is the message her inner voice would offer as a reminder. Even though many scholars and intellectuals mock the world of self-help, it is an important realm of self-recovery for the racially colonized mind. Speaking aloud daily affirmations to change long-imprinted, toxic messages is a useful strategy for cleansing the mind. It promotes vigilant awareness of the ways white-supremacist thinking (daily encoded in the world of advertisement, commercials, magazine images, etc.) enters our system and also empowers us to break its hold on our consciousness.

When I first chose to write books on the subject of love, I simply assumed that my audience would be interested readers of any race. Yet when I came to the table of decision makers in the publishing world, I was asked to identify who the audience would be. It was explained to me that it might be difficult for me to attract "white readers" since I was associated with black liberation. I believed that I could transcend the race-based consumerism that is often the norm in our society. (If a movie has only white characters, it is presumed to be marketed in the direction of all consumers; it is for everybody. However if the movie has only black characters, it is perceived to be directed at a black market.) When I wrote *All about Love: New Visions,* I never identified my race in the book, though clearly the photo on the back showed my color, because I wanted to demonstrate by this gesture that black writers who write specifically on the subject of race are not always only interested in race. I wanted to show that we are all complex thinkers who can be both specific in our focus and universal. The either/or thinking that is at the heart of the white-supremacist-based Western metaphysical dualism teaches people they must choose to like either black images or white images, or see books by white people as written for everybody and books by black people for black people. The inclusive nature of both/and thinking allows us to be inclusive. As a child I never thought that Emily Dickinson wrote her poems just for white readers (and she was truly the first poet whose work I loved). When I later read the work of Langston Hughes I never though he was writing just for black readers. Both poets wrote about the world they knew most intimately.

As my awareness of the way white-supremacist thinking shapes even our choices of what books we read, what books we want to display on our coffee tables, intensified, I developed strategies of resistance. When my second book on love, *Salvation: Black People and Love*, looked specifically at the experiences of black folks, I had to challenge the use of the phrase "black love" by white and black readers. I had to make the point that I was talking about the same ideas of love I had written about in the first book (which no one called a book about white love) but now focusing on the impact those ways of thinking about love had made on the consciousness of black people. The assumption that "whiteness" encompasses that which is universal, and therefore for everybody, while "blackness" is specific, and therefore "for colored only," is white-supremacist thought. And yet many liberal people, along with their more conservative peers, think this way not because they are "bad" people or are consciously choosing to be racist but because they have unconsciously learned to think in this manner. Such thinking, like so many other thought patterns and actions that help perpetuate and maintain white supremacy, can be easily unlearned.

Thirty years of talking about racism and white supremacy, giving lectures and facilitating anti-racism workshops has shown me how easy it is for individuals to change their thoughts and actions when they become aware and when they desire to use that awareness to alter behavior. White-supremacist backlash, which has sought to undermine both the legacy of civil rights and the new focus on critical race theory and practice, continues to push the notion that racist thinking, particularly in white minds, cannot be changed. This is just simply not true. Yet this false assumption gained momentum because there has been no collective demonstration on the part of masses of white people that they are ready to end race-based domination, especially when it comes to the everyday manifestation of white-supremacist thinking, of white power.

Clearly, the most powerful indicator that white people wanted to see institutionalized racism end was the overall societal support for desegregation and integration. The fact that many white people did not link this support to ending everyday acts of white-supremacist thought and practice, however, has helped racism maintain its hold on our culture. To break that hold we need continual anti-racism activism. We need to generate greater cultural awareness of the way white-supremacist thinking operates in our daily lives. We need to hear from the individuals who know, because they have lived anti-racist lives, what everyone can do to decolonize their minds, to maintain awareness, change behavior, and create beloved community.

COMMENT

Institutional racism as seen by hooks is subjectively valid; in other words, if one shares or views the world with the same perspective, prior knowledge and agenda for society as hooks, the information is true. The details noticed, highlighted and interpreted are the details which are visible through this perspective. This analysis does not seek to invalidate this knowledge production as untrue or invalid. However, because it is a subjective perspective it is not a perspective shared by everyone, it is not an inclusive production of knowledge. In other words, not only is the perspective narrow but the perspective privileges some and puts everyone else at a disadvantage; this is the original critique of "institutional racism."

In the excerpt, hooks uses "white supremacy to describe the system of race-based biases we live within, more than racism, (it) is inclusive of everyone." One can only assume she means that American society has a bias and preference for white people and their culture because society itself is immersed in and based on white supremacy. For this reason it is hard to pinpoint and identify patterns as white supremacist thought and institutionalization. However, it can be identified by specific behaviors that are obvious expressions of whiteness; e.g., dyeing one's hair blonde. Attempts to understand and promote anti–white supremacist behavior and thought are also tainted with white supremacist thinking, which makes overcoming white supremacy difficult, indeed. People of color have also internalized and normalized many values and behaviors that are what hooks considers white supremacist; in this way she believes her knowledge production to be all-inclusive; everyone lives with and through white supremacy. It is likely that this critique of hooks would also be considered to be complicit with white supremacist thinking.

It was possible to make this type of argument, which implicates everyone if one assumes that certain behaviors and cultural practices are exclusive to one race or culture. This author has echoed many of hooks' thoughts in his own classroom once upon a time in the Asian/Korean context and perspective. This approach does quickly become a discussion of which behaviors and thoughts belong to which culture or racial group. The static and exclusive cultural world this approach seems to assume is undermined, given that ideas, innovations, and behaviors have been shared all over the world and throughout history.

Instead of trying to decide what behavior and thought is indicative of this or that racial group, it might be remembered that ideas are ideas and preferences are preferences. Exposure to other groups of people presents an opportunity for more choices in paths of development; it also fosters attitudes of tolerance. It is a tricky endeavor to critique an individual's preference in the name of cultural purity or racial supremacy. People should be allowed to make choices without the fear of being accused of perpetuating something as negative as "white supremacy." Recall the example of the

Indian handloom industry. Introduction of modern machines was probably understood as "westernization"; however, the cost to India to maintain tradition was obsolescence and poverty. If cost and price are considered, many counterproductive cultural or racial practices all over the world could be challenged based on and driven by the choices of free people. Recall also the effect of modernization in Japanese society with regard to the rights of ordinary people, especially women. When Japan's government did not protect their traditional loom industry against western technology, quality of life for everyone dramatically improved. Certain traditions were kept, but they were kept voluntarily by the people practicing them. In other words, for Japan, adopting western modes of production meant change but also meant giving up their rigid and oppressive feudal way of life.

The inescapability of institutional racism in the form of white supremacy could be addressed through an analysis of language; the usage of English in America may have more to do with the perpetuation of white supremacy and may not have been considered by hooks. It is known that language is not just a method of communication, but it is also the means by which culture is preserved affirmed and transmitted. In other words, speaking the language of a group of people validates and perpetuates the perspectives and values generated by the people who speak that language. Speakers of multiple languages understand that grammar plays a key role in the formation of creativity, values, and perspectives. As long as one speaks the language of the dominant society, one will find oneself implicated in that system which privileges and favors certain beliefs and behaviors.

Understood this way, people are encouraged to do what they feel is required to live life in the way that best suits them as individuals. It is not necessary to negatively critique the attempts of whites to help others in the way they want. As a matter of fact, as long as the help is also voluntarily received, everyone can only benefit from the generosity and so-called selfishness of others.

Perhaps a more productive and tolerant approach to the matter of institutional racism can be had by examining why certain institutionally racist structures persist throughout society. In other words, white supremacy is only one form of institutional racism in a society that exhibits an infinite number of institutionally racist structures.

As discussed previously, subjective knowledge production gives privilege and advantage primarily to the producers of that knowledge and secondarily to anyone else who shares that perspective. Benefits of this knowledge production extend to those institutions and individuals who would benefit through the proposed legislation based on this knowledge production. This is not saying that this perspective is wrong; it is saying that the knowledge produced is only subjectively true. The nature of subjective knowledge production is that some people will arbitrarily gain and others will lose if society were to adopt this perspective.

This does not mean that what is identified as institutionally racist is morally better. It is likely that the signified problem of institutional racism is itself the product of legislated subjectivity. That is, what is identified as institutional racism is the result of subjectively produced knowledge and legislation. Systems and values of privilege which seem to be the object of critique, is in the opinion of this author, an aspect of life. This is because any rule or law which is established through the legislation of morality will empower some and disempower others. Because that system of privilege is now law, everyone is now coerced to accept that system of privilege. Often the realized benefits are confined to a narrow group of people and the cost is spread out to everyone else, thus the overall benefit and loss is not readily apparent, however, the system of privilege exists.

The conversation about institutional racism sacrifices the individual for the sake of saying something about an entire group of people. How one individual succeeds where another fails is not explained through this representation of racial dynamics. In other words, success or failure of an individual is not simply predictable or even addressed in this knowledge production. All success and failure are not due to the color of one's skin.

Institutional racism, described in the way above by hooks, is very narrow in its scope. Though some people criticize institutional racism as being too broad in its scope to be productive in explaining racism, this book maintains that it does not go far enough. The perspective of institutional racism is broad in the sense that it attempts to cover all of society; however, it is limited in the number of categorizations discussed and implicated in the theory. As bell hooks describes institutional racism, she only focuses on the white/black dynamic. This necessitates creative adaptation for anyone else not included in those racializations if it is to signify for other colored people; otherwise, it is irrelevant. Even for people who are black or white, one is automatically implicated as victim or victimizer, regardless of how one actually lives one's life. The level of generalization in the relevant racial projects ignores the individual and his or her unique situation and experience. The individual becomes either representative or an anomaly for everyone else in that same racial category. It is as if the individual does not matter in this knowledge production.

To reiterate an earlier point, everyone (no matter the racialization) has preferences and prejudices. Knowledge producers consider some preferences acceptable while others are arbitrarily deemed as unacceptable. What is and what is not acceptable is subjective. Whether those subjective opinions are right or wrong or good or evil is a subjective matter. Everyone acts based on their preferences and prejudices, and the actors must pay for those choices. Some people are willing to pay a premium in order to satisfy their preferences; this is their choice. In the free market, the problem is not necessarily the choices people decide to make; rather, problems arise when certain preferences are codified through regulation and the cost of preferences are removed by that same piece of legislation. The passing of legislation that removes the cost of various choices creates a system in which some people have advantages over others (chapter 10). In other words, costly decisions are no longer costly through standardization in pricing. In a strange twist, regulations do not create systems which are fairer; rather they support, foster, and maintain institutionally discriminatory systems which are at best, only subjectively fair. Instead of attempting to reform legislation by adding more legislation, all of the relevant legislation should eventually be repealed, perhaps gradually within a four-year time frame. Racialized thinking will always exist; attempts to do away with them will surely fail because racialization is the process of identity making. However, not codifying subjective perspectives into law allows people to act according to their free choices; this makes systems of privilege unstable and short lived. People may object to and dislike the choices which other people make, but that objection and dislike is only subjective. In a deregulated free market skin color and class are de-signified in favor of price and quality, where quality is always subjective.

There are also situations in society where the primary signified racialization is not skin color. In other words, the narrow view of hooks' institutional racism overlooks the situations where black and white workers collude to the disadvantage of many other people, including other black and white people. An example of this would be found in the auto industry and the racialized group of autoworkers where black and white autoworkers redefine themselves and create unity through the racialization of "autoworker." Autoworkers then racialize foreign car companies as negative and detrimental to the American way of life. By securing special treatment through protectionist tariffs, black and white autoworkers become exploiters of all other Americans by coercing them to buy cars at a much higher price. Import cars are taxed so that they are comparable or more expensive in price as compared to domestic cars. This protected price enables union autoworkers to maintain a higher salary than competition would normally allow. This system and knowledge production are institutionalized, and black and white autoworkers take advantage of it to the detriment of everyone else including other black Americans who must now buy cars at the much higher price point. By narrowly defining race in terms of black and white, and focusing on the signified events made visible through that perspective, other forms and expressions of institutionalized racism and exploitation are invisible and allowed to continue uncontested. In the discussion of the automotive industry, racial issues are conveniently reframed in terms of "American vs. Foreign." This allows people to overlook any previous existing racial understandings which may conflict with the immediate goal of imposing tariffs on imported cars. People, who might otherwise dislike a certain racialization of a person in America, forget that supporting tariffs on imports may help the very people in this country they normally dislike; these feelings of animosity can be along color lines and also along the lines of class and wealth. This means that legislation often will adversely affect the very people legislators claim to want to help. Corporations and many of their much maligned leaders and shareholders benefit from the tariffs which force people to buy their cars. The narrow xenophobic knowledge production of the car industry eclipses other racializations long enough for people in the auto industry to convince other people to support tariffs in general. This entire situation is further complicated by the fact that many Japanese cars are now made in America by Americans and many American cars are made over seas. Substitution of one form of discrimination with another goes against one of the rules of this book which is the prohibition of double standards or hypocrisy.

If one was really consumed by a hatred of foreigners then one would simply not buy their products no matter the price. However, in a free market and without the benefit of protectionism and tariffs, American cars might be much more expensive than the Japanese imports. One would be forced to pay more to maintain one's principles to only buy American products. If the price difference became sufficiently significant, then many anti-Japanese-car auto buyers would cave and buy the cheaper imports because the price of their own racism has become untenable. That person would also be less likely to express anti-Japanese or anti-foreigner sentiments. Eventually, the decrease in sales of American cars would demand change from the American auto industry to compete with the imports. In other words, their prices and quality would be forced to improve by their competition and the desire to stay in business, not through the force of law. The responsibility of the problem falls on the producers not the consumers. ALL Americans benefit from the lower priced high quality automobiles.

Tariffs serve to hide this cost of discrimination and protect and pre-serve the industry in its current inefficient and uncompetitive form. The American people are forced to buy into anti-foreign product mentality and hate foreigners more. At the same time Americans are forced to buy lower quality products at higher prices. Even with all of these advantages, American car companies are frequently in trouble. Chrysler required bail-outs in the form of loans from the government in 1979 and in 2011. In other words, through the bailouts, the government sustains systems of in-equality. Again, because government does not have any money of its own, it must tax Americans, including the working poor, to bail out multimillion dollar corporations.

The entire example of the auto industry in America should illustrate how current attempts to control and eliminate discrimination are limited in their effectiveness. Discriminated individuals may align themselves with a different racialization in order to exploit many other people. In other words, the system of discrimination critiqued by hooks is often used by discriminated people to discriminate against yet another group of people.

In spite of regulations and restrictions which were designed to prevent economic success by certain groups of people, these regulations often become the motivation for innovation or alternative methods of success. In the late 1800s and early 1900s many Asians took advantage of the op-portunities to work and make a living in the U.S. by working on plantations and railroads. When the railroad was completed many Chinese settled in California unable to return to China for political reasons. Discrimination in the 1850s and 1860s against Asians to protect white privilege resulted in the banning of Asians from schools; taxation and regulation of Chinese fish-ing and fishing nets; and restrictions and regulations for gold mining. Shut out of these occupations, many Asians turned to starting laundry services and restaurant businesses to generate an income.[1]

This is not an argument to condone and allow continuing the phenom-enon of legislating morality. The argument was made earlier that no one should be allowed to pass arbitrary laws based on subjective knowledge production. Rather, the point being made is that in spite of certain forms of discrimination, it is not the case that failure is the only result possible. Today when Asians signify the construct of "glass ceiling" (the situation where a person can see the top positions in various companies but are not promoted to those positions), the task to overcome this barrier by simply starting a rival company is made much more difficult by the protectionist

---

1   E. Allen Richardson, *Stranger in the Land: Pluralism and the Response to Diversity in the United States*, (New York: The Pilgrim Press, 1988), pg. 95.

character of regulations. Those regulations perform the role of protecting existing companies against more efficient and more motivated competition. The solution, therefore, should not be more regulation, rather the removal of regulations so that systems of privilege and discrimination are much more difficult to maintain should be the favored course of action.

Institutionally racist systems and businesses can only persist when they are protected by government regulations. This is because the price of arbitrary discrimination (especially discrimination based on characteristics which have nothing to do with actual production) is often higher than the prices the dynamics of the market can generate as demonstrated in the automotive example. As explained in the chapter which went over the free market, everyone seeks to gain advantages over others in the marketplace. Though many people may be offended by the choices of others, arbitrarily legislating morality does not do away with the offense; it merely takes away the cost of that particular behavior. If people were required to pay the price of their choices without the legislation of morality, society would be freer because people are allowed to make the choices which they want to make without the government imposed price manipulations and false messages. In other words, issues of institutional racism may exist, but a free market's flexibility mitigates their persistence, significance, and influence.

SUMMARY

Institutionalized racism is a construct made from a narrow perspective. Because it is a narrow form of knowledge production, it signifies specific relations of discrimination; however, it ignores many others. Institutionally racist systems require the legislation of morality to be established and to persist. Regulations which serve to protect the companies which arbitrarily discriminate must be removed in order to create a more just society.

QUESTIONS FOR DISCUSSION

1. In a country where there are no regulations to protect established companies/corporations, what would it take to break into a market?

2. How do you feel about how the free market deals with racism, that is, by indirectly addressing issues of racism by requiring people to have to pay for their racism?

WHO MAKES MORE: MEN OR WOMEN? 14

GOAL
For students to understand that knowledge, even when it comes to gender issues, is a matter of perspective

THERE HAS BEEN MUCH KNOWLEDGE PRODUCTION and will likely be much more regarding the issue of wage disparity particularly between men and women. It is believed by many who raise this type of comparison that wage disparity is wrong and an indication of some sort of prejudice which is also unjust. It is usual that this type of knowledge production is followed by a call for some sort of legislative action to correct the injustice of wage disparity.

Wage disparity does exist. This is not disputed by this book. Establishing or proving it is wrong or right is not the goal of this chapter. How one views wage disparity is subjective and proposals to end wage disparity often do not consider the unintended consequences of this type of legislation of morality. In other words, in the face of wage disparity, is there something to be done, and if so, what? Can the free market address this issue through voluntary cooperation and without coercive legislation? In keeping consistent with the basic rules of this book, whatever is proposed cannot be coercive nor can it be hypocritical or a double standard. The course of action which must be taken once one has identified some form of wage disparity should be broad and flexible enough to enable free choices without coercive legislation no matter how distasteful people may find those choices.

Here follows an excerpt from Thomas Sowell's book, *Economic Facts and Fallacies*.

EMPLOYER DISCRIMINATION

by Thomas Sowell

COMPARABILITY

In order to determine the existence or magnitude of sex discrimination by employers, as distinguished from other sex discrimination which may have occurred in education, or domestic differences between the sexes which affect job choices, we must compare women and men who have similar education, skills, job experience and other relevant characteristics.

Many statistics on male-female income differences do not do this but simply make gross comparisons of women and men in general as groups, either without regard to comparability or with very limited attempts to hold the differing variables constant. Thus a study in Britain found that women as a group earned 17 percent less per hour than men when both worked fulltime. However, this same study found that the pay differential was not due to women and men being paid different wages or salaries for doing the same job, but that women took lower-paying jobs more often than men, especially after returning to the labor force after having children. As young beginning workers, British women's incomes were 91 percent of that of British men but, as mothers, their incomes were just 67 percent of that of men who were fathers. Mothers' incomes declined as a percentage of male incomes more or less steadily until about a dozen years after giving birth, when it began to rise again, though never getting back to where it was before a child was born, perhaps indicating the permanent income loss due to interrupted careers.

In the United States, a study of graduates of the University of Michigan Law School found a similar pattern:

> The gap in pay between women and men was relatively small at the outset of their careers, but 15 years later, women graduates earned only 60 percent as much as men. Some of this difference reflected choices which workers had made, including the propensity of women lawyers to work shorter hours.

Attempting to control simultaneously for part-time versus full-time employment and for the effect of children and domestic responsibilities, another study found "that the gender pay gap is 5 percent for part-time workers age 21–35 without children, under 3 percent for full-time workers age 21–35 without children, and that *there is no pay gap* for full-time workers age 21–35 living alone." All these gaps represent the upper limit of the effect of employer discrimination *plus* whatever other factors might favor men, such as differences in education and in occupations involving physical strength or dangers. That the income gaps between women and men are so small without even taking these other factors into account suggests that employer discrimination by itself has far less influence on the gross income gaps between the sexes than gross statistics might suggest.

While comparing truly comparable individuals is something that must also be done when trying to determine the existence or effect of discrimination against ethnic or racial groups, achieving similar comparability between women and men is more challenging. That is because, while such factors as education and experience affect different racial or ethnic groups the same way—that is, blacks with more education earn more than blacks with less education, just as among whites, even if not to the same extent—the same factors can have *opposite* effects on women and men: As we have already noted, marriage and parenthood tend to lead to increased incomes for men and reduced incomes for women.

Nor are single women and single men comparable, when "single" people include people who have been married for years, and have then been divorced. That is because the long-term negative economic effects of marriage on women, such as the interruption or even cessation of full-time employment, do not disappear with a change in marital status and reentering the labor force with less experience than a man of the same age. By the same token, the *beneficial* economic effects of marriage for men do not disappear completely after a divorce, since past seniority and increased job skills continue to make the man a higher earner than a man who was never married or a woman who was never married.

To get comparability among people of both sexes who have not had their incomes affected by marriage means comparing women and men who were "never married" rather than simply "single." For purposes of separating out the effects of marriage, and the asymmetrical domestic arrangements which marriage often creates, from the effects of employer discrimination, the most comparable women and men are those who were never married. If male-female income gaps remain large among women and men who were never married, then obviously the economic effects of marriage do not explain sex differences in income. But if that differential changes substantially according to marital status and parenthood, then the employer is correspondingly less of a factor in income differences between women and men.

What are the facts?

As already noted, comparing never-married women and men who are past the child-bearing years and who both work full-time in the twenty-first century shows women of this description earning *more* than men of the same description. As far back as 1969, academic women who had never married earned more than academic men who had never married, while married academic women without children earned less and married academic women with children earned still less. For women in general—that is, not just academic women—those single women who had worked continuously since high school were in 1971 earning slightly *more* than men of the same description. All this was *before* affirmative action was defined as "under-representation" in a 1971 Executive Order which went into effect in 1972, and so represents what was happening under competitive labor market pressures before any major government intervention to advance women.

Both trends over time and studies of women at given times show the same pattern of a negative correlation between marital responsibilities (including children) and women's educational levels and career advancement. Whether in the earlier or the later era, women who were married and had children lagged furthest behind men in income, career advancement, or even working at all. A study published in 1956 showed that most women with Ph.D.s from Radcliffe were not working full-time and those who were averaged fewer children than those who worked part-time, intermittently, or not at all.

In gross terms—that is, ignoring differences between the sexes in continuous versus discontinuous employment, career choices, or full-time versus part-time employment, etc.—the ratio of female-to-male incomes in the general population remained relatively unchanged at about 60 percent during the decades of the 1960s and 1970s, and then began to rise significantly from the early 1980s, reaching 70 percent in 1990 and 77 percent in 2004. Finer breakdowns of the data to compare women and men of comparable ages, education, and employment histories showed the sexes much closer in earnings. Merely comparing full-time, year-round workers showed women's pay to be 81 percent of men's pay in 2005. Part-time workers not only earn less total pay, they are also paid less per hour and are less likely to be promoted. There have been, and continue to be, more women than men who are part-time workers.

Very substantial income differences between women and men in a particular field can co-exist with little or no income differences between women and men who are comparable within that field. For example, a study published in *The New England Journal of Medicine* found:

> In 1990, young male physicians earned 41 percent more per year than young female physicians…. However, after adjusting for differences in

specialty, practice setting, and other characteristics, no earnings difference was evident.

The young male physicians in this study worked over 500 hours a year more
than the young female physicians.

In general, it makes a difference whether the male-female income gap is com-
piled on an annual basis, a monthly basis or as per-hour earnings. Since women
tend to work fewer hours than men, the largest gap tends to be in annual income
and the smallest in per hour pay. For example, the U.S. Department of Labor has
reported weekly male-female earnings differences, showing women's earnings to
be 76.5 percent of that of men in 1999, for example, but women's hourly earnings
were 83.8 percent of that of men that same year. Comparing women and men
who were comparable in occupation, industry and other variables, the per-hour
difference shrank to 6.2 cents.

While there are factors tending to reduce the male-female income gap over
time, there are other factors tending to widen it. For example, as job experience
becomes more important in the economy and more highly rewarded, this tends
to widen the gap between men's incomes and women's incomes, since women
of a given age tend to have less job experience than men of the same age. Shifts
in demand from one industry to another and from one occupation to another
also affect male-female income gaps, since women and men continue to form
different proportions of the workforce in different industries and occupations.
Moreover, these proportions have changed over time: Nearly half of female college graduates in 1960 became teachers, while less than 10 percent did so by
1990. The net effect of conflicting trends on male-female earnings differentials
makes explanations of their income differences far from easy.

Although the male-female income gap has generally been declining over
time since the 1960s, within a given lifetime that gap tends to widen. That is,
young women tend to have earnings closer to the earnings of young men than
older women's earnings compared to older men. What happens in between is that
women's labor force participation rates are affected by domestic, and especially
child-rearing, responsibilities. A study in the *American Economic Review* showed:

> In March 2001, at ages 25–44, the prime period for career development,
> 34 percent of women with children under the age of six were out of the
> labor force, compared to 16 percent of women without children. Thirty
> percent of employed mothers worked part-time, compared to 11 per-
> cent of women with no children. Among men, however, the presence
> of children is associated with an increase in work involvement. Only 4

percent of men with children under the age of six are out of the labor force, and among employed fathers only 2 percent work part-time.

In short, having children has major effects on labor force participation rates—and *opposite* effects on women and men. Although younger women are of course more likely to have children, it is older women whose job qualifications have been most affected by the accumulated differences in job experience from that of men of similar ages. This difference is reflected in the wider male-female earnings gap in the older years. All this is particularly relevant to the notion of a "glass ceiling" restricting how high women are allowed to rise, especially in top management positions. These are positions usually reached after many years of experience. Empirically, the gaps between women and men are huge in both representation among high-level executives and in incomes at the executive levels, but shrink dramatically when comparing women and men of comparable experience, including continuous experience with a given company.

For example, only about 2.4 percent of top-level management positions were filled by women, according to a study in the *Industrial & Labor Relations Review,* and "the gender gap in compensation among top executives was at least 45%." Part of the reason for the compensation gap was that women were more likely to be executives in smaller corporations, whose executives tend to be paid less than executives in the largest corporations—and part of the reason for women being executives in smaller corporations is that this reflects their lesser experience. Taking these and other differences into account shrinks the male-female compensation gap considerably:

> Women in the sample were much younger, and had much less seniority in their company, than men. Part of the effect of age and seniority on the gender gap seems to be reflected in the size of companies women managed. All in all, we find that the unexplained gender compensation gap for top executives was less than 5% after one accounts for all observable differences between men and women.

Despite the complexities revealed by a closer examination of statistical data, lawsuits continue to be filed, claiming discrimination, based on purely numerical differences in the economic situations of women and men. As the *New York Times* reported in 2007:

> In the lawsuit, the lead plaintiff—a former assistant store manager who was upset about not being made a store manager—asserts that Costco discriminated against women in promotions because 13 percent of

the company's store managers were women, while nearly half of its employees were women.

This lawsuit was by no means unique. A similar claim was made against Wal-Mart in 2004, likewise based on statistical disparities. Back in 1973, the Equal Employment Opportunity Commission filed a sex discrimination lawsuit against Sears, based solely on statistical disparities, rather than on any woman who claimed that a man of lower qualifications than her own was hired or promoted when she was not. Yet this case went on for years, until it was finally decided in 1988 by the Seventh Circuit Court of Appeals, which pointed out that the EEOC had failed to come up with even "anecdotal evidence of discriminatory employment practices" or any "flesh and blood victims of discrimination." The court pointed out that the EEOC "did not present in evidence even one specific instance of discrimination" in a company with hundreds of stores from coast to coast.

Sears won that case but its legal victory obviously did not stop sex discrimination lawsuits against other companies based on statistical disparities. Employers who were not as large as Sears were in no financial position to fight a federal lawsuit for 15 years, and spend the $20 million that Sears spent defending this case, might well be forced to agree to a consent decree that would brand them in the public mind as guilty of sex discrimination. Moreover, the spread of cases like that, settled by employers not able to afford the cost of fighting through the courts for years, would be enough to convince many observers that sex discrimination was widespread and was the primary source of male-female economic differences.

SUMMARY AND IMPLICATIONS

Among the many factors which influence male-female economic differences, the most elusive is employer discrimination. Since no one is likely to admit to discriminating against women, which is both illegal and socially stigmatized, in principle discrimination can only be inferred indirectly from the disparities between women and men that remain after all the other factors have been taken into account. In practice, however, there is no way to take all other factors into account, since no one knows what they all are and statistics are not always available for all the factors we do know about. What we are left with, after taking into account all the factors that we are aware of and for which statistics are available, are residual differences which measure the upper limit of the *combined* effect of employer discrimination *plus* whatever other factors have been overlooked or not specified precisely. That residual is often much smaller than the gross income differences between women and men, sometimes is zero, and in a few instances women earn more than men whose measured characteristics are similar.

The empirical fact that most male-female economic differences are accounted for by factors other than employer discrimination does not mean that there have been no instances of discrimination, including egregious instances. But anecdotes about those egregious instances cannot explain the general pattern of male-female economic differences and their changes over time. Those changes are continuing. While in the period from 2000 to 2005 most women were still holding jobs making less than the weekly median wages, women were also 1.7 million out of 1.9 million new workers earning *above* the median wages.

While hard data are preferable to anecdotes, even hard data have their limitations. Statistics may not be available on all the factors that determine hiring, pay, or promotions. Nor can the direction of causation always be determined when the data are available. For example, the effect of marriage on women's economic opportunities and rewards may be estimated by comparing women who seem to be comparable in things that can be measured, but what if women who are more driven to pursue a career are less : likely to marry early or perhaps at all? That is not measurable, which is not to say that it is not important. Income differences between less driven and more driven women may be falsely attributed to marriage, when in these cases differences in marriage patterns may be an effect rather than a cause. In other words, it need not be marriage, as such, which accounts for income differences between married and unmarried women.

It can sometimes be difficult to distinguish income differences between the sexes caused by external barriers confronting women and differences caused by choices made by the women themselves. In addition to choices of educational specialties, occupations, and continuous or discontinuous employment, many married women have chosen to allow their husbands' best job opportunities to determine where the couple will live, with the wife then taking whatever her best option might be at that location, even if there would be better options for her somewhere else. Such wives' reduced occupational opportunities in such cases are in effect an investment in their husbands' enhanced occupational opportunities.

This is a special handicap for women in the academic world, where the wife of a man who teaches at Cornell University, for example, will not have a comparable academic institution in which she can pursue her own career within a hundred miles. It would be quite a coincidence if there was an opening in her field at Cornell at the same time when there was an opening there for her husband in his field. In some places, anti-nepotism policies would preclude her being hired, even if there were such an opening. While some professors have sufficient clout to make the hiring of a spouse a precondition for accepting an academic appointment at a given institution, such a precondition can reduce the number and quality of the institutions that will make an appointment to either husband or wife.

A more general indicator of wives' investments in their husbands' earning capacity is the changing ratio of husbands' earnings to their wives' earnings over time. As far back as 1981, one-third *of* all wives in the 25- to 34-year-old brackets had higher earnings than their husbands—but that percentage declined successively in older age brackets, so that less than 10 percent of wives who were age 65 or older had higher earnings than their husbands. In other words, the passage of time increased husbands' earnings more than the wives' earnings, another indication suggesting wives' investments in their husbands' earning capacity.

Given the numerous factors that impact the incomes and employment of women differently from the way they impact the incomes and employment of men, it can hardly be surprising that there have been substantial income differences between the sexes. Nor can all these differences be assumed to be negative on net balance for women—that is, taking other factors into account besides income. For example, the wives of affluent and wealthy men tend to work less and therefore to earn less. But the wife of a rich man is not poor, no matter how low her income might be. In homes where the income of the husband exceeds the income of the wife, the actual spending of that income cannot be determined by whose name is on what paycheck, and research indicates that the wife usually makes more of the decisions about how the pooled family income is spent than the husband does. Such ultimate realities are beyond the reach of most statistics—but whatever arrangements wives and husbands agree to between themselves are certainly no less important than what third party observers might prefer to see.

While fallacious inferences can be based on gross income data, the fallacy is not in the undisputed fact of male-female income differences but in the explanation of that fact. Much also depends on whether the social goal should be equal opportunity or equal incomes. As Professor Claudia Goldin, an economist at Harvard, put it:

> Is equality of income what we really want? Do we want everyone to have an equal chance to work 80 hours in their prime reproductive years? Yes, but we don't expect them to take that chance equally often.

Research by another female economist lends empirical support to that conclusion. Sylvia Ann Hewlett surveyed more than 2,000 women and more than 600 men. Her conclusions:

> About 37% of women take an off-ramp at some point in their career, meaning they quit their jobs—but just for an average of 2.2 years.

Another substantial number take scenic routes for a while—intentionally not ratcheting up their assignments. For instance, 36% of highly
qualified women have sought part-time jobs for some period, while
others have declined promotions or deliberately chosen jobs with
fewer responsibilities... The data show that highly qualified women
aren't afraid of hard work and responsibility. But it's hard to sustain a
73-hour workweek if you have serious responsibilities in other parts of
your life.

COMMENT

Sowell's argument, at the very least, is an example of knowledge production; one can "easily" produce statistics which support the agenda of any
particular knowledge production. It is not very difficult to produce "empirical evidence" to support a view which conflicts with existing conventional
wisdom. Conventional wisdom also has its empirically self-evident statistical facts to support its subjective view. Which set of facts and which perspective is the right one cannot be determined to everyone's satisfaction;
one's opinion and belief will be judged subjectively according to one's prior
knowledge, preference and ultimate goal. Everyone has facts. Because
facts are "cooked" or produced through subjective manipulation, facts of
this type cannot be the basis of legislation and government action. If action
is taken, people who disagree must now be coerced to agree or abide by
new regulation and legislation. The effect of this type of phenomenon is not
often considered by the legislating group of people.

Sowell's argument summarized is that, if one compares groups of men
and women who are single, were never married and have no children, one
will see that women make as much as or more than men. Sowell maintains
that if one is going to compare two groups of people, then similar groups
must be compared. Men benefit more materially when becoming a spouse
and parent. Women, however, are generally penalized both by marriage
and childbirth in terms of wages.

He believes that it would be misleading to make comparisons to illustrate
inequity if one compares lawyers with janitors; or people who have college
degrees with those who have do not have a high school diploma. A more
fair comparison would be between groups of individuals who have similar
relevant characteristics. Also, it is important to signify and disqualify those
characteristics, particularly those characteristics which are the result of

free choices, which affect each group differently. Sowell notes that marriage and childbirth affect men and women differently, even those who are
married to each other with the same type of job. To compare groups of men
and women which include people who have children and who are married or
both, would result in misleading information resulting in subjective moral
positioning.

Because of the different effects of marriage and parenthood on men
and women, Sowell maintains that a comparison should be made taking
into account those differences; "Single, never been married, never had
children" men must be compared with "single, never been married, never
had children" women. Showing how women can be seen as making as much
as or more than men, does not mean that men should organize for higher
wages. Rather he continues to maintain that wage disparities happen for
many reasons many of which do not necessitate regulation and legislation.
In this case, part of the wage disparity for men and women with the same
type of job comes as a result of the free choices of individuals. To reiterate an earlier argument, every choice has a cost whether one chooses to
acknowledge this or not. The person who makes a choice should be the one
who pays the cost of that choice. Attempts to remove the cost of various and
arbitrarily determined choices shift the cost of the choice onto others which
in turn creates a moral hazard. Because risk or cost of a choice has been
reduced, the motivation to make that choice increases, which increases the
frequency of that choice, which also results in increasing the cost passed
onto others.

What is interesting to note, except to those in scientific and statistical
fields, is that with the consideration of just 2 different variables or racializations, the conventional wisdom regarding the wages of men and women
is challenged. Nevertheless, what must be done, if anything, about wage
disparity is not altogether clear. Whether wage disparity discourse is wrong
or right, legitimate or illegitimate is not an issue in this book. Rather the
issue is whether anything can be coercively imposed on people that would
result in a greater good for all people and society. What is the trade off or
cost of such legislation?

The phenomenon of wage disparity, as such, is real and creates systems
of privilege and behavior which may or may not work out in favor of men
and women in any given work place. The difference in the price of the labor
of men and women for particular jobs makes very real the cost of discrimination based on sex. This is similar to the discussion on white privilege.
Employment based on arbitrary racializations which have little to do with
the actual job or productivity will impose an immediate penalty on that

business, bringing with it the threat of eventual failure against competition which does not discriminate arbitrarily or subjectively. To put it simply, as distasteful as this may sound, lower wages result in higher employment levels or lower unemployment levels. Following the same principle of the moral hazard, when the cost of something, in this case labor, is reduced, then people will consume or use more of it. Sexist employers who do not want to hire women at all will be forced to hire as many women as possible in order to remain competitive. Men will either have to seek employment elsewhere or endure higher unemployment levels. This is seen in the next chapter as well, where wage disparity between black and white workers is discussed.

The free choice of individuals should mean that people should be allowed to pay and be paid what they believe is fair; employers will make offers and employees will make decisions based on their situation. No one should be coerced to enter into any agreement; it must always be voluntary. If an arrangement is considered unfair, then one should be able to explore other options with other buyers and sellers in the market. In a free market there is always competition for labor. People will be paid what buyers believe that labor is worth. It is believed by many in free market economics that the tradeoff for higher wages is often higher unemployment.

Regulating wages, though well intentioned, is a form of price control which has many negative effects, the most important being inflexibility to changes in the labor and business market. Legislation often is focused narrowly to specific situations in a motionless and unchanging society; this is not reality. This type of knowledge production ignores the individual, both male and female and their unique situations. Focusing on a racialized collective imagines that most situations will be the same, and the exceptions are sacrificed for the majority. It should be remembered that each individual of each group, man or woman, can be put into many different racialized groups. It is through collectivism and generalization, these other racializations are subordinated for the sake of a single subjective perspective with regard to wage disparity. As was noted already, it is the competition for labor which protects the wages and jobs of both men and women.

SUMMARY

The knowledge used to determine whether men make more money than women is produced in a subjective manner. Rather than passing legislation on subjective knowledge production, no racial group should be permitted to have their perspective of morality legislated.

QUESTIONS FOR DISCUSSION

1. Has your perspective been challenged? Why or why not?

2. If you are male, does this knowledge production motivate you to have legislation protecting you against female discrimination?

3. If you are female, and males start to lobby against female gender discrimination, how would you react?

HOW MUCH CAN BE BLAMED ON DISCRIMINATION?[1]

15

GOAL

For students to understand that life is more complex than what racism can explain

Walter Williams is a professor of economics at the George Mason University and he wrote about the economic life of African Americans in his book *Race & Economics: How Much Can Be Blamed On Discrimination?* As the title of his book states, he examines the economic life of African Americans in U.S. history to see if there may be another reason for the economic situation of many African Americans today. Williams's argument is that market restrictions through regulation and legislation are far more detrimental to African Americans in America than discrimination based on color.

IS DISCRIMINATION A COMPLETE BARRIER TO ECONOMIC MOBILITY?

by Walter Williams

To observe racial discrimination is one thing. Quite another is to ask whether it is an insurmountable barrier to socioeconomic advancement. If a given level of

1   This chapter heading is taken from the title of a book by Walter Williams, *Race & Economics: How Much Can Be Blamed on Discrimination?* Hoover Institution Press Publication, 2011.

discrimination is not insurmountable, then spending resources to eliminate every vestige of it would be wasted, because those resources might be more productively used elsewhere to promote the same kind of advancement.

Racial as well as religious conflict has existed in varying degrees since the founding of the United States, and throughout the world for centuries. In addition to black Americans, the Irish, Italians, Jews, Puerto Ricans, Poles, Chinese, Japanese, Swedish, and most other ethnic groups have shared the experience of being discriminated against by one means or another.' The extent of discrimination they have faced has differed in degree and kind. Similarly, the response of these groups *to* discrimination has varied between and even within them.

As highly publicized as racial conflict is in the United States, what seems to be less appreciated is that such conflict is a phenomenon unique neither to this country nor to the twentieth century. Racial and ethnic preference, grouping, and conflict have been a permanent global feature of man's history.

In England, there has been widespread discrimination against West Indians, Pakistanis, and Indians. South Africa has a history of societal bifurcation and mutual hostility between Britons, Afrikaners, Asians, Coloreds, and black Africans, much of which continues today despite the end of apartheid.

Contrary to what is often thought, no racial or ethnic group has a monopoly on racial oppression and discrimination. Colored peoples racially discriminate against whites as well as other colored peoples. In Africa, black Africans often do so against Arabs, Syrians, Lebanese, Indians, and Chinese. Recent history has seen the expulsion en masse of some 50,000 Asians from Uganda. There have also been mass expulsions of Asians from Kenya. Although not nearly as extreme as in those two nations, Asians have encountered racial discrimination and hostility in the other countries of East Africa and Southern Africa, such as Tanzania, Zambia, and Malawi.

In addition, there is discrimination and conflict between people of identical racial stock but of different ethnic and religious groups. Widely known examples, which have resulted in large-scale murder, include Irish Catholics versus Irish Protestants; Igbos versus Kausa in Nigeria; Tutsis versus Hutus in Burundi; and Kikuyus and Juos in Kenya. The Tutsi massacre in 1972 saw an estimated 80,000 to 150,000 Hutus slaughtered; the atrocities included dismemberment and decapitation. According to a United Nations report, about 800,000 people were killed in the Rwandan genocide in 1994.

Other examples of ethnic conflict, some of it violent, can be found in Lebanon, with the Muslims versus Christians; Belgium, with the Flemings versus the Walloons;

Sri Lanka, with the Singhalese versus the Tamils; Israel with Palestinians versus Jews; and Canada, with English-speaking versus French-speaking populations.

CHINESE IN SOUTHEAST ASIA

In some countries of Southeast Asia, the minority Chinese population suffers the status of most-despised minority. In that region, the Chinese have always constituted a small presence—no more than 10 percent of the entire Southeast Asian population—and numbering less than 3 percent in countries such as Indonesia and the Philippines. The hostility of the indigenous populations has historically been manifested by massacre or deportation of segments of the Chinese population.

No less remarkable than the hostile racial climate the Chinese face in Southeast Asia is their considerable economic strength; through their roles as middlemen, merchants, and money handlers, they produce 30 to 40 percent of Indonesia's national product—at least ten times as much as their share of the population. A similarly disproportionate economic predominance can be seen in most other countries of Southeast Asia—for example, the Philippines, Malaysia, and Thailand. In Malaysia, where the Chinese constitute a much larger proportion of the population (37 percent), they own four-fifths of all retail establishments and three-fifths of all non-foreign-owned, corporate-equity capital invested in the country.

Numerous measures have been undertaken to reduce the economic predominance of the Chinese in Southeast Asia. These measures have ranged from affirmative action and outright expropriation of property to job-reservation laws and harsh business-licensing requirements. Despite measures to restrict the enterprise of the Chinese, their population clearly enjoyed a higher standard of living. Malays, for example, have never earned more than 57 percent of Chinese median income.

Despite anti-Chinese discriminatory laws, there is wholesale evasion of the anti-Chinese discriminatory laws. In many enterprises reserved for the indigenous population, what appears to be indigenous ownership and control is really a front or a stand-in for a Chinese owner. Such enterprises are often referred to as "Ali Baba" companies, with Ali being the apparent indigenous owner and Baba being the Chinese real owner. These scams survive with the connivance and participation of corrupt officials charged with the enforcement of the discriminatory laws.

RACIAL MALEVOLENCE AND ECONOMIC PROGRESS

No attempt is being made here to completely examine racial/ethnic hostility. I only want to (I) establish its widespread existence and (2) show that, despite handicaps wrought by discrimination, economic progress is possible. Obvious examples are the Chinese, Indians, and Jews—all despised aliens in racially hostile climates. A fuller examination would suggest that the same is true of Armenians, Greeks, and Jews in the successor states of the Ottoman Empire, and Igbos in Nigeria. The fact that such alien minorities sometimes make significant economic gains questions at least two assumptions made in the literature on race. Benevolence on behalf of the larger society is neither a necessary nor sufficient condition for an ethnic minority to achieve economic predominance; and economic progress can occur in the absence of what is traditionally considered political power.

Obviously, if the dominant racial group expropriates all the wealth of the non-preferred group, such as under a system of slavery, the latter has little or no chance to make economic progress. But in less extreme cases, the effect of racial hostility on group progress is not so clear.

The elimination of racial discrimination has been one prescription for economic progress and political power another. The experiences of the Chinese in Southeast Asia, Indians in Africa, and Armenians in the post- Ottoman Empire show that neither the elimination of racial discrimination nor political power is a *necessary* condition for group economic progress. In our own country, we have seen how Jews have prospered in the face of hostility. Although they now have significant political clout, their strongest socioeconomic progress occurred at a time when they were politically unimportant, even in areas where they were most highly concentrated.

Japanese-Americans and Chinese-Americans have always been and continue to be politically insignificant. On the West Coast, they were subjected to harsh persecution. The Chinese Exclusion Act of 1882, which proscribed citizenship, set the Japanese up for denial of land ownership. California, in 1913, enacted an anti-Japanese land law. Under its terms, a person ineligible for citizenship could not own agricultural land or lease it for more than three years. Over the ensuing years, ten other Western states adopted California's policy. The U.S. Supreme Court upheld the constitutionality of these state laws. During World War II, Japanese were interned, and their property was virtually confiscated.

Without a doubt, Japanese (and Chinese) have had experiences in the United States that, at least according to conventional wisdom, make them prime candidates for status as a disadvantaged group. Yet by almost any measure, they are one of the most "successful" ethnic groups in America. As early as 1975,

Japanese-Americans had the following characteristics: 19.5 percent of those employed were professional workers compared to 15.6 percent of white workers (the Chinese had 25 percent); their unemployment rate was 2.4 percent versus 4.1 percent for whites; similarly, in terms of labor-force participation rates and years of education, the Japanese and Chinese surpassed that of the white population. By contrast, although the Irish rank among the most politically successful of U.S. ethnic groups, by every measure of socioeconomic status they compare unfavorably to the Japanese, Jews, and Chinese.

The experience of several ethnic minority groups in the United States and elsewhere seriously calls into question arguments that disadvantaged minorities in the United States *must* acquire political power and need measures to "end racism" in order for socioeconomic growth to occur. The importance of recognizing that political power and/ or social benevolence is not a necessary condition for the socioeconomic progress of an ethnic group is not only an important intellectual exercise but also has practical importance, because all activities require resource expenditure. If, for example, resources are spent for political organization, they cannot be spent, perhaps more productively, elsewhere.

EARLY BLACK ECONOMIC ACHIEVEMENT

The portrayal of blacks as helpless victims of slavery and later gross discrimination has become part of the popular wisdom. But the facts of the matter do not square with that portrayal.

Despite the brutal and oppressive nature of slavery, slaves did not quietly acquiesce. Many found ways to lessen slavery's hardships and attain a measure of independence. During colonial days, slaves learned skills and found that they could earn a measure of independence by servicing ships as rope makers, coopers, and shipwrights. Some entered more skilled trades, such as silversmithing, gold beating, and cabinetmaking.

Typically, slaves turned over a portion of their earnings to their owners in exchange for de facto freedom. This practice, called self-hire, generated criticism. "As early as 1733–34, a Charles Town, South Carolina, grand jury criticized slaveholders for allowing their slaves 'to work out by the Week,' and 'bring in a certain Hire' which was not only Contrary to a Law subsisting, but a Great Inlet to Idleness, Drunkenness and other Enormities." Later, a group of Virginia planters said, "Many persons have suffered their slaves to go about to hire themselves and pay their masters for their hire,' and as a result 'certain' slaves lived free from their master's control." "Two ambitious Charles Town bricklayers, Tony and Primus, who spent their days building a church under the supervision of their master, secretly rented themselves to local builders at night and on weekends."

Many slaves exhibited great entrepreneurial spirit despite their handicaps. Even slave women were often found growing and selling produce in the South Carolina and Georgia Low Country. After putting in a day's work, some slaves were allowed to raise their own crops and livestock. These efforts allowed them to gain a presence in much of the marketing network on the streets and docks of port cities. Ultimately, the general assembly of South Carolina passed a law requiring that slave-grown crops and livestock be sold only to the master. However, the law was very difficult to enforce, particularly among blacks who had gained knowledge of the marketplace. Market activity by slaves was so great that North Carolina whites mounted a campaign to stop slave "dealing and Trafficking" altogether. In 1741, that state passed a law prohibiting slaves from buying, selling, trading, or bartering "any Commodities whatsoever" or to raise hogs, cattle, or horses "on any Pretense whatsoever."

During the colonial period, some slaves bought their freedom and acquired property. In Virginia's Northampton County, 44 out of 100 blacks had gained their freedom by 1664, and some had become landowners. During the late eighteenth century, blacks could boast of owning land. James Pendarvis owned 3,250 acres in St. Paul's Parish in the Charleston District of South Carolina. Pendarvis also possessed 113 slaves. Cabinetmaker John Gough owned several buildings in Charleston and others in the coastal South. During the late eighteenth and early nineteenth centuries, free blacks in Charleston had established themselves as relatively independent from an economic standpoint. As early as 1819, they comprised thirty types of workers, including ten tailors, eleven carpenters, twenty-two seamstresses, six shoemakers, and one hotel owner. Thirty years later, there were fifty types, including fifty carpenters, forty-three tailors, nine shoemakers, and twenty-one butchers.

New Orleans had the largest population of free blacks in the Deep South. Though they could not vote, they enjoyed more rights than blacks in other parts of the South—such as the right to travel freely and to testify in court against white people. "They owned some $2 million worth of property and dominated skilled crafts like bricklaying, cigar making, carpentry, and shoe making." New Orleans blacks also created privately supported benevolent societies, schools, and orphanages to assist their impoverished brethren.

Black entrepreneurs in New Orleans owned small businesses like liquor, grocery, and general stores capitalized with a few hundred dollars. There were also some larger businesses, for example, grocers like Francis Snaer, A. Blandin, and G. N. Ducroix, each of whom was worth over $10,000 ($209,000 in todays currency). One of the best-known black businesses was owned by Cecee Macarty, who inherited $12,000 and parlayed it into a business worth $155,000 at the time of her death in 1845. Another was Thorny Lafon, who started out with a small dry-goods store and later became a real estate dealer, amassing a fortune valued over $400,000 ($8 million today) by the time he died. Black control of the cigar industry enabled men like Lucien Mansion and Georges Alces to own sizable factories, with Alces hiring as many as 200 men. Twenty-two black men listed themselves as factory owners in the New Orleans registry of free Negroes, though it is likely that most of these were one-man shops.

Pierre A. D. Casenave, an immigrant from Santo Domingo, was among New Orleans' more notable businessmen. Having inherited $10,000, as a result of be-ing a confidential clerk of a white merchant-philanthropist, Casenave was in the "commission" business by 1853. By 1857, he was worth $30,000 to $40,000, and he had built an undertaking business, catering mostly to whites, that was worth $2 million in today's dollars.

Most free blacks in New Orleans were unskilled laborers. Males were employed on steamboats and as dockworkers and domestic servants, while females found work largely as domestic servants or washwomen. However, the ratio of skilled to unskilled workers among blacks was greater than among Irish and German workers. Indeed, free blacks dominated certain skilled crafts. According to J. D. B. DeBow, director of the 1850 census, in New Orleans that year there were 355 car-penters, 325 masons, 156 cigar makers, ninety-two shoemakers, sixty-one clerks, fifty-two mechanics, forty-three coopers, forty-one barbers, thirty-nine carmen, and twenty-eight painters.

In addition, there were free Negro blacksmiths (fifteen), butchers (eighteen), cabinetmakers (nineteen), cooks (twenty-five), overseers (eleven), ship carpenters (six), stewards (nine), and upholsterers (eight).Robert C. Reinders, a historian, says that DeBow may have exaggerated the data to show that New Orleans had more skilled blacks than elsewhere; however, other evidence points to free-black prominence in skilled trades—for example, 540 skilled blacks signing a register to stay in the state between 1842 and 1861. Plus, travelers spoke of "Negro artisans being served by Irish waiters and free Negro masons with Irish hod carriers."A few black skilled workers were relatively prosperous. Peter Howard, a porter, and C. Cruisin, an engraver, were each worth between $10,000 and $20,000. A. Tescault, a bricklayer, owned personal and real property valued at nearly $40,000.

By the end of the antebellum era, there was considerable property ownership among slaves in both the Upper and Lower South. Many amassed their resources through the "task" (or "hiring-out") system. In Richmond and Petersburg, Virginia, slaves worked in tobacco factories and earned $150 and up to $200 a year, plus all expenses. By 1850, slave hiring was common in hemp manufacturing and in the textile and tobacco industries. In Richmond, 62 percent of the male slave force was hired; in Lynchburg, 52 percent, in Norfolk, more than 50 percent, and in Louisville, 24 percent. Across the entire South, at least 100,000 slaves were hired out each year.

Self-hiring was another practice with a long tradition. It benefited both the slave and slave owner. The latter did not have to pay for the slave's lodging and clothing. Slaves, although obligated to pay their masters a monthly or yearly fee, could keep for themselves what they earned above that amount. Frederick Douglass explained that while employed as a Baltimore ship's caulker, "I was to be allowed all my time; to make bargains for work; to find my own employment, and collect my own wages; and in return for this liberty, I was to pay him [Douglass' master] three dollars at the end of each week, and to board and clothe myself, and buy my own calking [sic] tools." Self-hire, Douslass noted, was "another step in my career toward freedom.

Not every self-hire slave fared so well. Some were offered the prospect of buying themselves only to see the terms of the contract change. Slaves who earned larger sums than originally expected were required to pay the extra money to the master. Sometimes slaves who made agreements with their masters to pay a certain price for their freedom were sold shortly before the final payment was due.

So intense was the drive to earn money that some slaves were willing to work all day in the fields, then steal away under cover of darkness to work for wages, returning to the fields the next morning. Catahoula Parish (Louisiana) plantation owner John Liddell sought legal action, telling his lawyer, "I request that you would forthwith proceed to prosecute *John S. Sullivan* of Troy, Parish of Catahoula, for Hiring four of my Negro men, secretly, and without my knowledge or permission, at *midnight* on the 12th of August last 1849 (or between midnight and day)."

So common was the practice of self-hire that historians have described the people so employed as "Quasi-Free Negroes" or "Slaves Without Masters." In 1802, a French visitor to New Orleans noticed "a great many loose negroes about." Officials in Savannah, Mobile, and Charleston, and other cities talked about "nominal slaves," "quasi f.n [free Negroes]," and "virtually free negroes," who were seemingly oblivious to any law or regulation. In the Upper South—Baltimore, Washington, Norfolk, Louisville, Richmond, and Lexington, Virginia, for example—large numbers of quasi-free slaves contracted with white builders as skilled carpenters, coopers, and mechanics, while the less skilled worked as servants, hack drivers, and barbers. The quasi-free individuals, more entrepreneurial, established market stalls where they traded fish, produce, and other goods with plantation slaves and sold various commodities to whites. Historian Ira Berlin said, in describing the pre-staple crop period in the Low Country of South Carolina, "The autonomy of the isolated cow pen and the freedom of movement of stock raising allowed made a mockery of the total dominance that chattel bondage implied."

William Rosoe operated a small pleasure boat on the Chesapeake Bay. Ned Hyman, a North Carolina slave, amassed an estate "consisting of Lands chiefly, Live Stock, Negroes and money worth between $5,000 and $6,000 listed in his free Negro wife's name." Whites in his neighborhood said "he was a remarkable, uncommon Negro" and was "remarkably industrious, frugal & prudent…. In a word, his character as fair and as good—for honesty, truth, industry, humility, sobriety & fidelity—as any they (your memoralists) have ever seen or hear of."

Thomas David, a slave, owned a construction business in Bennettsville, South Carolina, where he built houses as well as "several larger buildings." He hired laborers, many of whom were slaves themselves, and taught them the necessary skills. This practice of slaves entering the market and competing successfully with whites became so prevalent that a group of the latter in New Hanover County, North Carolina, petitioned the state legislature to ban the practice. But despite statutes to the contrary, slaves continued to work as mechanics (as such workers were then called), contracting on their own "sometimes less than one half the rate that a regular bred white Mechanic could afford to do it."

In Tennessee, it was illegal for a slave to practice medicine; however, "Doctor Jack" did so with "great & unparalleled success," even though he was forced to give a sizable portion of his earnings to his owner, William Macon. After Macon died, Doctor Jack set up his practice in Nashville. Patients thought so much of his services that they appealed to the state legislature: "The undersigned citizens of Tennessee respectfully petition the Honourable Legislature of the State to repeal, amend or so modify the Act of 1831, chap. 103, S[ect]. 3, which prohibits Slaves from practicing medicine, as to exempt from its operation a Slave named Jack…"

Women were also found among slave entrepreneurs. They established stalls and small stores selling various products. They managed modest businesses as seamstresses, laundresses, and weavers. A Maryland slave recalled, "After my father was sold, my master gave my mother permission to work for herself, provided she gave him one half [of the profits]." She ran two businesses, a coffee shop at an army garrison, and a secondhand store selling trousers, shoes, caps, and other items. Despite protests by poor whites, she "made quite a respectable living."

With the increasing number of self-hire and quasi-free blacks came many complaints and attempts at restricting their economic activities. In 1826, Georgia prohibited blacks from trading "any quantity or amount whatever of cotton, tobacco, wheat, rye, oats, corn, rice or poultry or any other articles, except such as are known to be usually manufactured or vended by slaves." Tennessee applied similar restrictions to livestock. Virginia enacted legislation whereby an individual who bought or received any commodity from a slave would be given thirty-nine lashes "well laid on" or fined four times the value of the commodity.

Similar measures were enacted elsewhere. In addition to statutes against trading with slaves, there were laws governing master-slave relationships. North Carolina decreed in 1831 that a master who allowed a slave to "go at large as a freeman, exercising his or her own discre[t]ion in the employment of his or her time ... shall be fined in the discretion of the court." In 1835, the general assembly of North Carolina enacted a measure "for the better regulation of the slave labourers in the town and Port of Wilmington.... That if any slave shall hereafter be permitted to go at large, and make his own contracts to work, and labour in said town, by consent, and with the knowledge of his or her owner or master, the owner of the said slave shall forfeit and pay one hundred dollars... said slave shall receive such punishment as said commissioners or town magistrate shall think proper to direct to be inflicted, not exceeding twenty-five lashes."

Similar statutes were enacted in most slave states. In the 1830s, a South Carolina court of appeals ruled as follows: "if the owner without a formal act of emancipation permit his slave to go at large and to exercise all the rights and enjoy all the privileges of a free person of color, the slave becomes liable to seizure as a derelict."

A New Orleans newspaper, the *Daily Picayune,* complained that hired-out slaves had the liberty "to engage in business on their own account, to live according to the suggestions of their own fancy, to be idle or industrious, as the inclination for one or the other prevailed, provided only the monthly wages are regularly gained." In 1855, Memphis' *Daily Appeal* demanded the strengthening of an ordinance prohibiting slaves from hiring themselves out without a permit. One citizen complained that "to permit the negro to hire his own time sends a slave to ruin as property, debauches a slave, and makes him a strolling agent of discontent, disorder, and immorality among our slave population."

Much of the restrictive legislation was prompted or justified by the charge that some slaves were trafficking in stolen goods. But there was also concern that the self-hired and quasi-free would undermine the slavery system itself by breeding discontent and rebellion among slaves in general. Despite all the legal prohibitions, the self-hire and quasi-free practices prospered and expanded. Some slave owners who had sired children felt that, although they might not set those offspring free, they would allow them to be quasi-free and to own property. Other owners considered it simply sound policy to permit slaves a degree of freedom as a reward for good work. Even owners with a strong ideological commitment to the institution of slavery found it profitable to permit self-hire, particularly for their most talented and trusted bondsmen.

By the 1840s and '50s, many masters were earning good returns on slaves who found employment in Baltimore, Nashville, St. Louis, Savannah, Charleston, and New Orleans. In 1856, white builders in Smithfield, North Carolina, complained that they were being underbid by quasi-free blacks in the construction of houses and boats, and criticized white contractors who pursued such hiring practices. Whites in the Sumter District of South Carolina protested that "The law in relation to Slaves hiring their own time is not enforced with sufficient promptness and efficiency as to accomplish the object designed by its enactment."

The fact that self-hire became such a large part of slavery simply reflects the economics of the matter. Faced with fluctuating demands for the labor of slaves, it sometimes made sense for owners to let a slave hire himself out rather than to sit idle, in return for securing a portion of his outside earnings. Slaves favored hiring out because it gave them a measure of freedom; it also provided some income to purchase goods that would be otherwise unattainable.

FREE BLACKS IN THE NORTH

Free blacks played a significant economic role in northern cities. In 1838, a pamphlet entitled "A Register of Trades of Colored People in the City of Philadelphia and Districts" listed fifty-seven different occupations totaling 656 persons: bakers (eight), blacksmiths (twenty-three), brass founders (three), cabinetmakers and carpenters (fifteen), confectioners (five), and tanners (thirty-one). Black females engaged in businesses were also included in the register: dressmakers and tailoresses (eighty-one), dyers and scourers (four), and cloth fullers and glass/papermakers (two each).

Philadelphia was home to several very prosperous black businesses. Stephen Smith and William Whipper had one of the largest wood and coal yards in the city. As an example of the size of their business, they had, in 1849, "several thousand bushels of coal, 250,000 feet of lumber, 22 merchantmen cars running between Philadelphia and Baltimore, and $9,000 worth of stock in the Columbia bridge." At his death, Smith left an estate worth $150,000; he had earlier given an equal amount to establish the "Home for Aged and Infirm Colored Persons" in Philadelphia and had also donated the ground for the Mount Olive Cemetery for Colored People.

Another prosperous enterprise among early Philadelphia blacks was sailmaking. Nineteen black sailmaking businesses were recorded in the 1838 *Register.* James Forten (1766–1841), the most prominent of them, employed forty black and white workers in his factory in 1829. Stephen Smith was another black entrepreneur, a lumber merchant who was grossing $100,000 annually in sales by the 1850s. By 1854, Smith's net worth was estimated at $500,000, earning him a credit entry as the "King of the Darkies w. 100m. [with $100,000]"

Blacks dominated Philadelphia's catering business. Peter Augustine and Thomas Dorsey were the most prominent among them. Both men earned world-wide fame for their art, with Augustine often sending his terrapin as far away as Paris. Robert Bogle was a waiter who conceived of the catering idea in Philadelphia by contracting formal dinners for those who entertained in their homes. Nicolas Biddle, a leading Philadelphia financier and president of the Bank of United States, honored him by writing an "Ode to Ogle [sic]." Philadelphia blacks "... owned fifteen meeting houses and burial grounds adjacent, and one public hall." Their real estate holdings were estimated at $600,000 ($12 million today) and their personal property at more than $677,000." Henry and Sarah Gordon, two other black caterers, became so prosperous that they were able to contribute $66,000 to the "Home for the Aged and Infirm Colored Persons."

Blacks made their business presence felt in other northern cities as well. In 1769, ex-slave Emmanuel established Providence, Rhode Island's first oyster-and-ale house. In New York, Thomas Downing operated a successful restaurant to serve his Wall Street clientele before facing competition from two other blacks, George Bell and George Alexander, who opened similar establishments nearby. In 1865, Boston's leading catering establishment was owned and operated by a black. Thomas Dalton, also of Boston, was the proprietor of a prosperous clothing store valued at a half million dollars at the time of his death. John Jones of Chicago, who owned one of the city's leading tailoring establishments, left a fortune of $100,000.

Most blacks of course labored at low-skilled tasks. They nonetheless encountered opposition from whites. When the two races competed, or threatened to do so, violence often resulted. A commission looking into the causes of the 1834 Philadelphia riot, concluded as follows:

> An opinion prevails, especially among white laborers, that certain portions of our community, prefer to employ colored people, whenever they can be had, to the employing of white people; and in consequence of this preference, many whites, who are able and willing to work, are left without employment, while colored people are provided with work, and enabled comfortably to maintain their families; thus many white laborers, anxious for employment, are kept idle and indigent. Whoever mixed in the crowds and groups, at the late riots, must so often have heard those complaints, as to convince them, that ... they ... stimulated many of the most active among the rioters.

Racism and the fear of similar violence prompted New York City authorities to refuse licenses to black carmen and porters warning, "it would bring them into collision with white men of the same calling, and they would get their horses and carts 'dumped' into the dock and themselves abused and beaten.

The growth of the black labor force, augmented by emancipated and fugitive slaves, also contributed to white fears of black competition. In 1834, a group of Connecticut petitioners declared:

> The white man cannot labor upon equal terms with the negro. Those who have just emerged from the state of barbarism or slavery have few artificial wants. Regardless of the decencies of life, and improvement of the future, the black can afford to offer his services at lower prices than the white man.

The petitioners warned the legislature that if entry restrictions were not adopted, the (white) sons of Connecticut would be soon driven from the state by black porters, truckmen, sawyers, mechanics, and laborers of every description.

For their part, blacks soon faced increased competition from the nearly five million Irish, German, and Scandinavian immigrants who reached our shores between 1830 and 1860. Poverty-stricken Irish crowded into shantytowns and sought any kind of employment, regardless of pay and work conditions. One black observer wrote:

> These impoverished and destitute beings, transported from transatlantic shores are crowding themselves into everyplace of business and of labor, and driving the poor colored American citizen out. Along the wharves, where the colored man once done the whole business of shipping and unshipping—in stores where his services were once rendered, and in families where the chief places were filled by him, in all these situations there are substituted foreigners or white Americans.

Irish immigrants did not immediately replace black workers, because employers initially preferred black "humility" to Irish "turbulence." "Help Wanted" ads often read like this one in the *New York Herald* of May 13, 1853: "A Cook, Washer and Ironer: who perfectly understands her business; any color or country except Irish." The *New York Daily Sun* (May 11, 1853) carried: "Woman Wanted—To do general housework … English, Scotch, Welsh, German, or any country or color will answer except Irish." The *New York Daily Tribune,* on May 14, 1852, advertised: "Coachman Wanted—A Man who understands the care of horses and is willing to make himself generally useful, on a small place six miles from the city. A colored man preferred. No Irish need apply."

Indicative of racial preferences was the fact that, in 1853, black waiters *in New York* earned *more* than their white counterparts: $16 per month compared to $12. To increase their bargaining power and to dupe their white counterparts out of jobs, black waiters tricked the latter into striking for *$18* a day. When the strike ended, only the best white waiters were retained; the rest were replaced by blacks.

The mid-nineteenth century saw the early growth of the labor union movement. As I will discuss in more detail in a later chapter, the new unions directed considerable hostility at blacks and often excluded them from membership. When New York longshoremen struck in 1855 against wage cuts, black workers replaced them and violent clashes ensued. The *Frederick Douglass Paper* expressed little sympathy for white strikers: "[C]olored men can feel no obligation to hold out in a 'strike' with the whites, as the latter have never recognized them."

Abolitionist William Lloyd Garrison and many of his followers had similarly little sympathy with white attempts to form labor unions. They felt that employer desire for profit would override racial preferences. Garrison declared, "Place two mechanics by the side of each other, one colored and one white, he who works the cheapest and the best will get the most custom. In making a bargain, the color of the man will never be consulted." Demonstrating an economic understanding that's lost on many of today's black advocates, abolitionists urged blacks to underbid white workers rather than to combine with them. *New England Magazine* remarked:

> After all the voice of interest is louder, and speaks more to the purpose, than reason or philanthropy. When a black merchant shall sell his goods cheaper than his white neighbor, he will have the most customers.... When a black mechanic shall work cheaper and better than a white one, he will be more frequently employed.

During this period, black leadership exhibited a vision not often observed today, namely, lowering the price of goods or services is one of the most effective tools to compete. At a black convention in 1848, it was declared, "To be dependent is to be degraded. Men may pity us, but they cannot respect us." Black conventions repeatedly called upon blacks to learn agricultural and mechanical pursuits, to form joint-stock companies, mutual savings banks, and county associations in order to pool resources to purchase land and capital. In 1853, Frederick Douglass warned, "Learn trades or starve!"

Many blacks absorbed the lessons of competition. Virginia's Robert Gordon sold slack (fine screenings of coal) from his white father's coal yard, making what was then a small fortune of $ 15,000. By 1846, Gordon had purchased his freedom and moved to Cincinnati, where he invested those earnings in a coal yard and built a private dock on the waterfront. White competitors tried to run him out of business through ruthless price- cutting. Gordon cleverly responded by hiring fair-complexioned mulattos to purchase coal from price-cutting competitors, then used that coal to fill his own customers' orders. Gordon retired in 1865, invested his profits in real estate, and eventually passed his fortune to his daughter.

While still a slave, Frank McWorter set up a saltpeter factory in Kentucky's Pulaski County at the start of the War of 1812. After the war, he expanded his factory to meet the growing demand for gunpowder by westward-bound settlers. As a result of his enterprise, McWorter purchased his wife's freedom in 1817 and his own in 1819 for a total cost of $1,600.

Born a slave in Kentucky, Junius G. Graves went to Kansas in 1879. He worked on a farm for forty cents a day and by 1884 had amassed the sum of $2,200. Six years later, he owned 500 acres of land valued at $100,000. "Because of his success in producing a-greater-than-average-yield of potatoes per acre and because of his being the largest individual grower of potatoes, he was called 'The Negro Potato King.'"

Other examples of nineteenth-century black enterprise abound: William W. Browne founded the first black bank in Virginia; H. C. Haynes invented the Haynes Razor Strop in Chicago; A. C. Howard manufactured shoe polish (7,200 boxes per day) in Chicago.

LICENSING AS A STRATEGY OF EXCLUSION

As the Civil War approached, New Orleans' attitude toward free blacks changed with restrictions on the kind of businesses they could enter, along with licensure laws and an increasing hostile press. Some blacks saw migration as an alternative to the harassment. Haiti's emperor sent an agent to New Orleans to encourage them to take that option, and at least 281 "literate and respectable" free blacks migrated between in 1859–1860. Said the *Daily Picayune,* the most rabid of New Orleans' race-baiting newspapers:

> They [free Negroes] form the great majority of our regular settled masons, bricklayers, builders, carpenters, tailors, shoemakers etc., whose sudden emigration from this community would certainly be attended with some degree of annoyance; whilst we can count among them no small number of excellent musicians, jewelers, goldsmiths, tradesmen and merchants.

The newspaper went on to add that this population constituted a sober, industrious, and moral class, far advanced in education and civilization.

New Orleans was not the only city to enact licensure laws restricting economic activity of free blacks. A Washington, D.C., ordinance enacted in 1836 said:

> It shall not be lawful for the mayor to grant a license, for any purpose whatever, to any free negro or mulatto, except licenses to drive carts, drays, hackney carriages, or wagons.

The ordinance also prohibited licenses for blacks to operate taverns, restaurants, or any other eating establishment and from selling alcoholic beverages. A free black, Isaac N. Carey, who had been fined $50 for selling perfumery without a license, brought suit in the D.C. Circuit Court. In reversing the judgment against Carey, Chief Judge William Cranch said:

> It is said that colored persons are a distinct class, not entitled to equal rights with whites, and may be prohibited although whites may not. …Although free colored persons have not the same political rights which are enjoyed by free white persons, yet they have the same civil right, except so far as they are abridged by the general law of the land. Among these civil rights is the right to exercise any lawful and harmless trade, business, or occupation.

Two years later, the same court held that the Corporation of D.C. did have "a discretion to prohibit the granting of tavern licenses to colored persons."

During this early period, blacks came to dominate the very lucrative hackney business in the nation's capital. One visitor called the city "the very paradise of hackney coachmen," adding, "If these men do not get rich it must be owing to some culpable extravagance for their vehicles [which] are in continuous demand from the hour of dinner until five in the morning, and long distances and heavy charges are all in their favor."

In addition to black hackney owners, there were black barbers, restaurant owners, waiters, teachers, preachers, and skilled workers. Blacks became significant landowners in the district, paying taxes on over $600,000 worth of property on the eve of the Civil War. Two examples of black business success: James Wormley, who became proprietor of the famous Wormley Hotel; Alfred Jones and Alfred Lee, who made very good money as feed dealers.

SUMMARY

This brief historical overview has aimed simply to highlight several important principles that will be discussed in subsequent chapters. Gross racial discrimination alone has never been sufficient to prevent blacks from earning a living and bettering themselves by working as skilled or unskilled craftsmen and as business owners, accumulating considerable wealth. The fact that whites sought out blacks as artisans and workers, while patronizing black businesses, can hardly be said to be a result of white enlightenment. A far better explanation: market forces at work.

The relative color blindness of the market accounts for much of the hostility towards it. Markets have a notorious lack of respect for privilege, race, and class structures. White customers patronized black-owned businesses because their prices were lower or their product quality or service better. Whites hired black skilled and unskilled labor because their wages were lower or they made superior employees.

People have always sought to use laws to accomplish what they cannot accomplish through voluntary, peaceable exchange. As will be argued in subsequent chapters, restrictive laws harm blacks equally, whether they were written with the explicit intent—as in the past—to eliminate black competition or written—as in our time—with such benign goals as protecting public health, safety and welfare, and preventing exploitation of workers.

COMMENT

Williams is in no way condoning the attitudes and behaviors of racists no matter their color. As an African American himself, he is not condoning or advocating slavery, nor a return to the conditions of slavery. He is also not saying that slavery should have continued or that the conditions were favorable for slaves to achieve wealth. Rather, he is pointing out that resources may be better invested or spent on other endeavors that would have had a much better result than current social efforts of redistribution of wealth. By listing some of the early economic successes of African-American slaves through **self-hire** he shows how racism based on color can be overcome through the free market.

Williams points out that the free market cares less about one's skin color than the quality and price of the product one is selling; this includes labor and the quality of work that labor produces. Because African-American products were cheaper and of equal or better quality than other products, people patronized African-American businesses to the point that many African-Americans became wealthy. This was in spite of the discrimination and slavery that existed in the south at the time. Eventually the opportunity to save money or to make more money becomes stronger than the desire to maintain one's discrimination based on skin color against blacks; in other words, it was not worth it for many whites to maintain discrimination simply because the product had a connection with African Americans.

People who resented the success of the **quasi-free Negroes** and the cooperation of other whites during the time of slavery had their morality legislated for the rest of society. During the time of slavery and with the rise of the Jim Crow laws, many rules were passed to prevent African-American participation in money making endeavors. In spite of the discriminatory attitudes of many people, many other people continued to enjoy and consume the products of African-American entrepreneurs. Williams wrote elsewhere in the same book that extra-legal measures and legislation are only necessary when those prohibited behaviors are being carried out in a relatively free society. "... why would laws and extra-legal measures be necessary to restrict whites from hiring blacks or blacks from selling to whites, or whites serving blacks in restaurants, if whites did not want to make these transactions in the first place?"[1] This means that more and more laws were passed because people were doing the very things being prohibited. In the case of the south, blacks and whites were freely doing business with each other primarily because the price was right. This meant that people were not patronizing white businesses for one reason or another, cost or quality included. The legislation was passed because of and to prevent the ability for African Americans to become wealthy and to coerce everyone in society to give their business to whites only.

It should be clear by now that regulations and legislation function in ways that protect discriminatory behavior. Often legislation adversely affects the very racial groups well-intentioned people want to help; in the case of the antebellum South, the intentions were easy to see. Most if not all legislation removes the cost of arbitrary discrimination making discrimination more likely with consequences greater than most people can imagine. In the South, the higher cost of doing business with whites was removed through regulation and likely resulted in the South being in some ways somewhat economically behind the North. This should make people wonder if most legislation was and is needed in the first place. The argument of this book is that any legislation based on subjective knowledge

---

1   Williams, pg. 10.

production rather than inclusive knowledge production will have many unintended negative results for people and society. The core and original problem signified within a particular knowledge production, which gave rise to regulation may not have been as pervasive or as serious as the consequences of that regulation.

Today often forms of discrimination are codified under the guise of public safety. An example of this was the Flexner Report of 1910, which sought to eliminate poor quality medical training by standardizing medical school standards and education. By claiming to standardize medical education and the training of doctors, the American Medical Association, and the Federation of State Medical Boards formed a medical monopoly that imposed standards on medical education, which eventually shut down all ten African-American medical schools in the country.[2] What made this extremely problematic was that acceptance into any of the other medical schools was unlikely for African-American students. Interestingly, today the medical community praises the report named after Abraham Flexnor as critical for the start of modern medical education by doing away with private profit seeking medical schools. This of course, was done for the safety of the public. In the free market perspective, the Flexnor report does not deserve any praise at all.

Because government allows for the codification of subjective knowledge production by law, this type of legalization of discriminatory practices has continued and has become the norm today. The discriminatory aspect of legislation is hidden not only by focusing on a specific goal while ignoring the effects on other minority groups, but also by using racializations not signified as racial categories. Licensing laws, Williams points out, are also passed in the name of public safety but are in reality, "barriers to entry" that often target the working poor. The barriers serve efforts to block and limit entry into certain areas of the market with the purpose of cutting down competition for the protection of existing and established businesses. There are countless number of occupations that require licensing and training but do very little to prepare one for that particular field. Fields like local law enforcement, hair braiding, and food preparation have licensing regulations specifically designed to prevent people and competitive businesses from entering the market.

---

2   Todd Savitt, "Abraham Flexner and the Black Medical Schools," *Journal of the National Medical Association*, Vol. 98, No. 9, Septempter 2006, pg 1415–1424; Henry Jones, "How Medical Boards Nationalized Health Care," *Mises Daily*, Ludwig von Mises Institute, Feb 25, 2005, mises.org/daily/1749.

Legislation such as this does more harm to discriminated minorities than forms of overt racism and shrinks the size of the window of opportunity. Williams basically maintains that simple racial discrimination alone is not enough to prevent all forms of economic success. Racial discrimination codified by government legislation is how people are shut out and kept down in society.

SUMMARY

Williams believes that racial discrimination alone is not enough to control African Americans to keep them in poverty. Rather, it is government activity through legislation that can explain many of the problems one can see in the African-American community today. He believes that if there were no barriers to the free market for African Americans we would see much more wealth in that community.

QUESTIONS FOR DISCUSSION

1. How might the discussion of race change if the affluent in society were mostly people of color and the poor were white? (In fact, there are more poor whites in the U.S. than blacks if we go by the numbers and not by percentages.)

2. If there were *no* regulations in the marketplace, and people could not legislate their morality, where and how would people expend their energy?

CLOSING REMARKS 16

ALL OF THE KNOWLEDGE produced in this book has been from the perspective of a humanities professor who is theologically conservative and politically libertarian, trained in race theory and deconstruction. Though there is subjectivity in any knowledge production, the subjectivity here would be that of the general interest or the consumer. It is in the interest of the consumer to preserve freedom of choice for everyone and not just for the people with whom one agrees. If one believes that a person has the freedom to choose to live in the way that person chooses as long as s/he does not infringe on the rights of others, then that freedom must be available to everyone; it cannot be arbitrarily denied to others or subsets of the other. The arbitrary denial of free choice occurs through narrow subjective knowledge production and the legislation of morality.

As was explained in chapter 6, special interest groups are a kind of racial group. From their perspective they can make knowledge that may persuade many that their way of seeing society is the way everyone should, and so there ought to be a law making that the case. This is a common phenomenon today particularly in our current political process. Special interest groups exist in the political system and seek unequal treatment, advantages, and privileges for their cause that work against the general interest. Their influence in the legislative process create distortions in prices and risk assessment, which results in the creation of moral hazards, which in turn encourages high-risk choices for many other people often resulting in financial problems or even poverty for many of them; e.g. unfunded liabilities mentioned in chapter 8 and the housing crisis of 2008 as discussed in chapter 10.

The reality is that any system in society will dictate privilege and opportunity to a minority in society; some people are more gifted and able to succeed in one field over all others. Innovation constantly destabilizes existing systems of privilege, often rendering many of them irrelevant and eventually they are forgotten. The legislation of morality sustains failing systems and codifies obsolete systems of privilege through the use of force while discouraging innovation; numerous examples were given throughout the book, many of which can be summarized by the expression of "minimum standard." Minimum standards give the false impression of quality and safety while acting against innovation in areas that have those standards. This means that in a truly unregulated market, innovation is constant and fast paced, so much so that sometimes the bulk of society cannot keep pace; e.g. the field of internet technology.

Rather than increasing knowledge production to increase the legislation of morality so that more people can take a turn at manipulating the system to their advantage, the position of this book is to discourage all legislative activity based on subjective knowledge production that does not have an inclusive and broad vision of society. As discussed, rather than a narrow production of knowledge dictating truth to everyone else, maintaining a broad perspective makes it easier to maintain an open mind to new and conflicting ideas encountered in society. Because freedom is preserved in the absence of legislative activity, the variety of subjective productions of knowledge are tolerated because they can be ignored or adopted voluntarily. In other words, broad understanding of the process of subjectively produced knowledge increases the tolerance of people towards others.

A bonus to having a broad perspective is that people are better able to spot legislation that imposes double standards in any given field. Double standards in law create the kinds of systemic discrimination many scholars decry; e.g. protection for auto workers against the interest of consumers; or the protection of mortgage lenders against the interests of home owners.

Thus, when it comes to racial discrimination in the traditional sense of color, government activity often works against the minority's interests even and especially when that activity is supposedly in that minority's benefit. The minimum wage law discussed in chapter 10 is a good example of this phenomenon.

On the other hand, the free market is indifferent to one's racialization. It is the price system that enables people to be socially mobile and to accumulate wealth by making decisions for which they are responsible.

People, no matter their racialization, will generally choose the most cost effective option for themselves while preserving their own subjectively determined expected level of quality. The market does not care about one's racialization, only whether that person has a quality product to sell at the right price. The price system allows individuals to make choices according to their personal strengths and abilities, which lead to a tremendous explosion of innovative activity. The most recent and most revolutionary innovations are happening through the internet. The internet was a largely unregulated field that enabled many people to express their creativity in many ways that undermined and continues to destabilize entrenched corporate patterns of business. For example, YouTube, a video sharing website revolutionized digital movie making by providing film makers a cheap way to produce, market and get viewers for their work. It is the ultimate tool of empowerment of even the smallest minority of the individual. Whenever this type of innovation renders regulation irrelevant, politicians strive to quickly regulate the innovation for their own purposes. The recent legislation concerning "net neutrality" is a serious threat to this source of innovation and productive instability.[1]

It is not the interests of a single subjective racial project that should be the concern for everyone else in society. Rather, it is the diffusion of interests that preserve the freedoms of the general public. The diffusion of interests means also a diffusion of power. Concentration of power means a narrow perspective and understanding of life. Eventually as the legislative process continues its growth, all opposing and non-conforming perspectives will be regulated or criminalized. Without this kind of restrictive and oppressive legislation, society becomes freer and more tolerant. In the free market, no single racialization can maintain power for very long unless they continue to produce the kind of products everyone enjoys even with other options available to them. This freedom to choose must be preserved for everyone.

The advantage of a society that allows for free market dynamics is that there is no preset and predictable path of development; in other words success or failure is not pre-determined. Because the benefits of certain types of privilege are less of an issue, which career will result in a comfortable life also becomes more unpredictable. Thus, governments do not need to guide

---

1   Some may be quick to point out that that the internet was developed by the government; so government should continue in its form because sometimes they do something well. Andreas Antonopoulos explains why the government could not turn the internet into something profitable in his explanation of "dumb and smart" systems.   Andreas Antonopoulos, "Decentralization: Why Dumb Networks Are Better," *The Freeman*, July 1, 2015.

the direction of the economy or even of scientific research; the creative abilities of individuals pursuing their own self-interests result in a stable, developing and constantly changing society. Government activity often interferes with this type of progress through cronyism; favors to friends of people in power rather than investment for viable projects. The government has no money itself; the government taxes people and then uses that money for their own agenda. The resources would have been better spent if left in the hands of the consumers themselves. The Solyndra solar panel company fiasco is a good example of this type of government corruption; $528 million was given to a company that was run by a political insider to fulfill a campaign promise to promote green energy. The company failed after a couple of years and the money was wasted.[2]

With government out of the way, the creative energy of many people can be unleashed to develop ideas and systems that no politician in government could possibly imagine. Imaginative ways of overcoming existing problems often will unseat entrenched and less efficient businesses and their system of privilege. For example, internet shopping presents a serious challenge to traditional brick and mortar stores, including stores like Walmart, a business that is a favorite target of many anti-corporation special interest groups.

Change is the constant people must learn to embrace and assume. It is through change that many of the racial significations become de-signified. As people search for quality products at quality prices, the color of the person who produces those products become less and less of a factor in everyday life. In other words, race and racialization become a personal and private issue rather than a public one. This does not mean that knowledge production concerning race should stop; rather the point being made is that knowledge production should not be used to legislate morality.

Race and race making will always be a part of life primarily for the construction of personal identity. Almost all information that is learned by an individual results in an increased understanding or contextualization of the self. People can understand themselves by who they are not; people can also build their own character by determining who they wish to be like or aspire to be like.

Based on what is seen and signified, individuals make decisions and choices that affect the way they see others and the way they are seen by

2   Matthew L. Wald and Charlie Savage, "Furor Over Loans to Failed Solar Firm," *The New York Times*, online, September 14, 2011. http://www.nytimes.com/2011/09/15/us/politics/in-solyndra-loan-guarantees-white-house-intervention-is-questioned.html?_r=0

others. It is a complex dance that has no structure or predictability and is constantly changing as the world continually changes. Those few people who live their entire lives with very little change in habit and rhythm with the same racializations could be considered fortunate, or they could be strict conservatives protected by mountains of regulation. Change may not be welcomed by everyone, but it is part of life itself. Change happens in almost all areas of life—from technology to prior knowledge, in human life and business life, there is always change.

Everyone should learn to cope with this change; there is no exclusion or exemption from the dynamic of change. No matter if one is rich or poor, brown or yellow, man or woman, etc., people should learn to deal with change but in the way people feel most beneficial to themselves; there is no single way that this can be achieved. Racial categories tend to be static, but this does not mean that life lived by racialized people is static. In the free market there is room even for those who resist change; those individuals must only be willing to pay the price of their choices.

Poverty is another aspect of life in society; it cannot be eradicated. As was discussed in chapter 8, people are always finding new ways to become poor, just as people are always finding new ways to become rich. Rather than focus on the eradication of poverty, effort should be put into maintaining a system that enables people to rise out of poverty. Just who is poor, for how long, and how they get out of poverty is the subject of much knowledge production that leads to legislation. These endeavors almost always focus on racial generalizations, which are useless at the level of the individual and often exacerbate existing problems. The focus on poverty in this way fosters resentment against those who have wealth. In a free market, wealth is not necessarily a bad thing because it would have come from providing quality products and fair prices. In the free market everyone has the opportunity to be wealthy; everyone has the opportunity to exercise the power of choice. One need not wait for an election to have their choice validated. Instead in the market place one need only to go out and buy it.

Individuals should be given freedom from coercion to find solutions for their own situations *and* have the freedom to help others in the way they want and choose. Every choice has a cost; nearly every acquisition requires a trade-off. Rather than trying to remove or hide this system of cost, people and governments should simply give people their freedom to make voluntary transactions, for better or worse. This framework could be expressed as "mind your own business." This means that we may not like the choices others make, but this does not mean one should be allowed to disallow those choices made by others. We, as individuals, can only control how we live our own lives and influence our own families. Without the ability to legislate our morality we are left with the work of persuasion without coercion.

It is hoped that students will keep in mind the tool of deconstruction presented in this book to make their own self-interested choices and decisions for their own benefit to stay out of poverty or get out of poverty, should the need arise. In this way, individuals are not simply consumers of the knowledge produced by others for the benefit of others, but people become knowledge producers themselves, making knowledge for their own personal benefit. Using their own subjectively produced knowledge individuals will make choices based on their immediate situation rather than based on the hegemonic discourse of the time, including the knowledge of well intentioned knowledge producers. People should be treated as thinking and calculating beings who may or may not act and choose according to predictions based on a narrow production of knowledge.

THE IDEAL OF THE FREE MARKET

The free market in the material sense, with no government regulation, is an idealized place given our current political and social situation. It is like the "frictionless plane" of physics; it is a construct that does not exist in reality but serves as an extreme point to create an inclusive perspective that everyone may use equally. It can be used to reveal the hidden agendas and ultimate conclusions of various knowledge productions. It is a worthy goal towards which society should always move. If the free market became a reality in the U.S. as it was several times in history (e.g. Iceland and Ireland), then it would have standards and regulations, but not federal or governmental regulations. Not only would the standards arise from practical usage and experience over time, but our own personal sense of morality or religion would guide each individual's choice made in the free market. Most people will make their choices according to what they feel is best for themselves without infringing on the rights and property of others. In other words, people will act on their own self-interest.

Generally speaking, people are fanatical about what they believe is true. Legislation of a subjective morality to force others to agree is a recipe for a whole host of negative unintended consequences. Many of these consequences are seen today in the form of organizations that are monopolies run by the government. Among those negative consequences is a growing disrespect of the law, which includes the breaking of law as Friedman described in his videos. It is because our own religious beliefs trump the prescriptions and regulations of society, regardless of what society permits or prohibits. Prohibition and the current drug war are examples of laws' inability to change the personal beliefs, and actions, of individuals. Today, lines of intolerance are growing around political racializations because with election one has the power to coerce others to do things they otherwise would not do.

Thus, the free market not only exists for material goods, but it also exists for ideas, too. Governments often seek to control and regulate ideas through censorship and restrictive speech codes; consistent with the argument throughout the book, censorship ultimately only protects existing ideas against competition. Which ideas are good or bad can only be determined subjectively. To say that one idea is clearly better than another or that certain ideas are unsafe or dangerous and so must be banned is a dangerous road to travel. Ideas should be able to succeed or fail on their own just like private businesses. If an idea is a popular one, it will be used and spread on its own. If an idea is appealing to some people, then that idea will have its niche. If ideas are simply bad ideas, then the market will forget them quickly. Societies that do not enjoy freedom of choice for material goods also do not have the freedom to choose and subscribe to a variety of ideas and ideologies; this includes religious ideas or beliefs. When choosing between individual freedom and regulatory coercion, freedom is generally recognized as the better choice by most students.

Ideas should be allowed to compete against each other without censorship. Rather than censorship, respect for the beliefs of others while allowing for the process of persuasion, education, and knowledge sharing is a better principle to follow. Ideas are powerful. Knowledge production is influential. Certain ideas foster freedom and peace. Other ideas lead to oppression and discord. People should be allowed to choose the information they believe is best for them without regulation and restriction. People should also be taught to accept the responsibility of their choices, including the consequences of their ideology or religion.

Government activity should primarily be concerned with protecting individuals against powerful forces in society that would seek to plunder the rights and property of individuals. People should be educated and informed of the power of responsible free choice in a free society. If a free market–type setting became the underlying goal of intellectual and technological discourse, society would see an astounding level of creativity, opportunity, and material prosperity. This is because individuals living with actual problems would generate a variety of ways to address specific problems. From this variety, individuals in society would choose what works best for him or herself; choice would not be dictated by a distant politician who has a conflict of interest in that matter.

If this book has an agenda beyond disallowing the legislation of perspective, it would be the desire for all of society to be wealthy or to be on the road to wealth. When society functions with the principles of the free market, there is much opportunity and it is much easier to rise out of poverty. Jane Jacobs in her book *Death and Life of Great American Cities* laments that the problem of the slum in the 1960s prior to the war on poverty was that people were moving out too quickly.[3] Perhaps unwittingly, she stated that poverty for many people was a temporary situation. When this is the case, society is less concerned about the racialized "other" for negative reasons. In other words, it is harder to make knowledge that blames others when it is relatively easy to simply work out of poverty.

However, when poverty increases, violence against the weak others, the minorities, and individuals almost always occurs. Having suffered through a mild form of that discrimination as a child, I do not wish it for my children or anyone else. My own desire for a wealthy and prosperous community stems from the fact that hate and anger levels would be much lower among people in general. I personally believe the free market is the best way to achieve material prosperity, reduce the time spent in poverty, and foster peace among strangers. With the issue of race and poverty de-signified, we may focus on the thing that is truly important: the freedom to live life in a way that means the most for each of us.

---

3   Jane Jacobs, *The Death and Life of Great American Cities*, Vintage Books, 1992.

GLOSSARY

Absolute: something that does not change in meaning or interpretation, no matter the perspective.

Broken window fallacy: the belief that society is better off when property is damaged because people are employed to repair the damage. If this were true, then bombing an entire country is good for that country because of all the jobs created to repair everything and bury those who need to be buried. It would have been better if nothing was broken or bombed so that those resources can be used for productive endeavors of improvement, maintenance and innovation.

Caricature, racial: it is to ascribe a single race onto a person or to try to understand a person through one racial marker as if there is only one.

Central (economic) planning: or a planned economy is the situation where an individual or a small group of people make many economic decisions for the general interest.

Chess piece fallacy: the flawed idea that people can be controlled through law and regulations, and the mistaken idea that people will behave exactly as predicted by legislators and planners.

Collectivism: the idea that individuals belong to and are identified through a group or a particular racialization; in such a perspective the individual is designified and forgotten.

Competition: one of the two necessary aspects of the free market; it is the struggle against others for an objective, prize, customers, etc.

Conservative: a person or position that favors preserving things and traditions the way they are; an opponent to change.

Consumer: the racialization and perspective used to produce knowledge about the free market; a consumer is a user of products and services acquired in the market; everyone in the world is a consumer. Though it is a racialization it does not ignore each individual in that generalization.

Construct: the form that produced knowledge takes; knowledge is made, not discovered.

Corporatism: the system where government and big business cooperate with each other for mutual benefit; also known as crony capitalism.

Criminalization: making an otherwise peaceful person a criminal through arbitrary subjective legislation.

Crony capitalism: see corporatism.

Deconstruction: the process of taking constructs apart to see how they were made, from what perspective, for whose benefit or detriment, and for what purpose.

Discrimination: making distinction between different things.

Diversity: signified variety according to specific criteria; usually according to a single racial project.

Economics: the field of study that covers the production, distribution, and consumption of goods and services because resources are limited and have multiple alternative uses.

Economy: management of resources, especially when those resources are limited and have multiple alternative uses.

Exploitation: a non-voluntary transaction; a transaction in which required coercion was necessary to complete.

Fascism: the system where corporations are owned by private citizens but are controlled by the government.

Free market: a place where people can buy and sell anything to and from anyone at any price as long as people are willing to pay the price. The two most important aspects of a free market are voluntary cooperation, which means no coercion, and competition, which breeds innovation.

General interest: a generalization for consumers, representing everyone's interest as a whole yet preserving the individuality of consumers.

Generalize: to describe a complex situation or diverse group of people through one characteristic to provide context and reference.

Greed: a meaningless construct often understood to mean "wanting more than one needs." In this class, it is understood as wanting more than what one currently has, thus making it applicable to everyone eliminating the need to compensate for, regulate or eradicate it.

Hegemony: the conditions necessary in a given society for the achievement and consolidation of rule through a combination of coercion and consent. People are forced to believe things that are represented as good for them.

Identity: the understanding of oneself. The understanding, in this class, is through racial projects; the sum total of *all* racial categories one can be put into is one's identity. It is dynamic and never limited to one single racial project.

Impersonal: a characteristic of the free market where specific characteristics or racial projects of an individual do not matter when compared to the quality and price of what is being sold and/or one's ability to pay for it.

Incentive: something that incites action or greater effort; motivation based on self-interested calculation.

Individual: the smallest minority; a unique member of society whose rights and property are not subordinate to the general interest; but also whose rights and property is not superior to the general interest.

Innovation: the introduction of new and different ways of doing specific tasks in society, which result in increased productivity and often lower costs.

Institutional racism: the concept that racism is not just practiced by specific people but is a phenomenon that is systemic, shapes everyday social relations, and in which the meaning and practice of race changes over time.

Interest rate: the price of money.

Legislation of morality: the writing and passing of laws based on the subjective personal beliefs or religion of a large or small group of people.

Liberal: one who advocates change and who is generally opposed to preserving things the way they are; they oppose legislation and regulation in favor of innovation.

Meritocracy: government by merit. One is rewarded in society by the quality and amount of effort one exerts in life and society.

Monopoly: the undesirable situation where competition, and therefore choice, is absent and coercion reigns.

Moral hazard: a situation where misleading information makes certain choices seem more appealing and less risky than they actually are. Moral hazard motivates people to make riskier choices by passing the cost of the choices onto the general interest.

Object: the thing observed by subjects. Objects are the things that are studied, analyzed, and understood.

Other (n.): someone who is not me or not like me; who is other depends on the racialization being used.

Other (v.): the process of making someone an other (n.) through a racialization.

Perspective: point of view; what is seen from a location by someone looking at something else. Different people located in different places while looking at the same object will have different perspectives.

Planned economy: see "Central (economic) planning."

Poor: the state or condition of someone who has less than others; an arbitrary racialization based on a subjective point of view.

Politics: the activity of persuasion for the acquisition of power and or support for one's own goals and agenda.

Poverty: the state of being poor, which is usually subjectively defined.

Price: the messaging system of the free market. Prices dictate what to be sold, what and how much to buy, even what major students should choose.

Prior knowledge: all of the knowledge learned by an individual before encountering new knowledge; this is not limited to information, but includes experiences and observations.

Priority: the order of importance. Priorities illustrate the reality that not all things can be had all the time without cost and sacrifice.

Protectionism: the policy of protecting domestic industry against foreign competition; it works against the general interest by fostering localized monopolies.

Race: a category of people based on any identifiable characteristic.

Racial formation: Omi and Winant's theory of race; they define it as the "process by which racial categories are created, lived out, transformed and destroyed." It has two parts: racial project and hegemony.

Racial project: part of Omi and Winant's theory of racial formation; a specific interpretation or theory of race.

Racialization: making race based on a characteristic or to see someone through a racial project.

Racism: to identify and know someone through a single category and then expect that person in that category to act in a specific way and then treat that person differently because of that racialization.

Regulation: in society it is a rule or law to dictate, restrict and control behavior and order.

Religion: a system of belief. Defining it in this way means that there is nothing that is not religious.

Risk: the chance or probability of injury, loss, or failure.

Self-interest: a near synonym of greed; to act according to what is best for the self. This does not exclude the possibility of helping others as a part of one's self-interest.

Signify: the process of making something important. Simply pointing something out to learners as a thing to notice is the process of signification.

Socialization: training and conditioning for accepted patterns of behavior and thought; often mistaken for education.

Special interest: in racial terms the special interest is a racial project; smaller groups of people within the general population that act against and at the expense of the general interest.

Specific: the opposite of generalization; to focus on an individual as someone with an infinite number of racial markers.

Subject: grammatically understood as the one performing the action of the verb in a sentence. In knowledge production, the subject determines the perspective of the knowledge produced.

Subjective knowledge: knowledge that is produced from a perspective; this knowledge is not absolute and the information can only be subjectively true.

Subjectivity: the perspective of one performing the observation and reporting; implies specific location when viewing an object located in a specific location. The perspective of the subject is subjective.

Subsidy: money and funds provided by the government to reduce cost and risk. This often results in the creation of moral hazards.

Sweatshop: a subjective term used to describe certain working environments as undesirable and examples of worker exploitation.

Tariff: a tax imposed on import goods as part of protectionist knowledge production; it is what Friedman calls exploitation of the consumer.

Technical jargon: language and terms meant to be standardized to facilitate learning and understanding; often causes misunderstanding, creates distance, and shapes perception of what is studied.

Tolerance: a contradictory and hypocritical teaching where one is patient with and has a fair and permissive attitude towards different opinions and behaviors, unless those opinions and behaviors are signified as wrong. In the situation where one encounters behaviors or opinions that are signified as wrong, then one is free to be as intolerant as one desires.

TV: the way images and ideas are visually transmitted to a wide audience. It is not confined or restricted to any one form; any screen that conveys images can be considered a TV.

Unfair competition: the complaint made by businesses when forced to compete with businesses that sell products at a lower price with comparable or better quality.

Voluntary action: one of the two important aspects of the free market, it is any action, cooperation or transaction that occurs without coercion.

Voucher: money normally given to schools that is given to parents instead to enable parents to choose the best school for their children.

Welfare trap the situation where once someone is on welfare, it is difficult to come off of welfare because the benefits of staying on welfare are greater than coming off of it. People are also incentivised to reduce productivity in order to qualify for welfare benefits once one gets close to the government mandated poverty line.

White privilege: unearned advantages for being white. These advantages make it easier for whites to be successful and rise to positions of power in society.

BIBLIOGRAPHY

Aguirre, B.E., Rogelio Saenz, and Sean-Shong Hwang. "Remarriage and Intermarriage of Asians in the United States of America." *Journal Comparative Family Studies* 26, 2 (Summer 1995): 207–215.

Ahlstrom, Sydney E. *A Religious History of the American People*. New Haven: Yale University Press, 1972.

Alba, Richard D. *Ethnic Identity: The Transformation of White America*. New Haven: Yale University Press, 1990.

Allen, Theodore W. *The Invention of the White Race, Volume One: Racial Oppression and Social Control*. London: Verso, 1994.

Alumkal, Antony W. "Preserving Patriarchy: Assimilation, Gender Norms, and SecondGeneration Korean American Evangelicals." *Qualitative Sociology* 22, 2 (1999): 127–140.

Andersen, Margaret, and Patricia Hill Collins, eds. *Race, Class, and Gender: An Anthology*. Belmont: Wadsworth Publishing Company, 1995.

Antonopoulos, Andreas. "Decentralization: Why Dumb Networks Are Better," *The Freeman*, July 1, 2015.

Ashcroft, Bill, and Pal Ahluwalia. *Edward Said*. London: Routledge, 1999.

Bacon, Jean. "Constructing Collective Ethnic Identities: The Case of Second Generation Asian Indians." *Qualitative Sociology* 22, 2 (1999): 141–160.

Barker, Chris. *Television, Globalization and Cultural Identities*. Buckingham: Open University Press, 1999.

Bastiat, Frederic. *The Law*. Tribeca Books, 2012.

Bauman, Martin. "Shangri-La in Exile: Portraying Tibetan Diaspora Studies and Reconsidering Diaspora(s)." *Diaspora* 6, 3 (1997): 377–404.

Bell, Kay. *Dump Citizenship to Avoid Taxes?* May 3, 2012. www.bankrate. com.

Berger, Maurice. *White Lies: Race and the Myths of Whiteness.* New York: Farrar, Straus, Giroux, 1999.

Bielenberg, Andy, ed. *The Irish Diaspora.* Harlow: Pearson Education Limited, 2000.

Bourdieu, Pierre. *On Television.* Priscilla Parkhurst Ferguson, trans. New York: The New Press, 1996.

_____ *Language and Symbolic Power.* Edited by John B. Thompson. trans. Gino Raymond and Matthew Adamson. Cambridge: Harvard University Press, 1991.

Bourdieu, Pierre and Jean-Claude Passeron. *Reproduction in Education, Society and Culture.* Trans. Richard Nice. London: Sage Publications, 1990.

Bourdieu, Pierre and Loïc J. D. Wacquant. *An Invitation to Reflexive Sociology.* Chicago: The University of Chicago Press, 1992.

Brah, Avtar. *Cartographies of Diaspora: Contesting Identities.* London: Routledge, 1996.

Brettell, Caroline B., and James F. Hollifield, eds. *Migration Theory: Talking Across Disciplines,* New York: Routledge, 2000.

Brock, Rita Nakashima, and Rudy V. Busto. "Critical Reflections on Asian American Religious Identity." *Amerasia Journal* 22, 1 (1996): 161–195.

Brodkin, Karen. *How Jews Became White Folks and What That Says About Race in America.* New Brunswick NJ: Rutgers University Press, 1998.

Busto, Rudy V. "The Gospel According to the Model Minority? Hazarding an Interpretation of Asian American Evangelical College Students." *Amerasia Journal* 22, 1 (1996): 133–147.

Chong, Kelly H. "What It Means to Be Christian: The Role of Religion in the Construction of Ethnic Identity and Boundary Among Second-Generation Korean Americans," *Sociology of Religion* 59, 3 (Fall 1998): 259–286.

Chow, Rey. *Writing Diaspora: Tactics of Intervention in Contemporary Cultural Studies.* Bloomington: Indiana University Press, 1993.

Choy, Bong-youn. *Koreans in America.* Chicago: Nelson-Hall, 1979.

Chung, Chang-Su Ben. *Dual Cultural Ministry for Korean Immigrants Based upon Theology of Reconciliation.* Doctor of Ministry Thesis, McCormick Theological Seminary, 1994.

Coalter, Milton J., John M. Mulder, and Louis B. Weeks, eds. *The Presbyterian Predicament: Six Perspectives*. Louisville: Westminster/John Knox Press, 1990.

_____. *The Diversity of Discipleship: The Presbyterians and Twentieth-Century Christian Witness*. Louisville: Westminster/John Knox Press, 1991.

Cohen, Robin. *Global Diasporas: An Introduction*. Seattle: University of Washington Press, 1997.

Condon, Stephanie. "Senators Introduce 'STOCK ACT' to Stop 'Insider Trading' in Congress." November 15, 2011. www.cbsnews.com.

Copeland, E. Luther. *The Southern Baptist Convention and the Judgement of History: The Taint of an Original Sin*. Lanham: University Press of America, Inc., 1995.

Corbett, Julia Mitchell. *Religion in America. 3rd edition*. Upper Saddle River: Prentice Hall, 1997.

Cox, Chris, and Bill Archer. "Why $16 Trillion Only Hints at the True U.S. Debt: Hiding the Government's Liabilities from the Public Makes It Seem that We Can Tax Our Way out of Mounting Deficits. We Can't." November 28, 2012, online.wsj.com.

Craib, Ian. *Anthony Giddens*. London: Routledge, 1992.

Croucher, Sheila L. and Patrick J. Haney. "Marketing the Diasporic Creed." *Diaspora* 8, 3 (1999): 309–330.

Dreyfus, Hubert L. and Paul Rabinow. *Michel Foucault: Beyond Structuralism and Hermeneutics*. Chicago: The University of Chicago Press, 1983.

Dupuy, Alex. "Globalization, the Nation-State, and Imperialism." *Diaspora* 10, 1 (2001): 93–116.

Ebaugh, Helen Rose, and Janet Saltzman Chafetz. *Religion and the New Immigrants: Continuities and Adaptations in Immigrant Congregations*. Abridged student edition. Walnut Creek: Alta Mira Press, 2000.

Elwell, Walter A. *Evangelical Dictionary of Theology*. Grand Rapids: Baker Book House, 1984.

Epstein, Jim. "A Miracle Drug Cured Ed Levitt of Stage IV Lung Cancer, Then the FDA Withdrew It from the Market." December 3, 2013. reason.com

Eyermann, Craig. "More Perverse Incentives in ObamaCare," August 2, 2013. www.mygovcost.org.

Eze, Emmanuel Chukwudi, ed. *Race and the Enlightenment: A Reader*. Cambridge: Blackwell Publishers, 1997.

Fenton, John Y. *Transplanting Religious Traditions: Asian Indians in America*. New York: Praeger, 1988.

Finke, Roger, and Rodney Stark. *The Churching of America 1776–1990: Winners and Losers in Our Religious Economy.* New Brunswick: Rutgers University Press, 1992.

Foner, Nancy. "What's New About Transnationalism? New York Immigrants Today and at the Turn of the Century." *Diaspora* 6, 3 (1997): 355–376.

Fortier, Anne-Marie. "The Politics of 'Italians Abroad': Nation, Diaspora, and New Geographies of Identity," *Diaspora* 7, 2 (1998): 197–224.

Foucault, Michel. *Discipline and Punish: The Birth of the Prison.* trans. Alan Sheridan. New York: Vintage Books, 1977.

Friedman, Milton, and Rose Friedman. *Free to Choose: A Personal Statement.* New York: Harcourt Books, 1980.

Fugita, Stephen S., and David J. O'Brien. *Japanese American Ethnicity: The Persistence of Community.* Seattle and London: University of Washington Press, 1991.

Geertz, Clifford. *The Interpretation of Cultures: Selected Essays.* Basic Books, 1973.

Giddens, Anthony. *Modernity and Self-Identity: Self and Society in the Late Modern Age.* Stanford: Stanford University Press, 1991.

Gillespie, Nick, Todd Krainin, and Ajit Pai. "Net Neutrality Is a 'Solution That Won't Work to a Problem That Doesn't Exist,'" February 25, 2015. Reason.com.

Gilroy, Paul. *The Black Atlantic: Modernity and Double Consciousness.* Cambridge: Harvard University Press, 1993.

Glazer, Nathan, and Daniel Patrick Moynihan. *Beyond the Melting Pot: The Negroes, Puerto Ricans, Jews, Italians, and Irish of New York City.* Cambridge: The MIT Press and Harvard University Press, 1963.

Gordon, Milton M. *Assimilation in American Life: The Role of Race, Religion, and National Origins.* New York: Oxford University Press, 1964.

Greenhut, Steven M. *Abuse of Power: How the Government Misuses Eminent Domain,* Seven Locks Press. 2004.

Grosfoguel, Ramon, and Hector Cordero-Guzman. "International Migration in a Global Context: Recent Approaches to Migration Theory," *Diaspora* 7, 3 (1998).

Ha, Yong Joh. "The Korean Second Generation: The Eye of the Storm That Will Change America," Korean, *Light and Salt, overseas edition,* 2 (1999): 54–61.

Haarmann, Harold. *Language in Its Cultural Embedding: Explorations in the Relativity of Signs and Sign Systems.* Berlin: Mouton de Gruyter, 1990.

Hamamoto, Darrell Y. *Monitored Peril: Asian Americans and the Politics of TV Representation*. Minneapolis: University of Minnesota Press, 1994.

Han, Gil Soo. *Social Sources of Church Growth: Korean Churches in the Homeland and Overseas*. New York: University Press of America, 1994.

Hannaford, Ivan. *Race: The History of an Idea in the West*. Baltimore: The Johns Hopkins University Press, 1996.

Harris, Nigel. *Thinking the Unthinkable: The Immigration Myth Exposed*. London: I.B. Tauris Publishers, 2002.

Hasnas, John. "Have Markets Failed?" Video lecture to ReasonTV's Headquarters in Los Angeles, May 26, 2013.

Hatch, Nathan. O. *The Democratization of American Christianity*. New Haven: Yale University Press, 1989.

Hear, Nicholas Van. *New Diasporas: The Mass Exodus, Dispersal and Regrouping of Migrant Communities*. Seattle: University of Washington Press, 1998.

Held, David, and John B. Thompson, eds. *Social Theory of Modern Societies: Anthony Giddens and His Critics*. Cambridge: Cambridge University Press, 1989.

Herberg, Will. *Protestant Catholic Jew: An Essay in American Religious Sociology*. New York: Doubleday & Company, Inc., 1960.

Heyrman, Christine Leigh. *Southern Cross: The Beginnings of the Bible Belt*. Chapel Hill: The University of North Carolina Press, 1997.

Higgenbotham, Evelyn Brooks. *Righteous Discontent: The Women's Movement in the Black Baptist Church, 1880–1920*. Cambridge: Harvard University Press, 1993.

Hollinger, David A. *Postethnic America: Beyond Multiculturalism*. New York: Basic Books, 1995.

Hong, Grace Kyungwon. "Past Legacies, Future Projects: Asian Migration and the Role of the University Under Globalization." *Diaspora* 10, I (2001): 117–128.

Hong, Young-Gi. "Revisiting Church Growth in Korean Protestantism: A Theological Reflection." *International Review of Mission*. 89 (Apr 2000): 190–202.

Hsia, Jayjia. *Asian Americans in Higher Education and at Work*. Hillsdale: Lawrence Erlbaum Associates, Publishers, 1988.

Hsu, Ruth. "'Will the Model Minority Please Identify Itself?' American Ethnic Identity and Its Discontents. *Diaspora* 5, 1, (1996): 37–64.

Hurh, Won Moo, and Kwang Chung Kim, "Religious Participation of Korean Immigrants in the United States," *Journal of the Scientific Study of Religion* 29, 1 (1990): 19–34.

_____. *Korean Immigrants in America: A Structural Analysis of Ethnic Confinement and Adhesive Adaptation*. Rutherford: Associated University Presses, Inc., 1984.

Hurh, Won Moo, Hei Chu Kim, and Kwang Chung Kim. *Assimilation Patterns of Immigrants in the United States: A Case Study of Korean Immigrants in the Chicago Area*. Washington, D.C.: University Press of America, 1979.

Ignatiev, Noel. *How the Irish Became White*. New York: Routledge, 1995.

Ishii-Kuntz, Masako. "Intergenerational Relationships Among Chinese, Japanese, and Korean Americans." *Family Relations* 46, I (1997): 23–32.

Jacobs, Jane. *The Death and Life of Great American Cities*. New York: Vintage Books, 1961.

Jacobson, Matthew Frye. *Whiteness of a Different Color: European Immigrants and the Alchemy of Race*. Cambridge: Harvard University Press, 1998.

Jenkins, Richard. *Pierre Bourdieu*. London: Routledge, 1992.

Jon, Yung-Kyu Paul. *Transgeneration Ministry for Korean Immigrants in the United States*. Doctor of Ministry Thesis, McCormick Theological Seminary, 1991.

Jones, Henry. "How Medical Boards Nationalized Health Care," Mises Daily, Ludwig von Mises Institute, Feb 25, 2005, mises.org/daily/1749.

Kaplan, Caren. *Questions of Travel: Postmodern Discourses of Displacement*. Durham: Duke University Press, 1996.

Kaspersen, Lars Bo. *Anthony Giddens: An Introduction to a Social Theorist*, trans. Steven Sampson. Oxford: Blackwell Publishers, 2000.

Kazanjian, David. "Mass Mediating Diaspora: Iranian Exile Culture in Los Angeles," *Diaspora* 5, 2 (1996): 317–331.

Kennedy, Randall. *Interracial Intimacies: Sex, Marriage, Identity, and Adoption*. New York: Pantheon Books, 2003.

_____. *Nigger: The Strange Career of a Troublesome Word*. New York: Vintage Books, 2002.

Kerr, Dara. "Apple Loses Bid to Yank Court-Appointed Antitrust Monitor," February 10, 2014. news.cnet.com

Kibria, Nazli. "Introduction to the Special Issue." *Qualitative Sociology* 22, 2 (1999): 101–103.

Kim, Andrew E. "Korean Religious Culture and Its Affinity to Christianity: The Rise of Protestant Christianity in South Korea," *Sociology of Religion* 61, 2 (2000): 117–133.

Kim, Byong-suh. "The Explosive Growth of the Korean Church Today: A Sociological Analysis." *International Review of Mission* 74 (Jan 1985): 59–72.

Kim, Ai Ra. *Women Struggling for a New Life: The Role of Religion in the Cultural Passage from Korea to America.* New York: State University of New York Press, 1996.

Kim, Elaine H., and Eui-Young Yu, eds. *East to America: Korean American Life Stories.* New York: The New Press. 1996.

Kim, Eun-Young. "Career Choice Among Second-Generation Korean-Americans: Reflections of a Cultural Model of Success." *Anthropology and Education Quarterly* 24, 3 (1993): 224–248.

Kim, Hyung-chan, ed. *The Korean Diaspora: Historical and Sociological Studies of Korean Immigration and Assimilation in North America.* Santa Barbara: ABCClio, Inc., 1977.

Kim, Jacob. "Rewriting the Silent Exodus: Reconciliation and Identity for Koreans in Diaspora Space." Ph.D. dissertation, Temple University. 2003.

Kim, Sunoon. *The Truth of Eternal Life and the Wisdom of Life: Sermon Anthology vol. 2.* Seoul, Korea: Sung Kwang Publishing Co., 1996.

_____. *The Truth of Eternal Life and the Wisdom of Life: Sermon Anthology vol. 4.* Seoul, Korea: Sung Kwang Publishing Co., 1996.

Kim, Warren Y. *Koreans in America.* Po Chin Chai Printing Co. Ltd., 1971.

Koo, John H., and Andrew C. Nahm, eds. *An Introduction to Korean Culture.* Elizabeth: Hollym, 1997.

Kocieniewski, David. "G.E.'s Strategies Let It Avoid Taxes Altogether," *The New York Times*, March 24, 2011.

Korten, David C. *When Corporations Rule the World.* West Hartford: Kumarian Press, Inc., and Berrett–Koehler Publishers, Inc., 1995.

Kwon, Ho-Youn, Kwang Chung Kim, and R. Stephen Warner, eds. *Korean Americans and Their Religions: Pilgrims and Missionaries from a Different Shore.* University Park: The Pennsylvania State University Press, 2001.

Kwon, Victoria Hyonchu. *Entrepreneurship and Religion: Korean Immigrants in Houston, Texas.* New York: Garland Publishing, Inc., 1997.

Kwon, Victoria Hyonchu, Helen Rose Ebaugh, and Jacqueline Hagan. "The Structure and Functions of Cell Group Ministry in a Korean Christian Church." *Journal for the Scientific Study of Religion* 36, 2 (1997): 247–256.

Lal, Brij V. "The Odyssey of Indenture: Fragmentation and Reconstitution in the Indian Diaspora," *Diaspora* 5, 2 (1996): 167–187.

Lavie, Smadar and Ted Swedenburg, eds. *Displacement, Diaspora, and Geographies of Identity*. Durham: Duke University Press, 1996.

Lee, Helen. "Silent Exodus." *Christianity Today* 40 (August 12, 1996): 50–3.

Lee, Jung Young. *Korean Preaching: An Interpretation*. Nashville: Abingdon Press, 1997.

Lee, Seung Hoon. *Reconciliation Between First Generation and Second Generation in Korean Immigrant Church*. Doctor of Ministry Thesis, McCormick Theological Seminary, 1994.

Lee, Stacey J. *Unraveling the "Model Minority" Stereotype: Listening to Asian American Youth*. New York: Teachers College Press, 1996.

Lee, Timothy. "A Political Factor in the Rise of Protestantism in Korea: Protestantism and the 1919 March First Movement," *Church History* 69, 1 (Mar 2000): 116–142.

Levitt, Steven D., and Stephen J. Dubner. *Freakonomics: A Rogue Economist Explores the Hidden Side of Everything*. New York: First Harper Perennial, 2009.

Lincoln, Eric. *Coming Through the Fire: Surviving Race and Place in America*. Durham: Duke University Press, 1996.

Liu, Eric. *The Accidental Asian: Notes of a Native Speaker*. New York: Vintage Books, 1998.

Lowe, Lisa. *Immigrant Acts: On Asian American Politics*. Durham: Duke University Press, 1996.

_____ "Heterogeneity, Hybridity, Multiplicity: Marking Asian American Differences." *Diaspora* 1, 1 (1991): 24–44.

Lundell, In-Gyeong Kim. *Bridging the Gaps: Contextualization Among Korean Churches in America*. Peter Lang Publishing, 1995.

Ma, Sheng-Mei. *The Deathly Embrace: Orientalism and Asian American Identity*. Minneapolis: University of Minnesota Press, 2000.

Mandel, Maud. "One Nation Indivisible: Contemporary Western European Immigration Policies and the Politics of Multiculturalism." *Diaspora* 4, 1 (1995).

Marty, Martin E. *Protestantism in the United States: Righteous Empire*, second edition. New York: Charles Scribner's Sons, 1986.

McMaken, Ryan. "More Politics Means More Conflict," October 28, 2014, Mises Institute. mises.org.

Mestrovic, Stjepan G. *Anthony Giddens: The Last Modernist.* London: Routledge, 1998.

Min, Pyong Gap. *Changes and Conflicts: Korean Immigrant Families in New York* Boston: Allyn and Bacon, 1998.

———. "A Comparison of Korean Immigrant Protestant, Catholic, and Buddhist Congregations in New York," Unpublished paper, (March 1, 2002).

———. "Immigrants' Religion and Ethnicity: A Comparison of Korean Christian and Indian Hindu Immigrants," *Bulletin of the Royal Institute for Inter-Faith Studies 2* (2000): 1201–140.

———. "The Structure and Social Functions of Korean Immigrant Churches in the United States," *International Migration Review 26,* 4 (1992): 1370–1394.

Min, Pyong Gap, ed. *The Second Generation: Ethnic Identity Among Asian Americans.* New York: Alta Mira Press, 2002.

Min, Pyong Gap, and Rose Kim, ed. *Struggle for Ethnic Identity: Narratives by Asian American Professionals.* London: Alta Mira Press, 1999.

Murphy, Peter. "The Seven Pillars of Nationalism." *Diaspora 7,* 3 (1998): 369–416.

Myrdal, Gunnar. *An American Dilemma: The Negro Problem and Modern Democracy.* New York: Harper & Brothers, 1944.

Nakanishi, Don T., and Tina Yamano Nishida, eds. *The Asian American Educational Experience: A Source Book for Teachers and Students.* New York: Routledge, 1995.

Nauck, Bernhard. "Social Capital, Intergenerational Transmission and Intercultural Contact in Immigrant Families." *Journal of Comparative Family Studies 32,* 4 (Autumn 2001): 465–488.

Novak, Michael. *The Rise of the Unmeltable Ethnics.* New York: Macmillan, 1971.

O'Brien, Martin, Sue Penna, and Colin Hay. *Theorising Modernity: Reflexivity, Environment and Identity in Giddens' Social Theory.* London: Longman, 1999.

Omi, Michael, and Howard Winant. *Racial Formation in the United States: From the 1960s to the 1990s, second edition.* New York: Routledge, 1994.

Oropesa, R. S., and Nancy S. Landale. "In Search of the New Second Generation: Alternative Strategies for Identifying Second Generation

Children and Understanding Their Acquisition of English," *Sociological Perspectives* 40, 3 (1997): 429–455.

Park, Andrew Sung. *Racial Conflict and Healing: An Asian-American Theological Perspective.* New York: Orbis Books, 1998.

_____. *The Wounded Heart of God: The Asian Concept of Han and the Christian Doctrine of Sin.* Nashville: Abingdon Press, 1993.

Park, Edward J.W. "Friends or Enemies? Generational Politics in the Korean American Community in Los Angeles." *Qualitative Sociology* 22, 2 (1999): 161–175.

Park, Insook Han, and Lee-Jay Cho. "Confucianism and the Korean Family." *Journal of Comparative Family Studies* 26, 1 (Spring 1995): 117–134.

Park, Robert Ezra. *Race and Culture: Essays in the Sociology of Contemporary Man.* New York: The Free Press, 1964.

Park, Robert E., and Ernest W. Burgess. *Introduction to the Science of Sociology,* Chicago: University of Chicago Press, 1921.

Pasour Jr., Ernest C. "U.S. Agricultural Programs: Who Pays?" The Independent Institute, November 1, 2008, www.independent.org.

Pattie, Susan. "At Home in Diaspora: Armenians in America." *Diaspora* 3, 2 (1994): 185–197.

Pethokoukis, James. "Why a Single Mom Is Better Off with a $29,000 Job and Welfare than Taking a $69,000 Job," July 12, 2012. www.aei-ideas.org.

Pozzetta, George E., and Bruno Ramirez. *The Italian Diaspora: Migration Across the Globe.* Toronto: Multicultural History Society of Ontario, 1992.

Prado, C.G. *Starting with Foucault: An Introduction to Genealogy.* Oxford: Westview Press, 1995.

Richardson, E. Allen. *Strangers in the Land: Pluralism and the Response to Diversity in the United States.* New York: The Pilgrim Press, 1988.

Rosello, Mireille. "Interpreting Immigration Laws: 'Crimes of Hospitality' or 'Crimes Against Hospitality.'" *Diaspora* 8, 3, (1999): 209–224.

Rouse, Roger. "Mexican Migration and the Social Space of Postmodernism." *Diaspora* 1, 1 (1991) 8–23.

Rumbaut, Ruben G. "Paradoxes (and Orthodoxies) of Assimilation." *Sociological Perspectives* 40 (1997): 483–511.

Safran, William. "Comparing Diasporas: A Review Essay." *Diaspora* 8, 3 (1999): 255–292.

_____. "Diasporas in Modern Societies: Myths of Homeland and Return." *Diaspora* 1, 1 (1991): 83–99.

Said, Edward. *Culture and Imperialism.* New York: Vintage Books, 1993.

Savitt, Todd. "Abraham Flexner and the Black Medical Schools," *Journal of the National Medical Association*, Vol. 98, No. 9, September 2006, 1415–1424.

Schmidt, Leigh Eric. *Consumer Rights: The Buying and Selling of American Holidays*. Princeton: Princeton University Press, 1995.

Schnapper, Dominique. "From the Nation-State to the Transnational World: On the Meaning and Usefulness of *Diaspora* as a Concept." *Diaspora* 8, 3 (1999): 225–254.

Schweizer, Peter. *Extortion: How Politicians Extract Your Money, Buy Votes, and Line Their Own Pockets*, Houghton Mifflin Harcourt Trade. 2013.

Scott, James. *Seeing Like a State: How Certain Schemes to Improve the Human Condition Have Failed*. New Haven: Yale University Press, 1998.

_____. *Domination and the Arts of Resistance: Hidden Transcripts*. New Haven: Yale University Press, 1990.

Shim, D. "From Yellow Peril Through Model Minority to Renewed Yellow Peril." *Journal of Communication* 22, 4, (October 1998): 385–409.

Shin, Eui Hang, and Hyung Park. "An Analysis of Causes of Schisms in Ethnic Churches: The Case of Korean-American Churches." *Sociological Analysis* 49, 3 (1988): 234–248.

Shusterman, Richard, ed. *Bourdieu: A Critical Reader*. Malden: Blackwell Publishers, 1999.

Sollors, Werner. *Beyond Ethnicity: Consent and Descent in American Culture*. New York: Oxford University Press, 1986.

Song, Min-ho. "Constructing a Local Theology for a Second Generation Korean Ministry." *Urban Mission* (December 1997): 23–34.

_____. "The Korean Second Generation: The Present and Future of Ministry," Korean, *Light and Salt, overseas edition*, 2 (1999): 62–71.

Sowell Thomas. *Basic Economics*. New York: Basic Books, 2010.

_____. *The Economics and Politics of Race: An International Perspective*. New York: W. Morrow, 1983.

_____. *Economic Facts and Fallacies*. New York: Basic Books, 2008.

Stevens, Christine. "The Illusion of Social Inclusion: Cambodian Youth in South Australia." *Diaspora* 4, 1 (1995): 59–76.

Stephenson, Emily, and Patrick Temple-West, "Senators Weigh Tax 'Holiday' to Help Fund Highway Repairs," June 10, 2014. www.reuters.com.

Takaki, Ronald. *A Different Mirror: A History of Multicultural America*. Boston: Little, Brown and Company, 1993.

Tanner, Michael, and Charles Hughes, "The Work versus Welfare Trade-off: 2013; An Analysis of the Total Level of Welfare Benefits by State," Cato Institute, 2013.

Tanner, Michael D. "In Fighting the 'Job Lock,' Democrats Opened a Poverty Trap," March 1, 2014. www.cato.org.

Thies, Clifford F. "The Dead Zone: The Implicit Marginal Tax Rate," Ludwig von Mises Institute, November 9, 2009.

Tololyan, Khachig. "Elites and Institutions in the Armenian Transnation." Diaspora 9, 1 (2000): 107–136.

_____ "Diasporama." Diaspora 9, 2 (2000): 309–310.

_____ "Rethinking Diaspora(s): Stateless Power in the Transnational Moment." Diaspora 5, 1 (1996): 3–36.

_____. "The Nation-State and Its Others: In Lieu of a Preface." Diaspora 1, 1 (1991): 3–7.

Trueba, Henry T., Lilly Cheng, and Kenji Ima. Myth or Reality: Adaptive Strategies of Asian Americans in California. Washington DC: The Falmer Press, 1993.

Tuan, Mia. Forever Foreigners or Honorary Whites? The Asian Ethnic Experience Today. New Brunswick: Rutgers University Press, 1998.

_____ "Neither Real Americans nor Real Asians? Multigeneration Asian Ethnics Navigating the Terrain of Authenticity." Qualitative Sociology 22, 2 (1999): 105–125.

TuSmith, Bonnie. "Out on a Limb: Race and the Evaluation of Frontline Teaching." Amerasia Journal 27, 2 (2001): 1–17.

Tweed, Thomas. Our Lady of the Exile: Diasporic Religion at a Cuban Catholic Shrine in Miami. New York: Oxford University Press, 1997.

Vertovec, Steven. "Three Meanings of 'Diaspora,' Exemplified Among South Asian Religions," Diaspora 6, 3 (1997).

Veyne, Paul. Writing History: Essay on Epistemology. Mina Moore-Rinvolucri, trans. Middletown: Wesleyan University Press, 1971.

_____. Did the Greeks Believe in Their Myths? An Essay on the Constitutive Imagination. Paula Wissing, trans. Chicago: The University of Chicago Press, 1983.

Visweswaran, Kamala. "Diaspora by Design: Flexible Citizenship and South Asians in U.S. Racial Formations." Diaspora 6, 1 (1997): 5–30.

Warner, Stephen R., and Judith G. Wittner, eds. Gatherings in Diaspora: Religious Communities and the New Immigration. Philadelphia: Temple University Press, 1988.

White, Ronald C. Jr., Louis B. Weeks, and Garth M. Rosell. *American Christianity: A Case Approach.* Grand Rapids: William B. Eerdmans Publishing Company, 1986.

Williams, Peter W. *America's Religions: Traditions and Cultures.* Urbana: University of Chicago Press, 1998.

Williams, Raymond. *Religions of Immigrants from India and Pakistan: New Threads in the American Tapestry.* Cambridge: Cambridge University Press, 1988.

Williams, Walter. *Race & Economics: How Much Can Be Blamed on Discrimination?* Stanford: Hoover Institution Press Publication, 2011.

Winant, Howard. *Racial Conditions: Politics, Theory, Comparisons.* Minneapolis: University of Minnesota Press, 1994.

Winant, Howard. "Behind Blue Eyes: Contemporary White Racial Politics," in *Off White: Readings on Race, Power, and Society.* Michelle Fine et al., eds. New York: Routledge, 1997. Downloaded copy from http://www.soc.ucsb.edu/faculty/winant/whitness.html

_____."Racism Today: Continuity and Change in the Post–Civil Rights Era." Unpublished paper, downloaded from http://www.soc.ucsb.edu/faculty/winant/what_is_racism.html

Wood, Forrest G. *The Arrogance of Faith: Christianity and Race in America from the Colonial Era to the Twentieth Century.* Boston: Northeastern University Press, 1990.

Wood, Robert W. *Trending Now: Giving Up U.S. Citizenship*, May 9, 2013. www.forbes.com.

Winnick, Louis. "America's 'Model Minority,'" *Commentary* 90 (Aug 1990): 22–9.

Woods, Tom. *"Meltdown: A Free-Market Look at Why the Stock Market Collapsed, the Economy Tanked, and Government Bailouts Will Make Things Worse."* Regnery Publishing. 2009.

Wu, Jean, Yu-wen Shen, and Min Song, ed. *Asian American Studies: A Reader.* New Brunswick: Rutgers University Press, 2000.

Wuthnow, Robert. *God and Mammon in America.* New York: The Free Press, 1994.

_____. *Meaning and Moral Order: Explorations in Cultural Analysis.* Berkeley: University of California Press, 1987.

Yang, Fenggang. *Chinese Christians in America: Conversion, Assimilation, and Adhesive Identities.* University Park: The Pennsylvania State University Press, 1999.

Yang, Philip Q. "The 'Sojourner Hypothesis' Revisited." *Diaspora* 9: 2 (2000): 235–258.

Yang, Sungeun, and Paul C. Rosenblatt. "Shame in Korean Families." *Journal of Comparative Family Studies*. 32:3 (Summer 2001): 361–375.

Yau, Cecilia, ed. *A Winning Combination: ABC OBC: Understanding the Cultural Tensions in Chinese Churches*. Chinese Christian Mission, 1986.

Yoo, David K., ed. *New Spiritual Homes: Religion and Asian Americans*. Honolulu: University of Hawai'i Press, 1999.

Yu, Henry. *Thinking Orientals: Migration, Contact, and Exoticism in Modern America*. Oxford: Oxford University Press, 2001.

ARCHIVED SOURCES

"A Fall to Cheer," March 3, 2012. www.economist.com.

Robert Graboyes, "How to Grow the Supply of Healthcare." Interview with reason.tv, July 1, 2014.

Immigration and Naturalization Service: www.ins.usdoj.gov/graphics/aboutins/statistics/299.htm.

Income Mobility in the U.S. from 1996 to 2005: Report of the Department of the Treasury, November 13, 2007. www.treasury.gov/resource-center/tax-policy/Documents/incomemobilitystudy03-08revise.pdf

Institute for Research on Poverty website, "What Are Poverty Thresholds and Poverty Guidelines?" www.irp.wisc.edu/faqs/faq1.htm.

"Statement on the Mission of the Korean Churches in the New Millennium: Council of Presbyterian Churches in Korea, International Consultation on Korean Churches' Mission Around the World," Seoul, Korea, 23–27 May 1999. *International Review of Mission* 89, 353 (2000): 233–238.

JAMA Brochure. Conference held July 1–5, 2003; Georgia Institute of Technology, Atlanta Georgia.

Korean United Church of Philadelphia. "Korean American Ministry: Working Together Towards the 21st Century." Program. November 13–14, 1998.

Orthodox Presbyterian Church. "[The] Minutes of the Thirty-Ninth General Assembly, May 15–May 20 1972." Philadelphia: The Orthodox Presbyterian Church, 1972.

Personal website with information on the all-Japanese 442nd Regimental Combat Team. http://www.katonk.com/442nd/442/page1.html.

"Prohibited and Restricted Items," www.cbp.gov.

"Why Is There Corn in Your Coke?" November 19, 2012, LearnLiberty.
org.

NEWSPAPER SOURCES

"Prayer and Fasting in L.A." *The Korea Gospel Weekly*, in Korean, Feb 16,
2003, 1.

"A Forum to Dialogue Directly with Youth," *The Christian Herald USA*, in
Korean, Thursday, February 13, 2003, 10.

CPSIA information can be obtained at www.ICGtesting.com
Printed in the USA
LVOW01s0319270815

451667LV00007B/50/P